D1320121

WD

MASTERS OF THE ENGLISH NOVEL

MASTERS OF THE ENGLISH NOVEL

A STUDY OF PRINCIPLES AND PERSONALITIES

BY

RICHARD BURTON

Essay Index Reprint Series

BOOKS FOR LIBRARIES PRESS
FREEPORT, NEW YORK

First Published 1909
Reprinted 1969

STANDARD BOOK NUMBER:
8369-1252-7

LIBRARY OF CONGRESS CATALOG CARD NUMBER:
79-90620 CO

PRINTED IN THE UNITED STATES OF AMERICA

PREFACE

THE principle of inclusion in this book is the traditional one which assumes that criticism is only safe when it deals with authors who are dead. In proportion as we approach the living or, worse, speak of those still on earth, the proper perspective is lost and the dangers of contemporary judgment incurred. The light-minded might add, that the dead cannot strike back; to pass judgment upon them is not only more critical but safer.

Sometimes, however, the distinction between the living and the dead is an invidious one. Three authors hereinafter studied are examples: Meredith, Hardy and Stevenson. Hardy alone is now in the land of the living, Meredith having but just passed away. Yet to omit the former, while including the other two, is obviously arbitrary, since his work in fiction is as truly done as if he, like them, rested from his literary labors and the gravestone chronicled his day of death. For reasons best known to himself, Mr. Hardy seems to have chosen verse for the final expression of his personality. It is more than a decade since he published a novel. So far as age goes, he is the senior of Stevenson: " Desperate Remedies " appeared when the latter was a stripling

at the University of Edinburgh. Hardy is therefore included in the survey. I am fully aware that
to strive to measure the accomplishment of those
practically contemporary, whether it be Meredith
and Hardy or James and Howells, is but more or
less intelligent guess-work. Nevertheless, it is pleasant employ, the more interesting, perhaps, to the
critic and his readers because an element of uncertainty creeps into what is said. If the critic runs
the risk of *Je suis, J'y reste*, he gets his reward
in the thrill of prophecy; and should he turn out a
false prophet, he is consoled by the reflection that
it will place him in a large and enjoyable company.

Throughout the discussion it has been the intention to keep steadily before the reader the two main
ways of looking at life in fiction, which have led to
the so-called realistic and romantic movements. No
fear of repetition in the study of the respective
novelists has kept me from illustrating from many
points of view and taking advantage of the opportunity offered by each author, the distinction thus
set up. For back of all stale jugglery of terms,
lies a very real and permanent difference. The words
denote different types of mind as well as of art: and
express also a changed interpretation of the world of
men, resulting from the social and intellectual revolution since 1750.

No apology would appear to be necessary for
Chapter Seven, which devotes sufficient space to the

French influence to show how it affected the realistic tendency of all modern novel-making. The Scandinavian lands, Germany, Italy, England and Spain, all have felt the leadership of France in this regard and hence any attempt to sketch the history of the Novel on English soil, would ignore causes, that did not acknowledge the Gallic debt.

It may also be remarked that the method employed in the following pages necessarily excludes many figures of no slight importance in the evolution of English fiction. There are books a-plenty dealing with these secondary personalities, often significant as links in the chain and worthy of study were the purpose to present the complete history of the Novel. By centering upon indubitable masters, the principles illustrated both by the lesser and larger writers will, it is hoped, be brought home with equal if not greater force.

CONTENTS

MASTERS OF THE ENGLISH NOVEL

CHAPTER I

FICTION AND THE NOVEL

ALL the world loves a story as it does a lover.
It is small wonder then that stories have been
told since man walked erect and long before
transmitted records. Fiction, a conveniently broad
term to cover all manner of story-telling, is a hoary
thing and within historical limits we can but get
a glimpse of its activity. Because it is so diverse
a thing, it may be regarded in various ways: as a
literary form, a social manifestation, a comment
upon life. Main emphasis in this book is placed
upon its recent development on English soil under
the more restrictive name of Novel; and it is the
intention, in tracing the work of representative
novel writers, to show how the Novel has become
in some sort a special modern mode of expression
and of opinion, truly reflective of the *zeitgeist*.

The social and human element in a literary phenomenon is what gives general interest and includes
it as part of the *culturgeschichte* of a people. This

1

interest is as far removed from that of the literary specialist taken up with questions of morphology and method, as it is from the unthinking rapture of the boarding-school Miss who finds a current book " perfectly lovely," and skips intrepidly to the last page to see how it is coming out. Thoughtful people are coming to feel that fiction is only frivolous when the reader brings a frivolous mind or makes a frivolous choice. While it will always be legitimate to turn to fiction for innocent amusement, since the peculiar property of all art is to give pleasure, the day has been reached when it is recognized as part of our culture to read good fiction, to realize the value and importance of the Novel in modern education; and conversely, to reprimand the older, narrow notion that the habit means self-indulgence and a waste of time. Nor can we close our eyes to the tyrannous domination of fiction to-day, for good or bad. It has worn seven-league boots of progress the past generation. So early as 1862, Sainte-Beuve declared in conversation: " Everything is being gradually merged into the novel. There is such a vast scope and the form lends itself to everything." Prophetic words, more than fulfilled since they were spoken.

Of the three main ways of story-telling, by the epic poem, the drama and prose fiction, the epic seems to be the oldest; poetry, indeed, being the natural form of expression among primitive peoples.

The comparative study of literature shows that so far as written records go, we may not surely ascribe precedence in time either to fiction or the drama. The testimony varies in different nations. But if the name fiction be allowed for a Biblical narrative like the Book of Ruth, which in the sense of imaginative and literary handling of historical material it certainly is, the great antiquity of the form may be conceded. Long before the written or printed word, we may safely say, stories were recited in Oriental deserts, yarns were spun as ships heaved over the seas, and sagas spoken beside hearth fires far in the frozen north. Prose narratives, epic in theme or of more local import, were handed down from father to son, transmitted from family to family, through the exercise of a faculty of memory that now, in a day when labor-saving devices have almost atrophied its use, seems well nigh miraculous. Prose story-telling, which allows of ample description, elbow room for digression, indefinite extension and variation from the original kernel of plot, lends itself admirably to the imaginative needs of humanity early or late.

With the English race, fiction began to take constructural shape and definiteness of purpose in Elizabethan days. Up to the sixteenth century the tales were either told in verse, in the epic form of Beowulf or in the shrunken epic of a thirteenth century ballad like " King Horn "; in the verse narra-

tives of Chaucer or the poetic musings of Spenser.
Or else they were a portion of that prose romance
of chivalry which was vastly cultivated in the middle
ages, especially in France and Spain, and of which
we have a doughty exemplar in the Morte D'Arthur,
which dates nearly a century before Shakspere's
day. Loose construction and no attempt to deal
with the close eye of observation, characterize these
earlier romances, which were in the main conglomer-
ates of story using the double appeal of love and
war.

But at a time when the drama was paramount in
popularity, when the young Shakspere was writing
his early comedies, fiction, which was in the fulness
of time to conquer the play form as a popular
vehicle of story-telling, began to rear its head. The
loosely constructed, rambling prose romances of
Lyly of euphuistic fame, the prose pastorals of
Lodge from which model Shakspere made his forest drama, "As You Like It," the picaresque, harum-
scarum story of adventure, "Jack Wilton," the prototype of later books like "Gil Blas" and "Robinson Crusoe,"—these were the early attempts to give
prose narration a closer knitting, a more organic
form.

But all such tentative striving was only preparation; fiction in the sense of more or less formless
prose narration, was written for about two centuries
without the production of what may be called the

Novel in the modern meaning of the word. The broader name fiction may properly be applied, since, as we shall see, all novels are fiction, but all fiction is by no means Novels. The whole development of the Novel, indeed, is embraced within little more than a century and a half; from the middle of the eighteenth century to the present time. The term Novel is more definite, more specific than the fiction out of which it evolved; therefore, we must ask ourselves wherein lies the essential difference. Light is thrown by the early use of the word in critical reference in English. In reading the following from Steele's "Tender Husband," we are made to realize that the stark meaning of the term implies something new: social interest, a sense of social solidarity: "Our amours can't furnish out a Romance; they'll make a very pretty Novel."

This clearly marks a distinction: it gives a hint as to the departure made by Richardson in 1742, when he published "Pamela." It is not strictly the earliest discrimination between the Novel and the older romance; for the dramatist Congreve at the close of the seventeenth century shows his knowledge of the distinction. And, indeed, there are hints of it in Elizabethan criticism of such early attempts as those of Lyly, Nast, Lodge and others. Moreover, the student of criticism as it deals with the Novel must also expect to meet with a later confusion of nomenclature; the word being loosely applied to any

type of prose fiction in contrast with the short story
or tale. But here, at an early date, the severance
is plainly indicated between the study of contemporary society and the elder romance of heroism, super-
naturalism, and improbability. It is a difference
not so much of theme as of view-point, method and
intention.

For underlying this attempt to come closer to
humanity through the medium of a form of fiction,
is to be detected an added interest in personality for
its own sake. During the eighteenth century, commonly described as the Teacup Times, an age of
powder and patches, of etiquette, epigram and surface polish, there developed a keener sense of the
value of the individual, of the sanctity of the ego,
a faint prelude to the note that was to become so
resonant in the nineteenth century, sounding through
all the activities of man. Various manifestations in
the civilization of Queen Anne and the first Georges
illustrate the new tendency.

One such is the coffee house, prototype of the
bewildering club life of our own day. The eighteenth
century coffee house, where the men of fashion and
affairs foregathered to exchange social news over
their glasses, was an organization naturally fostering
altruism; at least, it tended to cultivate a feeling for
social relations.

Again, the birth of the newspaper with the Spectator Papers in the early years of the century, is

another such sign of the times: the newspaper being one of the great social bonds of humanity, for good or bad, linking man to man, race to race in the common, well-nigh instantaneous nexus of sympathy. The influence of the press at the time of a San Francisco or Messina horror is apparent to all; but its effect in furnishing the psychology of a business panic is perhaps no less potent though not so obvious. When Addison and Steele began their genial conversations thrice a week with their fellow citizens, they little dreamed of the power they set a-going in the world; for here was the genesis of modern journalism. And whatever its abuses and degradations, the fourth estate is certainly one of the very few widely operative educational forces to-day, and has played an important part in spreading the idea of the brotherhood of man.

That the essay and its branch form, the character sketch, both found in the Spectator Papers, were contributory to the Novel's development, is sure. The essay set a new model for easy, colloquial speech: just the manner for fiction which was to report the accent of contemporary society in its average of utterance. And the sketch, seen in its delightful efflorescence in the Sir Roger De Coverly papers series by Addison, is fiction in a sense: differing therefrom in its slighter framework, and the aim of the writer, which first of all is the delicate delineation of personality, not plot and the study of

the social complex. There is the absence of plot
which is the natural outcome of such lack of story
interest. A wide survey of the English essay from
its inception with Bacon in the early seventeenth
century will impress the inquirer with its fluid nature
and natural outflow into full-fledged fiction. The
essay has a way, as Taine says, of turning " spon-
taneously to fiction and portraiture." And as it is
difficult, in the light of evolution, to put the finger
on the line separating man from the lower order of
animal life, so is it difficult sometimes to say just
where the essay stops and the Novel begins. There
is perhaps no hard-and-fast line.

Consider Dr. Holmes' " Autocrat of the Breakfast
Table," for example; is it essay or fiction? There
is a definite though slender story interest and idea,
yet since the framework of story is really for the
purpose of hanging thereon the genial essayist's
dissertations on life, we may decide that the book
is primarily essay, the most charmingly personal,
egoistic of literary forms. The essay " slightly
dramatized," Mr. Howells happily characterizes it.
This form then must be reckoned with in the eighteenth century and borne in mind as contributory all
along in the subsequent development, as we try to get
a clear idea of the qualities which demark and limit
the Novel.

Again, the theater was an institution doing its
share to knit social feeling; as indeed it had been

in Elizabethan days: offering a place where many might be moved by the one thought, the one emotion, personal variations being merged in what is now called mob psychology, a function for centuries also exercised by the Church. Nor should the function of the playhouse as a visiting-place be overlooked.

So too the Novel came to express most inclusively among the literary forms this more vivid realization of *meum* and *tuum;* the worth of me and my intricate and inevitable relations to you, both of us caught in the coils of that organism dubbed society, and willingly, with no Rousseau-like desire to escape and set up for individualists. The Novel in its treatment of personality began to teach that the stone thrown into the water makes circles to the uttermost bounds of the lake; that the little rift within the lute makes the whole music mute; that we are all members of the one body. This germinal principle was at root a profoundly true and noble one; it serves to distinguish modern fiction philosophically from all that is earlier, and it led the late Sidney Lanier, in the well-known book on this subject, to base the entire development upon the working out of the idea of personality. The Novel seems to have been the special literary instrument in the eighteenth century for the propagation of altruism; here lies its deepest significance. It was a baptism which promised great things for the lusty young form.

We are now ready for a fair working definition of the modern Novel. It means a study of contemporary society with an implied sympathetic interest, and, it may be added, with special reference to love as a motor force, simply because love it is which binds together human beings in their social relations.

This aim sets off the Novel in contrast with past fiction which exhibits a free admixture of myth and marvel, of creatures human, demi-human and supernatural, with all time or no time for the enactment of its events. The modern story puts its note of emphasis upon character that is contemporary and average; and thus makes a democratic appeal against that older appeal which, dealing with exceptional personages—kings, leaders, allegorical abstractions—is naturally aristocratic.

There was something, it would appear, in the English genius which favored a form of literature—or modification of an existing form—allowing for a more truthful representation of society, a criticism (in the Arnoldian sense) of the passing show. The elder romance finds its romantic effect, as a rule, in the unusual, the strange and abnormal aspects of life, not so much seen of the eye as imagined of the mind or fancy. Hence, romance is historically contrasted with reality, with many unfortunate results when we come to its modern applications. The issue has been a Babel-like mixture of terms.

Or when the bizarre or supernatural was not the

basis of appeal, it was found in the sickly and absurd treatment of the amatory passion, quite as far
removed from the every-day experience of normal
human nature. It was this kind of literature, with
the French La Calprenède as its high priest,
which my Lord Chesterfield had in mind when he
wrote to his son under date of 1752, Old Style:
"It is most astonishing that there ever could have
been a people idle enough to write such endless
heaps of the same stuff. It was, however, the occupation of thousands in the last century; and is still
the private though disavowed amusement of young
girls and sentimental ladies." The chief trait of
these earlier fictions, besides their mawkishness, is
their almost incredible long-windedness; they have
the long breath, as the French say; and it may be
confessed that the great, pioneer eighteenth century
novels, foremost those of Richardson, possess a
leisureliness of movement which is an inheritance of
the romantic past when men, both fiction writers
and readers, seem to have Time; they look back to
Lyly, and forward (since history repeats itself here),
to Henry James. The condensed, breathless fiction
of a Kipling is the more logical evolution.

Certainly, the English were innovators in this field,
exercising a direct and potent influence upon foreign
fiction, especially that of France and Germany; it
is not too much to say, that the novels of Richardson and Fielding, pioneers, founders of the Eng-

lish Novel, offered Europe a type. If one reads the French fictionists before Richardson—Madame de La Fayette, Le Sage, Prevost and Rousseau—one speedily discovers that they did not write novels in the modern sense; the last named took a cue from Richardson, to be sure, in his handling of sentiment, but remained an essayist, nevertheless. And the greater Goethe also felt and acknowledged the Englishman's example. Testimonies from the story-makers of other lands are frequent to the effect upon them of these English pioneers of fiction.

It will be seen from this brief statement of the kind of fiction essayed by the founders of the Novel, that their tendency was towards what has come to be called " realism " in modern fiction literature. One uses this sadly overworked term with a certain sinking of the heart, yet it seems unavoidable. The very fact that the words " realism " and " romance " have become so hackneyed in critical parlance, makes it sure that they indicate a genuine distinction. As the Novel has developed, ramified and taken on a hundred guises of manifestation, and as criticism has striven to keep pace with such a growth, it is not strange that a confusion of nomenclature should have arisen. But underneath whatever misunderstandings, the original distinction is clear enough and useful to make: the modern Novel in its beginning did introduce a more truthful representation of human life than had obtained in the romantic

fiction deriving from the medieval stories. The
term "realism" as first applied was suitably descriptive; it is only with the subsequent evolution
that so simple a word has taken on subtler shades
and esoteric implications.

It may be roundly asserted that from the first
the English Novel has stood for truth; that it has
grown on the whole more truthful with each generation, as our conception of truth in literature has
been widened and become a nobler one. The obligation of literature to report life has been felt with
increasing sensitiveness. In the particulars of appearance, speech, setting and action the characters
of English fiction to-day produce a semblance of
life which adds tenfold to its power. To compare
the dialogue of modern masters like Hardy, Stevenson, Kipling and Howells with the best of the earlier
writers serves to bring the assertion home; the difference is immense; it is the difference between the
idiom of life and the false-literary tone of imitations
of life which, with all their merits, are still self-
conscious and inapt. And as the earlier idiom was
imperfect, so was the psychology; the study of
motives in relation to action has grown steadily
broader, more penetrating; the rich complexity of
human beings has been recognized more and more,
where of old the simple assumption that all mankind
falls into the two great contrasted groups of the
good and the bad, was quite sufficient. And, as a

natural outcome of such an easy-going philosophy, the study of life was rudimentary and partial; you could always tell how the villain would jump and were comfortable in the assurance that the curtain should ring down upon " and so they were married and lived happily ever afterwards."

In contrast, to-day human nature is depicted in the Novel as a curious compound of contradictory impulses and passions, and instead of the clear-cut separation of the sheep and the goats, we look forth upon a vast, indiscriminate horde of humanity whose color, broadly surveyed, seems a very neutral gray, —neither deep black nor shining white.   The white-robed saint is banished along with the devil incarnate; those who respect their art would relegate such crudities to Bowery melodrama.   And while we may allow an excess of zeal in this matter, even a confusion of values, there can be no question that an added dignity has come to the Novel in these latter days, because it has striven with so much seriousness of purpose to depict life in a more interpretative way.   It has seized for a motto the *Veritas nos liberavit* of the ancient philosopher. The elementary psychology of the past has been transferred to the stage drama, justifying Mr. Shaw's description of it as " the last sanctuary of unreality."   And even in the theater, the truth demanded in fiction for more than a century, is fast finding a place, and play-making, sensitive to the new desire, is changing in this respect before our eyes.

However, with the good has come evil too. In the modern seeking for so-called truth, the *nuda veritas* has in some hands become shameless as well,— a fact amply illustrated in the following treatment of principles and personalities.

The Novel in the hands of these eighteenth century writers also struck a note of the democratic,—a note that has sounded ever louder until the present day, when fiction is by far the most democratic of the literary forms (unless we now must include the drama in such a designation).   The democratic ideal has become at once an instinct, a principle and a fashion.   Richardson in his " Pamela " did a revolutionary thing in making a kitchen wench his heroine; English fiction had previously assumed that for its polite audience only the fortunes of Algernon and Angelina could be followed decorously and give fit pleasure.   His innovation, symptomatic of the time, by no means pleased an aristocratic on-looker like Lady Mary Wortley Montagu, who wrote to a friend: " The confounding of all ranks and making a jest of order has long been growing in England; and I perceive by the books you sent me, has made a very considerable progress.   The heroes and heroines of the age are cobblers and kitchen wenches. Perhaps you will say, I should not take my ideas of the manners of the times from such trifling

authors; but it is more truly to be found among
them, than from any historian; as they write merely
to get money, they always fall into the notions that
are most acceptable to the present taste. It has
long been the endeavor of our English writers to
represent people of quality as the vilest and silliest
part of the nation, being (generally) very low-born
themselves "—a quotation deliciously commingled of
prejudice and worldly wisdom.

But Richardson, who began his career by writing
amatory epistles for serving maids, realized (and
showed his genius thereby), that if the hard fortunes
and eventful triumph of the humble Pamela could
but be sympathetically portrayed, the interest on
the part of his aristocratic audience was certain to
follow,—as the sequel proved.

He knew that because Pamela was a human being
she might therefore be made interesting; he adopted,
albeit unconsciously, the Terentian motto that nothing human should be alien from the interests of his
readers. And as the Novel developed, this interest
not only increased in intensity, but ever spread until
it depicted with truth and sympathy all sorts and
conditions of men. The typical novelist to-day prefers to leave the beaten highway and go into the
by-ways for his characters; his interest is with the
humble of the earth, the outcast and alien, the under
dog in the social struggle. It has become well-nigh
a fashion, a fad, to deal with these picturesque and

once unexploited elements of the human passion-play.

This interest does not stop even at man; influenced by modern conceptions of life, it overleaps the line of old supposed to be impassable, and now includes the lower order of living things: animals have come into their own and a Kipling or a London gives us the psychology of brutekind as it has never been drawn before—from the view-point of the animal himself. Our little brothers of the air, the forest and the field are depicted in such wise that the world returns to a feeling which swelled the heart of St. Francis centuries ago, as he looked upon the birds he loved and thus addressed them:

" And he entered the field and began to preach to the birds which were on the ground; and suddenly those which were in the trees came to him and as many as there were they all stood quietly until Saint Francis had done preaching; and even then they did not depart until such time as he had given them his blessing; and St. Francis, moving among them, touched them with his cape, but not one moved."

It is because this modern form of fiction upon which we fix the name Novel to indicate its new features has seized the idea of personality, has stood for truth and grown ever more democratic, that it has attained to the immense power which marks it at the present time. It is justified by historical facts; it has become that literary form most closely revealing the contours of life, most expressive of its average experience, most sympathetic to its heart-throb. The thought should prevent us from regarding it as merely the syllabub of the literary feast, a kind of after-dinner condiment. It is not necessary to assume the total depravity of current taste, in order to account for the tyranny of this latest-born child of fiction. In the study of individual writers and developing schools and tendencies, it will be well to keep in mind these underlying principles of growth: personality, truth and democracy; a conception sure to provide the story-maker with a new function, a new ideal. The distinguished French critic Brunetière has said: " The novelist in reality is nothing more than a witness whose evidence should rival that of the historian in precision and trust-worthiness. We look to him to teach us literally to see. We read his novels merely with a view to finding out in them those aspects of existence which escape us, owing to the very hurry and stir of life, an attitude we express by saying that for a novel to be recognized as such, it must offer an historical or documentary value, a value precise and deter-mined, particular and local, and as well, a general and lasting psychologic value or significance."

It may be added, that while in the middle eighteenth century the novel-writing was tentative and hardly more than an avocation, at the end of the nineteenth, it had become a fine art and a profession. It did

not occur to Richardson, serious-minded man that
he was, that he was formulating a new art canon
for fiction.   Indeed, the English author takes himself less and less seriously as we go back in time.
It was bad form to be literary when Voltaire visited
Congreve and found a fine gentleman where he
sought a writer of genius: complaining therefore
that fine gentlemen came cheap in Paris; what he
wished to see was the creator of the great comedies.
In the same fashion, we find Horace Walpole, who
dabbled in letters all his days and made it really
his chief interest, systematically underrating the professional writers of his day, to laud a brilliant amateur who like himself desired the plaudits of the
game without obeying its exact rules.   He looked
askance at the fiction-makers Richardson and Fielding, because they did not move in the polite circles
frequented by himself.

The same key is struck by lively Fanny Burney
in reporting a meeting with a languishing lady of
fashion who had perpetrated a piece of fiction with
the alarming title of " The Mausoleum of Julia ":
" My sister intends, said Lady Say and Sele, to
print her Mausoleum, just for her own friends and
acquaintances."

" Yes? said Lady Hawke, I have never . printed
yet."

And a little later, the same spirit is exhibited by
Jane Austen when Madame de Sévigné sought her:

Miss Austen suppressed the story-maker, wishing
to be taken first of all for what she was: a country
gentlewoman of unexceptionable connections. Even
Walter Scott and Byron plainly exhibit this dislike
to be reckoned as paid writers, men whose support
came by the pen. In short, literary professionalism
reflected on gentility. We have changed all that
with a vengeance and can hardly understand the
earlier sentiment; but this change of attitude has
carried with it inevitably the artistic advancement
of modern fiction. For if anything is certain it is
that only professional skill can be relied upon to
perfect an art form. The amateur may possess gift,
even genius; but we must look to the professional
for technique.

One other influence, hardly less effective in molding
the Novel than those already touched upon, is found
in the increasing importance of woman as a central
factor in society; indeed, holding the key to the
social situation. The drama of our time, in so frequently making woman the protagonist of the piece,
testifies, as does fiction, to this significant fact:
woman, in the social and economic readjustment that
has come to her, or better, which she is still under-
going, has become so much more dominant in her
social relations, that any form of literature truthfully mirroring the society of the modern world must
regard her as of potent efficiency. And this is so
quite apart from the consideration that women make

up to-day the novelist's largest audience, and that, moreover, the woman writer of fiction is in numbers and popularity a rival of men.

It would scarcely be too much to see a unifying principle in the evolution of the modern Novel, in the fact that the first example in the literature was Pamela, the study of a woman, while in representative latter-day studies like " Tess of the D'Urbervilles," " The House of Mirth," " Trilby " and " The Testing of Diana Mallory " we again have studies of women; the purpose alike in time past or present being to fix the attention upon a human being whose fate is sensitively, subtly operative for good or ill upon a society at large. It is no accident then, that woman is so often the central figure of fiction: it means more than that, love being the solar passion of the race, she naturally is involved. Rather does it mean fiction's recognition of her as the creature of the social biologist, exercising her ancient function amidst all the changes and shifting ideas of successive generations. Whatever her superficial changes under the urge of the time-spirit, Woman, to a thoughtful eye, sits like the Sphinx above the drifting sands, silent, secret, powerful and obscure, bent only on her great purposive errand whose end is the bringing forth of that Overman who shall rule the world. With her immense biologic mission, seemingly at war with her individual career, and destructive apparently of that emancipation which is the present dream of her champions, what a type, what a motive this for fiction, and in what a manifold and stimulating way is the Novel awakening to its high privilege to deal with such material.   In this view, having these wider implications in mind, the rôle of woman in fiction, so far from waning, is but just begun.

This survey of historical facts and marshaling of a few important principles has prepared us, it may be hoped, for a clearer comprehension of the developmental details that follow.   It is a complex growth, but one vastly interesting and, after all, explained by a few, great substructural principles: the belief in personality, democratic feeling, a love for truth in art, and a realization of the power of modern Woman. The Novel is thus an expression and epitome of the society which gave it birth.

CHAPTER II

EIGHTEENTH CENTURY BEGINNINGS:
RICHARDSON

THERE is some significance in the fact that Samuel Richardson, founder of the modern novel, was so squarely a middle-class citizen of London town. Since the form he founded was, as we have seen, democratic in its original motive and subsequent development, it was fitting that the first shaper of the form should have sympathies not too exclusively aristocratic: should have been willing to draw upon the backstairs history of the servants' hall for his first heroine.

To be sure, Mr. Richardson had the not uncommon failing of the humble-born: he desired above all, and attempted too much, to depict the manners of the great; he had naïve aristocratical leanings which account for his uncertain tread when he would move with ease among the boudoirs of Mayfair. Nevertheless, in the honest heart of him, as his earliest novel forever proves, he felt for the woes of those social underlings who, as we have long since learned, have their microcosm faithfully reflecting the greater world they serve, and he did his best work in that intimate portrayal of the feminine heart, which is not of a class but typically human; he knew Clarissa Harlowe quite as well as he did Pamela; both were of interest because they were women. That acute contemporary, Lady Mary Wortley Montagu, severely reprimands Richardson for his vulgar lapses in painting polite society and the high life he so imperfectly knew; yet in the very breath that she condemns " Clarissa Harlowe " as " most miserable stuff," confesses that " she was such an old fool as to weep over " it " like any milkmaid of sixteen over the ballad of the Lady's Fall "—the handsomest kind of a compliment under the circumstances. And with the same charming inconsistency, she declares on the appearance of " Sir Charles Grandison " that she heartily despises Richardson, yet eagerly reads him— " nay, sobs over his works in the most scandalous manner."

Richardson was the son of a carpenter and himself a respected printer, who by cannily marrying the daughter of the man to whom he was apprenticed, and by diligence in his vocation, rose to prosperity, so that by 1754 he became Master of The Stationers' Company and King's Printer, doing besides an excellent printing business.

As a boy he had relieved the dumb anguish of serving maids by the penning of their love letters; he seemed to have a knack at this vicarious manner of love-making and when in the full maturity of fifty years, certain London publishers requested him to write for them a narrative which might stand as a model letter writer from which country readers should know the right tone, his early practice stood him in good stead. Using the epistolary form into which he was to throw all his fiction, he produced " Pamela," the first novel of analysis, in contrast with the tale of adventure, of the English tongue. It is worth remarking that Richardson wrote this story at an age when many novelists have well-nigh completed their work; even as Defoe published his masterpiece, " Robinson Crusoe," at fifty-eight. But such forms as drama and fiction are the very ones where ripe maturity, a long and varied experience with the world and a trained hand in the technique of the craft, go for their full value. A study of the chronology of novel-making will show that more acknowledged masterpieces were written after forty than before. Beside the eighteenth century examples one places George Eliot, who wrote no fiction until she had nearly reached the alleged dead-line of mental activity: Browning with his greatest poem, " The Ring and the Book," published in his forty-eighth year; Du Maurier turning to fiction at sixty, and De Morgan still later. Fame came to Richardson then late in life, and never man enjoyed it more. Ladies with literary leanings (and the kind is independent of periods) used to drop into his place beyond Temple Bar—for he was a bookseller

as well as printer, and printed and sold his own
wares—to finger his volumes and have a chat about
poor Pamela or the naughty Lovelace or impeccable
Grandison. For how, in sooth, could they keep away
or avoid talking shop when they were bursting with
the books just read?

And much, too, did Richardson enjoy the prosperity his stories, as well as other ventures, brought
him, so that he might move out Hammersmith way
where William Morris and Cobden Sanderson have
lived in our day, and have a fine house wherein to
receive those same lady callers, who came in increasing flocks to his impromptu court where sat the
prim, cherub-faced, elderly little printer. It is all
very quaint, like a Watteau painting or a bit of
Dresden china, as we look back upon it through the
time-mists of a century and a half.

In spite of its slow movement, the monotony of
the letter form and the terribly utilitarian nature
of its morals, " Pamela " has the essentials of interesting fiction; its heroine is placed in a plausible
situation, she is herself life-like and her struggles
are narrated with a sympathetic insight into the
human heart—or better, the female heart. The gist
of a plot so simple can be stated in few words:
Mr. B., the son of a lady who has benefited Pamela
Andrews, a serving maid, tries to conquer her virtue
while she resists all his attempts—including an abduction, Richardson's favorite device—and as a re-

ward of her chastity, he condescends to marry her, to her very great gratitude and delight. The English Novel started out with a flourish of trumpets as to its moral purpose; latter-day criticism may take sides for or against the novel-with-a-purpose, but that Richardson justified his fiction writing upon moral grounds and upon those alone is shown in the descriptive title-page of the tale, too prolix to be often recalled and a good sample in its long-windedness of the past compared with the terse brevity of the present in this matter: " Published in order to cultivate the principles of virtue and religion in the mind of youth of both sexes "; the author of " Sanford and Merton " has here his literary progenitor. The sub-title, " or Virtue Rewarded," also indicates the homiletic nature of the book. And since the one valid criticism against all didactic aims in story-telling is that it is dull, Richardson, it will be appreciated, ran a mighty risk. But this he was able to escape because of the genuine human interest of his tales and the skill he displayed with psychologic analysis rather than the march of events. The close-knit, organic development of the best of our modern fiction is lacking; leisurely and lax seems the movement. Modern editions of " Pamela " and " Clarissa Harlowe " are in the way of vigorous cutting for purposes of condensation. Scott seems swift and brief when set beside Richardson. Yet the slow convolutions and involutions serve to acquaint us intimately with the characters; dwelling with them longer, we come to know them better.

It is a fault in the construction of the story that instead of making Pamela's successful marriage the natural climax and close of the work, the author effects it long before the novel is finished and then tries to hold the interest by telling of the honeymoon trip in Italy, her cool reception by her husband's family, involving various subterfuges and difficulties, and the gradual moral reform she was able to bring about in her spouse. It must be conceded to him that some capital scenes are the result of this post-hymeneal treatment; that, to illustrate, where the haughty sister of Pamela's husband calls on the woman she believes to be her husband's mistress. Yet there is an effect of anti-climax; the main excitement—getting Pamela honestly wedded—is over. But we must not forget the moral purpose: Mr. B.'s spiritual regeneration has to be portrayed before our very eyes, he must be changed from a rake into a model husband; and with Richardson, that means plenty of elbow-room. There is, too, something prophetic in this giving of ample space to post-marital life; it paves the way for much latter-day probing of the marriage misery.

The picture of Mr. B. and Pamela's attitude towards him is full of irony for the modern reader; here is a man who does all in his power to ruin her and, finding her adamant, at last decides to do the next best thing—secure her by marriage. And instead of valuing him accordingly, Pamela, with a kind of spaniel-like fawning, accepts his august hand. It must be confessed that with Pamela (that is, with Richardson), virtue is a market commodity for sale to the highest bidder, and this scene of barter and sale is an all-unconscious revelation of the low standard of sex ethics which obtained at the time. The suggestion by Sidney Lanier that the sub-title should be: "or Vice Rewarded," "since the rascal Mr. B. it is who gets the prize rather than Pamela," has its pertinency from our later and more enlightened view. But such was the eighteenth century. The exposure of an earlier time is one of the benefits of literature, always a sort of ethical barometer of an age—all the more trustworthy in reporting spiritual ideals because it has no intention of doing so.

That Richardson succeeds in making Mr. B. tolerable, not to say likable, is a proof of his power; that the reader really grows fond of his heroine—especially perhaps in her daughterly devotion to her humble family—speaks volumes for his grasp of human nature and helps us to understand the effect of the story upon contemporaneous readers. That effect was indeed remarkable. Lady Mary, to quote her again, testifies that the book "met with very extraordinary (and I think undeserved) success. It has been translated into French and Italian; it was all the fashion at Paris and Versailles and is still the joy of the chambermaids of all nations." Again she writes, " it has been translated into more languages than any modern performances I ever heard of." A French dramatic version of it under the same title appeared three years after the publication of the novel and a little later Voltaire in his " Nanine" used the same motif. Lady Mary's reference to chambermaids is significant; it points to the new sympathy on the part of the novelist and the consequent new audience which the modern Novel was to command; literally, all classes and conditions of mankind were to become its patrons; and as one result, the author, gaining his hundreds of thousands of readers, was to free himself forever of the aristocratic Patron, at whose door once on a time, he very humbly and hungrily knelt for favor. To-day, the Patron is hydra-headed; demos rules in literature as in life.

The sentimentality of this pioneer novel which now seems old-fashioned and even absurd, expressed Queen Anne's day. " Sensibility," as it was called, was a favorite idea in letters, much affected, and later a kind of cult. A generation after Pamela, in Mackenzie's " Man of Feeling," weeping is unrestrained in English fiction; the hero of that lachrymose tale incurred all the dangers of influenza because of his inveterate tendency toward damp emotional effects; he was perpetually dissolving in

" showers of tears." In fact, our novelists down
to the memory of living man gave way to their
feelings with far more abandon than is true of
the present repressive period. One who reads Dickens' " Nicholas Nickleby " with this in mind, will
perhaps be surprised to find how often the hero
frankly indulges his grief; he cries with a freedom
that suggests a trait inherited from his mother of
moist memory. No doubt, there was abuse of this
" sensibility " in earlier fiction: but Richardson was
comparatively innocuous in his practice, and Coleridge, having the whole sentimental tendency in view,
seems rather too severe when he declared that " all
the evil achieved by Hobbes and the whole school
of materialists will appear inconsiderable if it be compared with the mischief effected and occasioned by
the sentimental philosophy of Sterne and his numerous imitators." The same tendency had its vogue
on both the English and French stage—the *Comédie
larmoyante* of the latter being vastly affected in London and receiving in the next generation the good-
natured satiric shafts of Goldsmith. It may be possible that at the present time, when the stoicism of
the Red Indian in inhibiting expression seems to be
an Anglo-Saxon ideal, we have reacted too far from
the gush and the fervor of our forefathers. In
any case, to Richardson belongs whatever of merit
there may be in first sounding the new sentimental
note.

Pope declared that " Pamela," was as good as twenty sermons—an innocently malignant remark, to be sure, which cuts both ways! And plump, placid Mr. Richardson established warm epistolary relations with many excellent if too emotional ladies, who opened a correspondence with him concerning the conductment of this and the following novels and strove to deflect the course thereof to soothe their lacerated feelings. What novelist to-day would not appreciate an audience that would take him *au grand sérieux* in this fashion! What higher compliment than for your correspondent—and a lady at that—to state that in the way of ministering to her personal comfort, Pamela must marry and Clarissa must not die! Richardson carried on a voluminous letter-writing in life even as in literature, and the curled darlings of latter-day letters may well look to their laurels in recalling him. A certain Mme. Belfair, for example, desires to look upon the author of those wonderful tales, yet modestly shrinks from being seen herself. She therefore implores that he will walk at an hour named in St. James Park—and this is the novelist's reply:

" I go through the Park once or twice a week to my little retirement; but I will for a week together be in it, every day three or four hours, till you tell me you have seen a person who answers to this description, namely, short—rather plump—fair wig, lightish cloth coat, all black besides; one hand gen-

erally in his bosom, the other a cane in it, which
he leans upon under the skirts of his coat; . . .
looking directly fore-right as passers-by would imagine, but observing all that stirs on either hand
of him; hardly ever turning back; of a light brown
complexion, smoothish faced and ruddy cheeked, looking about sixty-five; a regular, even pace, a gray
eye, sometimes lively—very lively if he have hope
of seeing a lady whom he loves and honors!"

Such innocent philandering is delicious; there is
a flavor to it that presages the "Personals" in
a New York newspaper. "Was ever lady in such
humor wooed?" or shall we say it is the novelist,
not the lady, who is besieged!

"Pamela" ran through five editions within a year
of its appearance, which was a conspicuous success
in the days of an audience so limited when compared
with the vast reading public of later times. The
smug little bookseller must have been greatly pleased
by the good fortune attending his first venture into
a new field, especially since he essayed it so late in
life and almost by accident. His motive had been in
a sense practical; for his publishers had requested
him to write a book "on the useful concerns of
life"—and that he had done so, he might have
learned any Sunday in church, for divines did not
hesitate to say a kind word from the pulpit about
so unexceptionable a work.

One of the things Richardson had triumphantly

demonstrated by his first story was that a very slight texture of plot can suffice for a long, not to say too long, piece of fiction, if only a free hand be given the story-teller in the way of depicting the intuitions and emotions of human beings; dealing with their mind states rather than, or quite as much as, their actions. This was the modern note, and very speedily was the lesson learned; the time was apt for it. From 1742, the date of " Pamela," to 1765 is but a quarter century; yet within those narrow time-limits the English Novel, through the labors of Richardson and Fielding, Smollett, Sterne and Goldsmith, can be said to have had its birth and growth to a lusty manhood and to have defined once and for all the mold of this new and potent form of prose art. By 1773 a critic speaks of the " novel-writing age "; and a dozen years later, in 1785, novels are so common that we hear of the press " groaning beneath their weight,"—which sounds like the twentieth century. And it was all started by the little printer; to him the praise. He received it in full measure; here and there, of course, a dissident voice was heard, one, that of Fielding, to be very vocal later; but mostly they were drowned in the chorus of adulation. Richardson had done a new thing and reaped an immediate reward; and—as seldom happens, with quick recognition—it was to be a permanent reward as well, for he changed the history of English literature.

One would have expected him to produce another
novel post-haste, following up his maiden victory
before it could be forgotten, after the modern manner.   But those were leisured days and it was half
a dozen years before " Clarissa Harlowe " was
given to the public.   Richardson had begun by taking a heroine out of low life; he now drew one from
genteel middle class life; as he was in " Sir Charles
Grandison," the third and last of his fictions, to
depict a hero in the upper class life of England.
In Clarissa again, plot was secondary, analysis, sentiment, the exhibition of the female heart under
stress of sorrow, this was everything.   Clarissa's
hand is sought by an unattractive suitor; she rebels—
a social crime in the eighteenth century; whereat, her
whole family turn against her—father, mother, sister,
brothers, uncles and aunts—and, wooed by Lovelace,
a dashing rake who is in love with her according to
his lights, but by no means intends honorable matri-
mony, she flies with him in a chariot and four, to find
herself in a most anomalous position, and so dies
broken-hearted; to be followed in her fate by Lovelace, who is represented as a man whose loose principles are in conflict with a nature which is far from
being utterly bad.   The narrative is mainly developed through letters exchanged between Clarissa and
her friend, Miss Howe.   There can hardly be a more
striking testimony to the leisure enjoyed by the
eighteenth century than that society was not bored

by a story the length of which seems almost in-
terminable to the reader to-day. The slow movement is sufficient to preclude its present prosperity.
It is safe to say that Richardson is but little read
now; read much less than his great contemporary,
Fielding. And apparently it is his bulk rather than
his want of human interest or his antiquated manner
that explains the fact. The instinct to-day is
against fiction that is slow and tortuous in its on-
ward course; at least so it seemed until Mr. De
Morgan returned in his delightful volumes to the
method of the past. Those are pertinent words
of the distinguished Spanish novelist, Valdes: " An
author who wishes to be read not only in his life,
but after his death (and the author who does not
wish this should lay aside his pen), cannot shut
his eyes, when unblinded by vanity, to the fact that
not only is it necessary to be interesting to save
himself from oblivion, but the story must not be a
very long one. The world contains so many great and
beautiful works that it requires a long life to read
them all. To ask the public, always anxious for
novelty, to read a production of inordinate length,
when so many others are demanding attention, seems
to me useless and ridiculous. . . . The most noteworthy instance of what I say is seen in the cele-
brated English novelist, Richardson, who, in spite
of his admirable genius and exquisite sensibility and
perspicuity, added to the fact of his being the father

of the modern Novel, is scarcely read nowadays, at least in Latin countries. Given the indisputable beauties of his works, this can only be due to their extreme length. And the proof of this, that in France and Spain, to encourage the taste for them, the most interesting parts have been extracted and published in editions and compendiums."

This is suggestive, coming from one who speaks by the book. Who, in truth, reads epics now—save in the enforced study of school and college? Will not Browning's larger works—like "The Ring and the Book "—suffer disastrously with the passing of time because of a lack of continence, of a failure to realize that since life is short, art should not be too long? It may be, too, that Richardson, newly handling the sentiment which during the following generation was to become such a marked trait of imaginative letters, revelled in it to an extent unpalatable to our taste; "rubbing our noses," as Leslie Stephen puts it, "in all her (Clarissa's) agony,"—the tendency to overdo a new thing, not to be resisted in his case. But with all concessions to length and sentimentality, criticism from that day to this has been at one in agreeing that here is not only Richardson's best book but a truly great Novel. Certainly one who patiently submits to a ruminant reading of the story, will find that when at last the long-deferred climax is reached and the awed and penitent Lovelace describes the death-bed

moments of the girl he has ruined, the scene has
a great moving power. Allowing for differences of
taste and time, the vogue of the Novel in Richardson's day can easily be understood, and through all
the stiffness, the stilted effect of manner and speech,
and the stifling conventions of the *entourage*, a sweet
and charming young woman in very piteous distress
emerges to live in affectionate memory. After all,
no poor ideal of womanhood is pictured in Clarissa.
She is one of the heroines who are unforgettable,
dear. Mr. Howells, with his stern insistence on truth
in characterization, declares that she is " as freshly
modern as any girl of yesterday or to-morrow.
' Clarissa Harlowe,' in spite of her eighteenth century costume and keeping, remains a masterpiece in
the portraiture of that ever-womanly which is of all
times and places."

Lovelace, too, whose name has become a synonym
for the fine gentleman betrayer, is drawn in a way
to make him sympathetic and creditable; he is far
from being a stock figure of villainy. And the
minor figures are often enjoyable; the friendship
of Clarissa with Miss Howe, a young woman of
excellent good sense and seemingly quite devoid of
the ultra-sentiment of her time, preludes that between Diana and her "Tony" in Meredith's great
novel. As a general picture of the society of the
period, the book is full of illuminations and side-
lights; of course, the whole action is set on a stage

that bespeaks Richardson's narrow, middle class morality, his worship of rank, his belief that worldly goods are the reward of well-doing.

As for the contemporaneous public, it wept and praised and went with fevered blood because of this fiction. We have heard how women of sentiment in London town welcomed the book and the opportunity it offered for unrestrained tears. But it was the same abroad; as Ik Marvel has it, Rousseau and Diderot over in France, philosophers as they professed to be, "blubbered their admiring thanks for ' Clarissa Harlowe.' " Similarly, at a later day we find caustic critics like Jeffrey and Macaulay writing to Dickens to tell how they had cried over the death of Little Nell—a scene the critical to-day are likely to stigmatize as one of the few examples of pathos overdone to be found in the works of that master. It is scarcely too much to say that the outcome of no novel in the English tongue was watched with such bated breath as was that of " Clarissa Harlowe " while the eight successive books were being issued.

Richardson chose to bask for another half dozen years in the fame of his second novel, before turning in 1754 to his final attempt, " Sir Charles Grandison," wherein it was his purpose to depict the perfect pattern of a gentleman, " armed at all points " of social and moral behavior. We must bear in mind that when " Clarissa " was published he was

sixty years of age and to be pardoned if he did
not emulate so many novel-makers of these brisker
mercantile times and turn off a story or so a year.

By common confession, this is the poorest of
his three fictions.   In the first place, we are asked
to move more steadily in the aristocratic atmosphere
where the novelist did not breathe to best advantage.
Again, Richardson was an adept in drawing women
rather than men and hence was self-doomed in elect-
ing a masculine protagonist.   He is also off his
proper ground in laying part of the action in Italy.
His beau ideal, Grandison, turns out the most impossible prig in English literature.   He is as insufferable as that later prig, Meredith's Sir Willoughby in "The Egotist," with the difference that
the author does not know it, and that you do not believe in him for a moment; whereas Meredith's creation is appallingly true, a sort of simulacrum of us
all.   The best of the story is in its portrayal of wom-
ankind; in particular, Sir Charles' two loves, the English Harriet Byron and the Italian Clementina, the
last of whom is enamored of him, but separated by
religious differences.   Both are alive and though
suffering in the reader's estimation because of their
devotion to such a stick as Grandison, nevertheless
touch our interest to the quick.   The scene in which
Grandison returns to Italy to see Clementina, whose
reason, it is feared, is threatened because of her
grief over his loss, is genuinely effective and affecting.

The mellifluous sentimentality, too, of the novelist seems to come to a climax in this book; justifying Taine's satiric remark that "these phrases should be accompanied by a mandolin." The moral tag is infallibly supplied, as in all Richardson's tales—though perhaps here with an effect of crescendo. We are still long years from that conception of art which holds that a beautiful thing may be allowed to speak for itself and need not be moraled down our throats like a physician's prescription. Yet Fielding had already, as we shall see, struck a wholesome note of satiric fun. The plot is slight and centers in an abduction which, by the time it is used in the third novel, begins to pall as a device and to suggest paucity of invention. The novel has the prime merit of brevity; it is much shorter than "Clarissa Harlowe," but long enough, in all conscience, Harriet being blessed with the gift of gab, like all Richardson's heroines. "She follows the maxim of Clarissa," says Lady Mary with telling humor, "of declaring all she thinks to all the people she sees without reflecting that in this mortal state of imperfection, fig-leaves are as necessary for our minds as our bodies." It is significant that this brilliant contemporary is very hard on Richardson's characterization of women in this volume (which she says "sinks horribly"), whereas never a word has she to say in condemnation of the hero, who to the present critical eye seems the biggest blot on the

performance. How can we join the chorus of praise
led by Harriet, now her ladyship and his loving
spouse, when it chants: " But could he be otherwise
than the best of husbands who was the most dutiful
of sons, who is the most affectionate of brothers,
the most faithful of friends, who is good upon principle in every relation in life?" Lady Mary is
also extremely severe on the novelist's attempt to
paint Italy; when he talks of it, says she, "it is
plain he is no better acquainted with it than he is
with the Kingdom of Mancomingo." It is probable
that Richardson could not say more for his Italian
knowledge than did old Roger Ascham of Archery
fame, when he declared: "I was once in Italy, but
I thank God my stay there was only nine days."
" Sir Charles Grandison" has also the substantial
advantage of ending well: that is, if to marry Sir
Charles can be so regarded, and certainly Harriet
deemed it desirable.

It is pleasant to think of Richardson, now well
into the sixties, amiable, plump and prosperous, surrounded for the remainder of his days—he was to
die seven years later at the ripe age of seventy-five—
by a bevy of admiring women, who, whether literary
or merely human, gave this particular author that
warm and convincing proof of popularity which,
to most, is worth a good deal of chilly posthumous
fame which a man is not there to enjoy. Looking
at his work retrospectively, one sees that it must

always have authority, even if it fall deadly dull upon our ears to-day; for nothing can take away from him the distinction of originating that kind of fiction which, now well along towards its second century of existence, is still popular and powerful. Richardson had no model; he shaped a form for himself. Fielding, a greater genius, threw his fiction into a mold cast by earlier writers; moreover, he received his direct impulse away from the drama and towards the novel from Richardson himself.

The author of " Pamela " demonstrated once and for all the interest that lies in a sympathetic and truthful representation of character in contrast with that interest in incident for its own sake which means the subordination of character, so that the persons become mere subsidiary counters in the game. And he exhibited such a knowledge of the subtler phases of the nooks and crannies of woman's heart, as to be hailed as past-master down to the present day by a whole school of analysts and psychologues; for may it not be said that it is the popular distinction of the nineteenth century fiction to place woman in the pivotal position in that social complex which it is the business of the Novel to represent? Do not our fiction and drama to-day—the drama a belated ally of the Novel in this and other regards— find in the delineation of the eternal feminine under new conditions of our time, its chief, its most significant motif? If so, a special gratitude is due

the placid little **Mr. Richardson** with his **Pamelas,
Clarissas** and **Harriets.** He found fiction unwritten
so far as the chronicles of contemporary society were
concerned, and left it in such shape that it was
recognized as the natural quarry of all who would
paint manners; a field to be worked by Jane Austen,
Dickens and Thackeray, Trollope and George Eliot,
and a modern army of latter and lesser students of
life. His faults were in part merely a reflection of
his time; its low-pitched morality, its etiquette which
often seems so absurd. Partly it was his own, too;
for he utterly lacked humor (save where unconscious) and never grasped the great truth that in
literary art the half is often more than the whole;
The Terentian *ne quid nimis* had evidently not been
taken to heart by Samuel Richardson, Esquire, of
Hammersmith, author of "Clarissa Harlowe" in
eight volumes, and Printer to the Queen. Again and
again one of Clarissa's bursts of emotion under the
tantalizing treatment of her seducer loses its effect
because another burst succeeds before we (and she)
have recovered from the first one. He strives to
give us the broken rhythm of life (therein showing
his affinity with the latter day realists) instead of
that higher and harder thing—the more perfect
rhythm of art; not so much the truth (which cannot be literally given) as that seeming-true which
is the aim and object of the artistic representation.
Hence the necessity of what Brunetière calls in an

admirable phrase, the true function of the novel—
" to be an abridged representation of life." Construction in the modern sense Richardson had not
studied, naturally enough, and was innocent of the
fineness of method and the sure-handed touches of
later technique. And there is a kind of drawing-
room atmosphere in his books, a lack of ozone which
makes Fielding with all his open-air coarseness a
relief. But judged in the setting of his time, this
writer did a wonderful thing not only as the Father
of the Modern Novel but one of the few authors
in the whole range of fiction who holds his conspicuous place amid shifting literary modes and
fashions, because he built upon the surest of all
foundations—the social instinct, and the human
heart.

If the use of the realistic method alone denoted
the Novel, Defoe, not Richardson, might be called its
begetter. " Robinson Crusoe," more than twenty
years before " Pamela," would occupy the primate
position, to say nothing of Swift's " Gulliver's Travels," antedating Richardson's first story by some
fifteen years. Certainly the observational method,
the love of detail, the grave narrative of imagined
fact (if the bull be permitted) are in this earlier
book in full force. But " Robinson Crusoe " is not
a rival because it does not study man-in-society;
never was a story that depended less upon this kind
of interest. The position of Crusoe on his desert

isle is so eminently unsocial that he welcomes the
black man Friday and quivers at the human quality
in the famed footprints in the sand.   As for Swift's
chef d'œuvre, it is a fairy-tale with a grimly realistic manner and a savage satiric intention.   To
speak of either of these fictions as novels is an
example of the prevalent careless nomenclature.   Between them and "Pamela" there yawns a chasm.
Moreover, "Crusoe" is a frankly picaresque tale belonging to the elder line of romantic fiction, where
incident and action and all the thrilling haps of Ad-
venture-land furnish the basis of appeal rather than
character analysis or a study of social relations.
The personality of Crusoe is not advanced a whit by
his wonderful experiences; he is done entirely from
the outside.

Richardson, therefore, marks the beginning of the
modern form.   But that the objection to Defoe as
the true and only begetter of the Novel lies in his
failure, in his greatest story, to center the interest
in man as part of the social order and as human
soul, is shown by the fact that his less known, but
remarkable, story "Moll Flanders," picaresque as it
is and depicting the life of a female criminal, has
yet considerable character study and gets no small
part of its appeal for a present-day reader from the
minute description of the fall and final reform of the
degenerate woman.   It is comparatively crude in
characterization, but psychological value is not en-

tirely lacking. However, with Richardson it is almost all. It was of the nature of his genius to make
psychology paramount: just there is found his
modernity. Defoe and Swift may be said to have
added some slight interest in analysis pointing towards the psychologic method, which was to find full
expression in Samuel Richardson.

CHAPTER III

EIGHTEENTH CENTURY BEGINNINGS: FIELDING

It is interesting to ask if Henry Fielding, barrister, journalist, tinker of plays and man-about-town, would ever have turned novelist, had it not been for Richardson, his predecessor. So slight, so seemingly accidental, are the incidents which make or mar careers and change the course of literary history. Certain it is that the immediate cause of Fielding's first story was the effect upon him of the fortunes of the virtuous Pamela. A satirist and humorist where Richardson was a somewhat solemn sentimentalist, Fielding was quick to see the weakness, and—more important,—the opportunity for caricature, in such a tale, whose folk harangued about morality and whose avowed motive was a kind of hard-surfaced, carefully calculated honor, for sale to the highest bidder. It was easy to recognize that Pamela was not only good but goody-goody. So Fielding, being thirty-five years of age and of uncertain income—he had before he was thirty squandered his mother's estate,—turned himself, two years after " Pamela " had appeared, to a new field and

concocted the story known to the world of letters as:
" The Adventures of Joseph Andrews and His Friend
Abraham Adams."

This Joseph purports to be the brother of Pamela
(though the denouement reveals him as more gently
born) and is as virtuous in his character of serving-
man as the sister herself; indeed, he outvirtues her.
Fielding waggishly exhibits him in the full exercise
of a highly-starched decorum rebuffing the amatory
attempts of sundry ladies whose assault upon the
citadel of his honor is analogous to that of Mr. B.,—
who naturally becomes Squire Booby in Fielding's
hands—upon the long suffering Pamela. Thus,
Lady Booby, in whose employ Joseph is footman,
after an invitation to him to kiss her which has been
gently but firmly refused, bursts out with: " Can a
boy, a stripling, have the confidence to talk of his
virtue? "

" Madam," says Joseph, " that boy is the brother
of Pamela and would be ashamed that the chastity of
his family, which is preserved in her, should be stained
in him."

The chance for fun is palpable here. But something unexpected happened: what was begun as burlesque, almost horse-play, began to pass from the
key of shallow, lively satire, broadening and deepening into a finer tone of truth. In a few chapters,
by the time the writer had got such an inimitable
personage as Parson Adams before the reader, it was

seen that the book was to be more than a *jeu d'esprit*: rather, the work of a master of characterization. In short, Joseph Andrews started out ostensibly to poke good-natured ridicule at sentimental Mr. Richardson: it ended by furnishing contemporary London and all subsequent readers with a notable example of the novel of mingled character and incident, entertaining alike for its lively episodes and its broadly genial delineation of types of the time. And so he soon had the town laughing with him at his broad comedy.

In every respect Fielding made a sharp contrast with Richardson. He was gentle-born, distinguished and fashionable in his connections: the son of younger sons, impecunious, generous, of strong often unregulated passions,—what the world calls a good fellow, a man's man—albeit his affairs with the fair sex were numerous. He knew high society when he choose to depict it: his education compared with Richardson's was liberal and he based his style of fiction upon models which the past supplied, whereas Richardson had no models, blazed his own trail. Fielding's literary ancestry looks back to " Gil Blas " and " Don Quixote," and in English to " Robinson Crusoe." In other words, his type, however much he departs from it, is the picturesque story of adventure. He announced, in fact, on his title-page that he wrote " in imitation of the manner of Cervantes."

Again, his was a genius for comedy, where Rich-

ardson, as we have seen, was a psychologist. The
cleansing effect of wholesome laughter and an outdoor
gust of hale west wind is offered by him, and with it
go the rude, coarse things to be found in Nature
who is nevertheless in her influence so salutary, so
necessary, in truth, to our intellectual and moral
health. Here then was a sort of fiction at many removes from the slow, analytic studies of Richardson:
buoyant, objective, giving far more play to action
and incident, uniting in most agreeable proportions
the twin interests of character and event. The very
title of this first book is significant. We are invited
to be present at a delineation of two men,—but these
men are displayed in a series of adventures. Unquestionably, the psychology is simpler, cruder, more
elementary than that of Richardson. Dr. Johnson,
who much preferred the author of " Pamela " to the
author of " Tom Jones " and said so in the hammer-
and-tongs style for which he is famous, declared to
Bozzy that " there is all the difference in the world
between characters of nature and characters of
manners: and there is the difference between the characters of Fielding and those of Richardson.
Characters of manners are very entertaining; but
they are to be understood by a more superficial
observer than characters of nature, where a man must
dive into the recesses of the human heart."

And although we may share Boswell's feeling that
Johnson estimated the compositions of Richardson

too highly and that he had an unreasonable prejudice against Fielding—since he was a man of magnificent biases—yet we may grant that the critic-god made a sound distinction here, that Fielding's method is inevitably more external and shallow than that of an analyst proper like Richardson; no doubt to the great joy of many weary folk who go to novels for the rest and refreshment they give, rather than for their thought-evoking value.

The contrast between these novelists is maintained, too, in the matter of style: Fielding walks with the easy undress of a gentleman: Richardson sits somewhat stiff and pragmatical, carefully arrayed in full-bottomed wig, and knee breeches, delivering a lecture from his garden chair. Fielding is a master of that colloquial manner afterwards handled with such success by Thackeray: a manner " good alike for grave or gay," and making this early fiction-maker enjoyable. Quite apart from our relish of his vivid portrayals of life, we like his wayside chatting. For another difference: there is no moral motto or announcement: the lesson takes care of itself. What unity there is of construction, is found in the fact that certain characters, more or less related, are seen to walk centrally through the narrative: there is little or no plot development in the modern sense and the method (the method of the type) is frankly episodic.

In view of what the Novel was to become in the

nineteenth century, Richardson's way was more modern, and did more to set a seal upon fiction than Fielding's: the Novel to-day is first of all psychologic and serious. And the assertion is safe that all the later development derives from these two kinds written by the two greatest of the eighteenth century pioneers, Richardson and Fielding: on the one hand, character study as a motive, on the other the portrayal of personality surrounded by the external factors of life. The wise combination of the two, gives us that tangle of motive, act and circumstance which makes up human existence.

With regard to the morals of the story, a word may here be said, having all Fielding's fiction in mind. Of the suggestive prurience of much modern novelism, whether French or French-derived, he, Fielding, is quite free: he deals with the sensual relations with a frank acknowledgment of their physical basis. The truth is, the eighteenth century, whether in England or elsewhere, was on a lower plane in this respect than our own time. Fielding, therefore, while he does no affront to essential decency, does offend our taste, our refinement, in dealing with this aspect of life. We have in a true sense become more civilized since 1750: the ape and tiger of Tennyson's poem have receded somewhat in human nature during the last century and a half. The plea that since Fielding was a realist depicting society as it was in his day, his license is legitimate, whereas Richardson was giving a sort of sentimentalized stained-glass picture of it not as it was but, in his opinion, should be,—is a specious one; it is well that in literature, faithful reflector of the ideals of the race, the beast should be allowed to die (as Mr. Howells, himself a staunch realist, has said), simply because it is slowly dying in life itself. Fielding's novels in unexpurgated form are not for household reading to-day: the fact may not be a reflection upon him, but it is surely one to congratulate ourselves upon, since it testifies to social evolution. However, for those whose experience of life is sufficiently broad and tolerant, these novels hold no harm: there is a tonic quality to them.—Even bowdlerization is not to be despised with such an author, when it makes him suitable for the hands of those who otherwise might receive injury from the contact. The critic-sneer at such an idea forgets that good art comes out of sound morality as well as out of sound esthetics. It is pleasant to hear a critic of such standing as Brunetière in his " L'Art et Morale " speak with spiritual clarity upon this subject, so often turned aside with the shrug of impatient scorn.

The episodic character of the story was to be the manner of Fielding in all his fiction. There are detached bits of narrative, stories within stories— witness that dealing with the high comedy figures of Leonora and Bellamine—and the novelist does not bother his head if only he can get his main characters

in motion,—on the road, in a tavern or kitchen
brawl, astride a horse for a cross-country dash after
the hounds. Charles Dickens, whose models were of
the eighteenth century, made similar use of the episode in his early work, as readers of " Pickwick "
may see for themselves.

The first novel was received with acclaim and
stirred up a pretty literary quarrel, for Richardson
and his admiring clique would have been more than
human had they not taken umbrage at so obvious a
satire. Recriminations were hot and many.

Mr. Andrew Lang should give us in a dialogue between dead authors, a meeting in Hades between the
two: it would be worth any climatic risk to be present
and hear what was said; Lady Mary, who may once
more be put on the witness-stand, tells how, being
in residence in Italy, and a box of light literature
from England having arrived at ten o'clock of the
night, she could not but open it and " falling upon
Fielding's works, was fool enough to sit up all night
reading. I think ' Joseph Andrews ' better than his
Foundling "—the reference being, of course, to
" Tom Jones "; a judgment not jumping with that
of posterity, which has declared the other to be his
masterpiece; yet not an opinion to be despised, coming from one of the keenest intellects of the time.
Lady Mary, whose cousin Fielding was, had a clear
eye alike for his literary merits and personal foibles
and faults, but heartily liked him and acted as his

literary mentor in his earlier days; his maiden play was dedicated to her and her interest in him was more than passing.

The Bohemian barrister and literary hack who had made a love-match half a dozen years before and now had a wife and several children to care for, must have been vastly encouraged by the favorable reception of his first essay into fiction; at last, he had found the kind of literature congenial to his talents and likely to secure suitable renown: his metier as an artist of letters was discovered, as we might now choose to express it; he would hardly have taken himself so seriously. It was natural that he should publish the next year a three volume collection of his miscellany, which contained his second novel, " Mr. Jonathan Wild The Great," distinctly the least liked of his four stories, because of its bitter irony, its almost savage tone, the gloom which surrounds the theme, a powerful, full-length portrayal of a famous thief-taker of the period, from his birth to his bad end on a Newgate gallows. Mr. Wild is a sort of foreglimpse of the Sherlock Holmes-Raffles of our own day.

Fielding's wife died this year and it may be that sorrow for her fatal illness was the subjective cause of the tone of this gruesomely attractive piece of fiction; but there is some reason for believing it to be an earlier work than " Joseph Andrews "; it belongs to a more primitive type of story-making, because of its sensational features: its dependence for interest upon the seamy side of aspects of life exhibited like magic lantern slides with little connection, but spectacular effects. The satire of the book is directed at that immoral confusion between greatness and goodness, the rascally Jonathan being pictured in grave mock-heroics as in every way worthy—and the sardonic force at times almost suggests the pen of Dean Swift.

But such work was but a prelude to what was to follow. When the world thinks of Henry Fielding it thinks of " Tom Jones," it is almost as if he had written naught else. " The History of Tom Jones, A Foundling " appeared six years after " Jonathan Wild," the intermediate time (aside from the novel itself) being consumed in editing journals and officiating as a Justice of the Peace: the last a rôle it is a little difficult, in the theater phrase, to see him in. He was two and forty when the book was published: but as he had been at work upon it for a long while (he speaks of the thousands of hours he had been toiling over it), it may be ascribed to that period of a man's growth when he is passing intellectually from youth to early maturity; everything considered, perhaps the best productive period. His health had already begun to break: and he was by no means free of the harassments of debt. Although successful in his former attempt at fiction, novel writing was but an aside with him, after all;

he had not during the previous six years given regular time and attention to literary composition, as a modern story-maker would have done under the stimulus of like encouragement. The eighteenth century audience, it must be borne in mind, was not large enough nor sufficiently eager for an attractive new form of literature, to justify a man of many trades like Fielding in devoting his days steadily to the writing of fiction. There is to the last an effect of the gifted amateur about him; Taine tells the anecdote of his refusal to trouble himself to change a scene in one of his plays, which Garrick begged him to do: " Let them find it out," he said, referring to the audience. And when the scene was hissed, he said to the disconsolate player: " I did not give them credit for it: they have found it out, have they? " In other words, he was knowing to his own poor art, content if only it escaped the public eye. This is some removes from the agonizing over a phrase of a Flaubert.

Like the preceding story, " Tom Jones " has its center of plot in a life history of the foundling who grows into a young manhood that is full of high spirits and escapades: likable always, even if, judged by the straight-laced standards of Richardson, one may not approve. Jones loves Sophia Western, daughter of a typical three-bottle, hunting squire: of course he prefers the little cad Blifil, with his money and position, where poor Tom has neither:

equally of course Sophia (whom the reader heartily
likes, in spite of her name) prefers the handsome
Jones with his blooming complexion and many amatory adventures. And, since we are in the simple-
minded days of fiction when it was the business of
the sensible novelist to make us happy at the close,
the low-born lover, assisted by Squire Allworthy, who
is a *deus ex machina* a trifle too good for human
nature's daily food, gets his girl (in imitation of
Joseph Andrews) and is shown to be close kin to
Allworthy—tra-la-la, tra-la-lee, it is all charmingly simple and easy! The beginners of the English
novel had only a few little tricks in their box in the
way of incident and are for the most part innocent
of plot in the Wilkie Collins sense of the word. The
opinion of Coleridge that the "Oedipus Tyrannus,"
"The Alchemist" and "Tom Jones" are "the three
most perfect plots ever planned" is a curious comment upon his conception of fiction, since few stories
have been more plotless than Fielding's best book.
The fact is, biographical fiction like this is to be
judged by itself, it has its own laws of technique.

The glory of "Tom Jones" is in its episodes, its
crowded canvas, the unfailing verve and variety of
its action: in the fine open-air atmosphere of the
scenes, the sense of the stir of life they convey: most
of all, in an indescribable manliness or humanness
which bespeaks the true comic force—something of
that same comic view that one detects in Shakspere

and Molière and Cervantes. It means an open-eyed
acceptance of life, a realization of its seriousness yet
with the will to take it with a smile: a large tolerancy
which forbids the view conventional or parochial or
aristocratic—in brief, the view limited. There is
this in the book, along with much psychology so
superficial as to seem childish, and much interpretation that makes us feel that the higher possibilities
of men and women are not as yet even dreamed of.
In this novel, Fielding makes fuller use than he had
before of the essay link: the chapters introductory
to the successive books,—and in them, a born essayist, as your master of style is pretty sure to be,
he discourses in the wisest and wittiest way on topics
literary, philosophical or social, having naught to
do with the story in hand, it may be, but highly
welcome for its own sake. This manner of pausing
by the way for general talk about the world in terms
of Me has been used since by Thackeray, with delightful results: but has now become old-fashioned,
because we conceive it to be the novelist's business to
stick close to his story and not obtrude his personality at all. Thackeray displeases a critic like Mr.
James by his postscript harangues about himself as
Showman, putting his puppets into the box and shut-
ting up his booth: fiction is too serious a matter to
be treated so lightly by its makers—to say nothing
of the audience: it is more, much more than mere
fooling and show-business. But to go back to the

eighteenth century is to realize that the novel is being newly shaped, that neither novelist nor novel-reader is yet awake to the higher conception of the genre. So we wax lenient and are glad enough to get these resting-places of chat and charm from Fielding: it may not be war, but it is nevertheless magnificent.

Fielding in this fiction is remarkable for his keen observation of every-day life and character, the average existence in town and country of mankind high and low: he is a truthful reporter, the verisimilitude of the picture is part of its attraction. It is not too much to say that, pictorially, he is the first great English realist of the Novel. For broad comedy presentation he is unsurpassed: as well as for satiric gravity of comment and illustration. It may be questioned, however, whether when he strives to depict the deeper phases of human relations he is so much at home or anything like so happy. There is no more critical test of a novelist than his handling of the love passion. Fielding essays in "Tom Jones" to show the love between two very likable flesh-and-blood young folk: the many mishaps of the twain being but an embroidery upon the accepted fact that the course of true love never did run smooth. There is a certain scene which gives us an interview between Jones and Sophia, following on a stormy one between father and daughter, during which the Squire has struck his child to the ground and left her there with blood and tears streaming down her face. Her disobedience in not accepting the addresses of the unspeakable Blifil is the cause of the somewhat drastic parental treatment. Jones has assured the Squire that he can make Sophia see the error of her ways and has thus secured a moment with her. He finds her just risen from the ground, in the sorry plight already described. Then follows this dialogue:

" ' O, my Sophia, what means this dreadful sight? '

" She looked softly at him for a moment before she spoke, and then said:

" ' Mr. Jones, for Heaven's sake, how came you here? Leave me, I beseech you, this moment.'

" ' Do not,' says he, ' impose so harsh a command upon me. My heart bleeds faster than those lips. O Sophia, how easily could I drain my veins to preserve one drop of that dear blood.'

" ' I have too many obligations to you already,' answered she, ' for sure you meant them such.'

" Here she looked at him tenderly almost a minute, and then bursting into an agony, cried:

" ' Oh, Mr. Jones, why did you save my life? My death would have been happier for us both.'

" ' Happy for us both! ' cried he. ' Could racks or wheels kill me so painfully as Sophia's—I cannot bear the dreadful sound. Do I live but for her? '

" Both his voice and look were full of irrepressible tenderness when he spoke these words; and at the same time he laid gently hold on her hand, which she did not withdraw from him; to say the truth, she hardly knew what she did or suffered. A few moments now passed in silence between these lovers, while his eyes were eagerly fixed on Sophia, and hers declining toward the ground; at last she recovered strength enough to desire him again to leave her, for that her certain ruin would be the consequence of their being found together; adding:

"'Oh, Mr. Jones, you know not, you know not what hath passed this cruel afternoon.'

"'I know all, my Sophia,' answered he; 'your cruel father hath told me all, and he himself hath sent me hither to you.'

"'My father sent you to me!' replied she: 'sure you dream!'

"'Would to Heaven,' cried he, 'it was but a dream. Oh! Sophia, your father hath sent me to you, to be an advocate for my odious rival, to solicit you in his favor. I took any means to get access to you. O, speak to me, Sophia! Comfort my bleeding heart. Sure no one ever loved, ever doted, like me. Do not unkindly withhold this dear, this soft, this gentle hand—one moment perhaps tears you forever from me. Nothing less than this cruel occasion could, I believe, have ever conquered the respect and love with which you have inspired me.'

" She stood a moment silent, and covered with

confusion; then, lifting up her eyes gently towards him, she cried:

"'What would Mr. Jones have me say?'

We would seem to have here a writer not quite in his native element. He intends to interest us in a serious situation. Sophia is on the whole natural and winning, although one may stop to imagine what kind of an agony is that which allows of so mathematical a division of time as is implied in the statement that she looked at her lover—tenderly, too, forsooth!—"almost a minute." The mood of mathematics and the mood of emotion, each excellent in itself, do not go together in life as they do in eighteenth century fiction. But in the general impression she makes, Sophia, let us concede, is sweet and realizable. But Jones, whom we have long before this scene come to know and be fond of—Jones is here a prig, a bore, a dummy. Sir Charles Grandison in all his woodenness is not arrayed like one of these. Consider the situation further: Sophia is in grief; she has blood and tears on her face—what would any lover,—nay, any respectable young man do in the premises? Surely, stanch her wounds, dry her eyes, comfort her with a homely necessary handkerchief. But not so Jones: he is not a real man but a melodramatic lay-figure, playing to the gallery as he spouts speeches about the purely metaphoric bleeding of his heart, oblivious of the disfigurement of his sweetheart's visage from real blood. He insults her by addressing her in the

third person, mouths sentiments about his " odious
rival " (a phrase with a superb Bowery smack to
it!) and in general so disports himself as to make
an effect upon the reader of complete unreality.
This was no real scene to Fielding himself: why then
should it be true: it has neither the accent nor the
motion of life. The novelist is being " literary," is
not warm to his work at all. When we turn from
this attempt to the best love scenes in modern hands,
the difference is world-wide. And this unreality—
which violates the splendid credibility of the hero in
dozens of other scenes in the book,—is all the worse
coming from a writer who expressly announces his
intention to destroy the prevalent conventional hero
of fiction and set up something better in his place.
Whereas Tom in the quoted scene is nothing if not
conventional and drawn in the stock tradition of
mawkish heroics. The plain truth is that with Fielding love is an appetite rather than a sentiment and he
is only completely at ease when painting its rollick-
ing, coarse and passional aspects.

In its unanalytic method and loose construction
this Novel, compared with Richardson, is a throw-
back to a more primitive pattern, as we saw was the
case with Fielding's first fiction. But in another
important characteristic of the modern Novel it surpasses anything that had earlier appeared: I refer
to the way it puts before the reader a great variety
of human beings, so that a sense of teeming exist-

ence is given, a genuine imitation of the spatial complexity of life, if not of its depths. It is this effect, afterwards conveyed in fuller measure by Balzac, by Dickens, by Victor Hugo and by Tolstoy, that gives us the feeling that we are in the presence of a master of men, whatever his limitations of period or personality.

How delightful are the subsidiary characters in the book! One such is Partridge, the unsophisticated schoolmaster who, when he attends the theater with Tom and hears Garrick play " Hamlet," thinks but poorly of the player because he only does what anybody would do under the circumstances! Allworthy and Blifil one may object to, each in his kind, for being conventionally good and bad, but in numerous male characters in less important rôles there is compensation: the gypsy episode, for example, is full of raciness and relish. And what a gallery of women we get in the story: Mrs. Honour the maid, and Miss Western (who in some sort suggests Mrs. Nickleby), Mrs. Miller, Lady Bellaston, Mrs. Waters and other light-of-loves and dames of folly, whose dubious doings are carried off with such high good humor that we are inclined to overlook their misdeeds. There is a Chaucerian freshness about it all: at times comes the wish that such talent were used in a better cause. A suitable sub-title for the story, would be: Or Life in The Tavern, so large a share do Inns have in its unfolding. Fielding would have yielded hearty assent to Dr. Johnson's dictum that a good inn stood for man's highest felicity here below: he relished the wayside comforts of cup and bed and company which they afford.

" Tom Jones " quickly crossed the seas, was admired in foreign lands. I possess a manuscript letter of Heine's dated from Mainz in 1830, requesting a friend to send him this novel: the German poet represents, in the request, the literary class which has always lauded Fielding's finest effort, while the wayfaring man who picks it up, also finds it to his liking. Thus it secures and is safe in a double audience. Yet we must return to the thought that such a work is strictly less significant in the evolution of the modern Novel, because of its form, its reversion to type, than the model established by a man like Richardson, who is so much more restricted in gift.

Fielding's fourth and final story, " Amelia," was given to the world two years later, and but three years before his premature death at Lisbon at the age of forty-nine—worn out by irregular living and the vicissitudes of a career which had been checkered indeed. He did strenuous work as a Justice these last years and carried on an efficacious campaign against criminals: but the lights were dimming, the play was nearly over. The pure gust of life which runs rampant and riotous in the pages of " Tom Jones " is tempered in " Amelia " by a quieter, sad-

der tone and a more philosophic vision.   It is in
this way a less characteristic work, for it was of
Fielding's nature to be instantly responsive to good
cheer and the creature comforts of life.   When she
got the news of his death, Lady Mary wrote of him:
" His happy constitution (even when he had, with
great pains, half demolished it) made him forget
everything when he was before a venison pastry or
over a flask of champagne; and I am persuaded
he has known more happy moments than any prince
upon earth.   His natural spirits gave him rapture
with his cook-maid and cheerfulness in a garret."
Here is a kit-kat showing the man indeed: all his
fiction may be read in the light of it.   The main
interest in " Amelia " is found in its autobiographical flavor, for the story, in describing the fortunes—
or rather misfortunes—of Captain Booth and his
wife, drew, it is pretty certain, upon Fielding's own
traits and to some extent upon the incidents of his
earlier life.   The scenes where the Captain sets up
for a country gentleman with his horses and hounds
and speedily runs through his patrimony, is a transcript of his own experience: and Amelia herself
is a sort of memorial to his well-beloved first wife
(he had married for a second his honest, good-
hearted kitchen-maid), who out of affection must
have endured so much in daily contact with such
a character as that of her charming husband.   In
the novel, Mrs. Booth always forgives, even as the

Captain ever goes wrong. There would be something sad in such a clear-eyed comprehension of one's own weakness, if we felt compelled to accept the theory that he was here drawing his own likeness; which must not be pushed too far, for the Captain is one thing Fielding never was—to wit, stupid. There is in the book much realism of scene and incident; but its lack of animal spirits has always militated against the popularity of " Amelia "; in fact, it is accurate to say that Fielding's contemporary public, and the reading world ever since, has confined its interest in his work to " Joseph Andrews " and " Tom Jones."

The pathos of his ending, dying in Portugal whither he had gone on a vain quest for health, and his companionable qualities whether as man or author, can but make him a more winsome figure to us than proper little Mr. Richardson; and possibly this feeling has affected the comparative estimates of the two writers. One responds readily to the sentiment of Austin Dobson's fine poem on Fielding:

> " Beneath the green Estrella trees,
>   No artist merely, but a man
>   Wrought on our noblest island-plan,
>   Sleeps with the alien Portuguese."

And in the same way we are sympathetic with Thackeray in the lecture on the English humorists: " Such a brave and gentle heart, such an intrepid and courageous spirit, I love to recognize in the manly, the English Harry Fielding." Imagine any later critic calling Richardson " Sam! " It is inconceivable.

Such then were the two men who founded the English Novel, and such their work. Unlike in many respects, both as personalities and literary makers, they were, after all, alike in this: they showed the feasibility of making the life of contemporary society interesting in prose fiction. That was their great common triumph and it remains the keynote of all the subsequent development in fiction. They accomplished this, each in his own way: Richardson by sensibility often degenerating into sentimentality, and by analysis—the subjective method; Fielding by satire and humor (often coarse, sometimes bitter) and the wide envisagement of action and scene—the method objective. Richardson exhibits a somewhat straitened propriety and a narrow didactic tradesman's morality, with which we are now out of sympathy. Fielding, on the contrary, with the abuse of his good gift for tolerant painting of seamy human nature, gives way often to an indulgence of the lower instincts of mankind which, though faithfully reflecting his age, are none the less unpleasant to modern taste. Both are men of genius, Fielding's being the larger and more universal: nothing but genius could have done such original

things as were achieved by the two.   Nevertheless,
set beside the great masters of fiction who were to
come, and who will be reviewed in these pages, they
are seen to have been excelled in art and at least
equaled in gift and power.   So much we may properly claim for the marvelous growth and ultimate
degree of perfection attained by the best novel-makers of the nineteenth and twentieth centuries.   It
remains now to show what part was played in the
eighteenth century development by certain other
novelists, who, while not of the supreme importance
of these two leaders, yet each and all contributed
to the shaping of the new fiction and did their share
in leaving it at the century's end a perfected instrument, to be handled by a finished artist like Jane
Austen.   We must take some cognizance, in special,
of writers like Smollett and Sterne and Goldsmith
—potent names, evoking some of the pleasantest
memories open to one who browses in the rich meadow
lands of English literature.

CHAPTER IV

DEVELOPMENTS; SMOLLETT, STERNE AND OTHERS

THE popularity of Richardson and Fielding showed itself in a hearty public welcome: and also in that sincerest form of flattery, imitation. Many authors began to write the new fiction. Where once a definite demand is recognized in literature, the supply, more or less machine-made, is sure to follow.

In the short quarter of a century between " Pamela " and " The Vicar of Wakefield," the Novel got its growth, passed out of leading strings into what may fairly be called independence and maturity: and by the time Goldsmith's charming little classic was written, the shelves were comfortably filled with novels recent or current, giving contemporary literature quite the air so familiar to-day. Only a little later, we find the *Gentleman's Magazine*, a trustworthy reporter of such matters, speaking of " this novel-writing age." The words were written in 1773, a generation after Richardson had begun the form. Still more striking testimony, so far back as 1755, when Richardson's maiden story was but a dozen years old, a writer in " The Connoisseur " is facetiously proposing to establish a factory for the fashioning of novels, with one, a master workman, to furnish plots and subordinates to fill in the details—an anticipation of the famous literary *menage* of Dumas *père*.

Although there was, under these conditions, inevitable imitation of the new model, there was a deeper reason for the rapid development. The time was ripe for this kind of fiction: it was in the air, as we have already tried to suggest. Hence, other fiction-makers began to experiment with the form, this being especially true of Smollett. Out of many novelists, feeble or truly called, a few of the most important must be mentioned.

I

The Scotch-born Tobias Smollett published his first fiction, " Roderick Random," eight years after " Pamela " had appeared, and the year before " Tom Jones "; it was exactly contemporaneous with " Clarissa Harlowe." A strict contemporary, then, with Richardson and Fielding, he was also the ablest novelist aside from them, a man whose work was most influential in the later development. It is not unusual to dismiss him in a sentence as a coarser Fielding. The characterization hits nearer the bull's eye than is the rule with such sayings, and more vulgar than the greater writer he certainly is, brutal where Fielding is vigorous: and he exhibits and exaggerates the latter's tendencies to the picaresque, the burlesque and the episodic. His fiction is of the elder school in its loose fiber, its external method of dealing with incident and character. There is little or nothing in Smollett of the firm-knit texture and subjective analysis of the moderns. Thus the resemblances are superficial, the differences deeper-going and palpable. Smollett is often violent, Fielding never: there is an impression of cosmopolitanism in the former— a wider survey of life, if only on the surface, is given in his books. By birth, Smollett was of the gentry; but by the time he was twenty he had seen service as Surgeon's Mate in the British navy, and his after career as Tory Editor, at times in prison, literary man and traveler who visited many lands and finally, like Fielding, died abroad in Italy, was checkered enough to give him material and to spare for the changeful bustle, so rife with action and excitement, of his four principal stories. Like the American Cooper, he drew upon his own experiences for his picture of the navy; and like a later American, Dr. Holmes, was a physician who could speak by the card of that side of life.

Far more closely than Fielding he followed the " Gil Blas " model, depending for interest primarily upon adventures by the way, moving accidents by flood and field. He declares, in fact, his intention

to use Le Sage as a literary father and he translated
" Gil Blas."   In striking contrast, too, with Fielding
is the interpretation of life one gets from his books;
with the author of " Tom Jones " we feel, what we
do in greater degree with Shakespeare and Balzac,
that the personality of the fiction-maker is healthily
merged in his characters, in the picture of life.   But
in the case of Dr. Smollett, there is a strongly individual satiric bias: less of that largeness which
sees the world from an unimplicated coign of vantage, whence the open-eyed, wise-minded spectator
finds it a comedy breeding laughter under thoughtful
brows.   We seem to be getting not so much scenes
of life as an author's setting of the scene for his own
private reasons.   Such is at least the occasional
effect of Smollett.   Also is there more of bitterness,
of savagery in him: and where Fielding was broad
and racily frank in his handling of delicate themes,
this fellow is indecent with a kind of hardness and
brazenness which are amazing.   The difference between plain-speaking and unclean speaking could
hardly be better illustrated.   It should be added, in
justice, that even Smollett is rarely impure with the
alluring saliency of certain modern fiction.

In the first story, " The Adventures of Roderick
Random " (the cumbrous full titles of earlier fiction
are for apparent reasons frequently curtailed in the
present treatment), published when the author was
twenty-seven, he avails himself of a residence of some

years in Jamaica to depict life in that quarter of
the world at a time when the local color had the
charm of novelty.   The story is often credited with
being autobiographic, as a novelist's first book is
likely to be; since, by popular belief, there is one
story in all of us, namely, our own.   Its description
of the hero's hard knocks does, indeed, suggest the
fate of a man so stormily quarrelsome throughout
his days: for this red-headed Scot, this "hack of
genius," as Henley picturesquely calls him, was
naturally a fighting man and, whether as man or
author, attacks or repels sharply: there is nothing
uncertain in the effect he makes.   His loud vigor
is as pronounced as that of a later Scot like Carlyle;
yet he stated long afterward that the likeness between himself and Roderick was slight and superficial.   The fact that the tale is written in the first
person also helps the autobiographic theory: that
method of story-making always lends a certain credence to the narrative.   The scenes shift from western Scotland to the streets of London, thence to
the West Indies: and the interest (the remark applies to all Smollett's work) lies in just three things
—adventure, diversity of character, and the realistic picture of contemporary life—especially that
of the navy on a day when, if Smollett is within
hailing distance of the facts, it was terribly corrupt.
Too much credit can hardly be given him for first
using, so effectively too, the professional sea-life of

his country: a motive so richly productive since
through Marryat down to Dana, Herman Melville,
Clark Russell and many other favorite writers, both
British and American. In Smollett's hands, it is
a strange muddle of religion, farce and smut, but
set forth with a vivid particularity and a gusto of
high spirits which carry the reader along, willy-nilly.
Such a book might be described by the advertisement
of an old inn: " Here is entertainment for man and
beast." As to characterization, if a genius for it
means the creation of figures which linger in the
familiar memory of mankind, Smollett must perforce
be granted the faculty; here in his first book are
Tom Bowling and Strap—to name two—the one
(like Richardson's Lovelace) naming a type: the
other standing for the country innocent, the meek
fidus Achates, both as good as anything of the same
class in Fielding. The Welsh mate, Mr. Morgan,
for another of the sailor sort, is also excellent. The
judgment may be eccentric, but for myself the character parts in Smollett's dramas seem for variety
and vividness often superior to those of Fielding.
The humor at its best is very telling. The portraits,
or caricatures, of living folk added to the story's
immediate vogue, but injure it as a permanent contribution to fiction.

A fair idea of the nature of the attractions offered
(and at the same time a clear indication of the sort
of fiction manufactured by the doughty doctor) may

be gleaned from the following *précis*—Smollett's own
—of Chapter XXXVIII: " I get up and crawl into
a barn where I am in danger of perishing through
the fear of the country people.   Their inhumanity.
I am succored by a reputed witch.   Her story.   Her
advice.   She recommends me as a valet to a single
lady whose character she explains."   This promises
pretty fair reading: of course, we wish to read on
and to learn more of that single lady and the hero's
relation to her.   Such a motive, which might be
called, " The Mistakes of a Night," with details too
crude and physical to allow of discussion, is often
overworked by Smollett (as, in truth, it is by Fielding, to modern taste): the eighteenth century had
not yet given up the call of the Beast in its fiction—
an element of bawdry was still welcome in the print
offered reputable folk.

The style of Smollett in his first fiction, and in
general, has marked dramatic flavor: his is a gift of
forthright phrase, a plain, vernacular smack characterizes his diction.   To go back to him now is
to be surprised perhaps at the racy vigor of so faulty
a writer and novelist.   A page or so of Smollett,
after a course in present-day popular fiction, reads
very much like a piece of literature.   In this respect, he seems full of flavor, distinctly of the major
breed: there is an effect of passing from attenuated
parlor tricks into the open, when you take him up.
Here, you can but feel, is a masculine man of

letters, even if it is his fate to play second fiddle to Fielding.

Smollett's initial story was a pronounced success with the public—and he aired an arrogant joy and pooh-poohed insignificant rivals like Fielding. His hand was against every man's when it came to the question of literary prowess; and like many authors before and since, one of his first acts upon the kind reception of " Roderick Random," was to get published his worthless blank-verse tragedy, " The Regicide," which, refused by Garrick, had till then languished in manuscript and was an ugly duckling beloved of its maker. Then came Novel number two, " The Adventures of Peregrine Pickle," three years after the first: an unequal book, best at its beginning and end, full of violence, not on the whole such good art-work as the earlier fiction, yet very fine in spots and containing such additional sea-dogs as Commodore Trunnion and Lieutenant Hatchway, whose presence makes one forgive much. The original preface contained a scurrilous reference to Fielding, against whom he printed a diatribe in a pamphlet dated the next year. The hero of the story, a handsome ne'er-do-well who has money and position to start the world with, encounters plenty of adventure in England and out of it, by land and sea. There is an episodic book, " Memoirs, supposed to be written by a lady of quality," and really giving the checkered career of Lady Vane, a fast gentlewoman of the time, done for pay at her request, which is illustrative of the loose state of fictional art in its unrelated, lugged-in character: and as well of eighteenth century morals in its drastic details. We have seen that Fielding was frankly episodic in handling a story; Smollett goes him one better: as may most notoriously be seen also in the unmentionable Miss Williams' story in " Roderick Random "—in fact, throughout his novels.   Pickle, to put it mildly, is not an admirable young man.   An author's conception of his hero is always in some sort a give-away: it expresses his ideals; that Smollett's are sufficiently low-pitched, may be seen here. Plainly, too, he likes Peregrine, and not so much excuses his failings as overlooks them entirely.

After a two years' interval came " The Adventures of Ferdinand, Count Fathom," which was not liked by his contemporaries and is now seen to be definitely the poorest of the quartette.   It is enough to say of it that Fathom is an unmitigable scoundrel and the story, mixed romance and melodrama, offers the reader dust and ashes instead of good red blood. It lacks the comic verve of Smollett's typical fiction and manipulates virtue and vice in the cut-and-dried style of the penny-dreadful.   Even its attempts at the sensational leave the modern reader, bred on such heavenly fare as is proffered by Stevenson and others, indifferent-cold.

It is a pleasure to turn from it to what is gen-

erally conceded to be the best novel he wrote, as it
is his last: " The Expedition of Humphrey Clinker,"
which appeared nearly twenty years later, when the
author was fifty years old. " The Adventures of
Sir Launcelot Graves," written in prison a decade
earlier, and a poor satire in the vein of Cervantes,
can be ignored, it falls so much below Smollett's
main fiction. He had gone for his health's sake to
Italy and wrote " Humphrey Clinker " at Leghorn,
completing it only within a few weeks of his death.
For years he had been degenerating as a writer, his
physical condition was of the worst: it looked as if
his life was quite over. Yet, by a sort of leaping-up
of the creative flame out of the dying embers of the
hearth, he wrought his masterpiece.

It was thrown into letter form, Richardson's framework, and has all of Smollett's earlier power of
characterization and brusque wit, together with a
more genial, mellower tone, that of an older man not
soured but ripened by the years. Some of its main
scenes are enacted in his native Scotland and possibly this meant strength for another Scot, as it
did for Sir Walter and Stevenson. The kinder interpretation of humanity in itself makes the novel
better reading to later taste; so much can not honestly be said for its plain speaking, for as Henley
says in language which sounds as if it were borrowed
from the writer he is describing, " the stinks and
nastinesses are done with peculiar gusto." The idea

of the story, as usual a pivot around which to re-
volve a series of adventures, is to narrate how a
certain bachelor, country gentleman, Matthew
Bramble, a *malade imaginaire*, yet good-hearted and
capable of big laughter—" the most risible misan-
thrope ever met with," as he is limned by one of
the persons of the story—travels in England, Wales
and Scotland in pursuit of health, taking with him
his family, of whom the main members include his
sister, Tabitha (and her maid, Jenkins), and his
nephew, not overlooking the dog, Chowder. Clinker,
who names the book, is a subsidiary character, merely
a servant in Bramble's establishment. The crotchety
Bramble and his acidulous sister, who is a forerunner
of Mrs. Malaprop in the unreliability of her spelling,
and Lieutenant Lishmahago, who has been compli-
mented as the first successful Scotchman in fiction—
all these are sketched with a verity and in a vein
of genuine comic invention which have made them
remembered. Violence, rage, filth—Smollett's beset-
ting sins—are forgotten or forgiven in a book which
has so much of the flavor and movement of life.
The author's medical lore is made good use of in
the humorous descriptions of poor Bramble's ail-
ments. Incidentally, the story defends the Scotch
against the English in such a pronounced way that
Walpole calls it a " party novel "; and there is,
moreover, a pleasant love story interwoven with the
comedy and burlesque. One feels in leaving this

fiction that with all allowance for his defects, there
is more danger of undervaluing the author's powers
and place in the modern Novel than the reverse.

Fielding and Smollett together set the pace for
the Novel of blended incident and character: both
were, as sturdy realists, reactionary from the sentimental analysis of Richardson and express an instinct contrary to the self-conscious pathos of a
Sterne or the idyllic romanticism of a Goldsmith.
Both were directly of influence upon the Novel's
growth in the nineteenth century: Fielding especially
upon Thackeray, Smollett upon Dickens.   If Smollett had served the cause in no other way than in
his strong effect upon the author of " The Pickwick
Papers," he would deserve well of all critics: how the
little Copperfield delighted in that scant collection
of books on his father's bookshelf, where were " Roderick Random," " Peregrine Pickle " and " Humphrey Clinker," along with " Tom Jones," " The
Vicar of Wakefield," " Gil Blas " and " Robinson
Crusoe "—" a glorious host," says he, " to keep me
company.   They kept alive my fancy and my hope
of something beyond that time and place."   And of
Smollett's characters, who seem to have charmed him
more than Fielding's, he declares: " I have seen Tom
Pipes go clambering up the church-steeple: I have
watched Strap with the knapsack on his back stop-
ping to rest himself upon the wicket gate: and I
know that Commodore Trunnion held that Club with

Mr. Pickle in the parlor of our little village ale house." Children are shrewd critics, in their way, and what an embryo Charles Dickens likes in fiction is not to be slighted. But as we have seen, Smollett can base his claims to our sufferance not by indirection through Dickens, but upon his worth; many besides the later and greater novelist have a liking for this racy writer of adventure, and creator of English types, who was recognized by Walter Scott as of kin to the great in fiction.

II

In the fast-developing fiction of the late eighteenth century, the possible ramifications of the Novel from the parent tree of Richardson enriched it with the work of Sterne, Swift and Goldsmith. They added imaginative narratives of one sort or another, which increased the content of the form by famous things and exercised some influence in shaping it. The remark has in mind " Tristram Shandy," " Gulliver's Travels " and " The Vicar of Wakefield." And yet, no one of the three was a Novel in the sense in which the evolution of the word has been traced, nor yet are the authors strictly novelists.

Laurence Sterne, at once man of the world and clergyman, with Rabelais as a model, and himself a master of prose, possessing command of humor and pathos, skilled in character sketch and essay-philosophy, is not a novelist at all. His aim is not to depict the traits or events of contemporary society, but to put forth the views of the Reverend Laurence Sterne, Yorkshire parson, with many a quaint turn and whimsical situation under a thin disguise of story-form. Of his two books, " Tristram Shandy " and " The Sentimental Journey," unquestionable classics, both, in their field, there is no thought of plot or growth or objective realization: the former is a delightful *tour de force* in which a born essayist deals with the imaginary fortunes of a person he makes as interesting before his birth as after it, and in passing, sketches some characters dear to posterity: first and foremost, Uncle Toby and Corporal Trim. It is all pure play of wit, fancy and wisdom, beneath the comic mask—a very frolic of the mind. In the second book the framework is that of the travel-sketch and the treatment more objective: a fact which, along with its dubious propriety, may account for its greater popularity. But much of the charm comes, as before, from the writer's touch, his gift of style and ability to unloose in the essay manner a unique individuality.

In his life Sterne, like Swift, exhibited most unclerical traits of worldliness and in his work there is the refined, suggestive indelicacy, not to say indecency, which we are in the habit nowadays of charging against the French, and which is so much worse than the bluff, outspoken coarseness of a Field-

ing or a Smollett.   At times the line between Sterne
and Charles Lamb is not so easy to draw in that,
from first to last, the elder is an essayist and humorist, while the younger has so much of the eighteenth
century in his feeling and manner.   In these modern
times, when so many essayists appear in the guise
of fiction-makers, we can see that Sterne is really the
leader of the tribe: and it is not hard to show how
neither he nor they are novelists divinely called.
They (and he) may be great, but it is another greatness.   The point is strikingly illustrated by the statement that Sterne was eight years publishing the
various parts of " Tristram Shandy," and a man of
forty-six when he began to do so.   Bona fide novels
are not thus written.   Constructively, the work is
a mad farrago; but the end quite justifies the means.
Thus, while his place in letters is assured, and the
touch of the cad in him (Goldsmith called him " the
blackguard parson ") should never blind us to his
prime merits, his significance for our particular study
—the study of the modern Novel in its development
—is comparatively slight.   Like all essayists of rank
he left memorable passages: the world never tires of
" God tempers the wind to the shorn lamb," and
pays it the high compliment of ascribing it to holy
writ: nor will the scene where the recording angel
blots out Uncle Toby's generous oath with a tear,
fade from the mind; nor that of the same kindly
gentleman letting go the big fly which has, to his

discomfiture, been buzzing about his nose at dinner:
" ' Go,' says he, lifting up the latch and opening his
hand as he spoke to let it escape. ' Go, poor devil,
get thee gone, why should I hurt thee? The world
surely is wide enough to hold both thee and me ' "—
a touch so modern as to make Sterne seem a century
later than Fielding. These are among the precious
places of literature. This eighteenth century divine has in advance of his day the subtler sensibility
which was to grow so strong in later fiction: and
if he be sentimental too, he gives us a sentimentality
unlike the solemn article of Richardson, because of
its French grace and its relief of delicious humor.

III

Swift chronologically precedes Sterne, for in 1726,
shortly after " Robinson Crusoe " and a good fifteen
years before " Pamela," he gave the world that
unique lucubration, " Gulliver's Travels," allegory,
satire and fairy story all in one. It is certainly
anything but a novel. One of the giants of English
letters, doing many things and exhibiting a sardonic
personality that seems to peer through all his work,
Swift's contribution to the coming Novel was above
all the use of a certain grave, realistic manner of
treating the impossible: a service, however, shared
with Defoe. He gives us in a matter-of-fact chronicle style the marvelous happenings of Gulliver in

Lilliputian land or in that of the Brobdingnagians. He and Defoe are to be regarded as pioneers who suggested to the literary world, just before the Novel's advent, that the attraction of a new form and a new method, the exploitation of the truth that, "The proper study of mankind is man," could not (and should not) kill the love of romance, for the good and sufficient reason that romance meant imagination, illusion, charm, poetry. And in due season, after the long innings enjoyed by realism with its triumphs of analysis and superfaithful transcriptions of the average life of man, we shall behold the change of mood which welcomes back the older appeal of fiction.

IV

It was the enlargement of this sense of romance which Oliver Goldsmith gave his time in that masterpiece in small, " The Vicar of Wakefield ": his special contribution to the plastic variations connected with the growing pains of the Novel. Whether regarded as poet, essayist, dramatist or story-maker, Dr. Goldsmith is one of the best-loved figures of English letters, as Swift is one of the most terrible. And these lovable qualities are nowhere more conspicuous than in the idyllic sketch of the country clergyman and his family. Romance it deserves to be called, because of the delicate idealization in the setting and in the portrayal of the Vicar himself—a man who not only

preached God's love, " but first he followed it himself." And yet the book—which, by the bye, was
published in 1766 just as the last parts of " Tristram
Shandy " were appearing in print—offers a good
example of the way in which the more romantic depiction of life, in the hands of a master, inevitably
blends with realistic details, even with a winning
truthfulness of effect. Some of the romantic charm
of " The Vicar of Wakefield," we must remember,
inheres in its sympathetic reproduction of vanished
manners, etiquette and social grace; a sweet old-
time grace, a fragrance out of the past, emanates
from the memory of it if read half a lifetime ago.
An elder age is rehabilitated for us by its pages,
even as it is by the canvases of Romney and Sir
Joshua. And with this more obvious romanticism
goes the deeper romanticism that comes from the
interpretation of humanity, which assumes it to be
kindly and gentle and noble in the main. Life, made
up of good and evil as it is, is, nevertheless, seen
through this affectionate time-haze, worth the living.
Whatever their individual traits, an air of country
peace and innocence hovers over the Primrose household: the father and mother, the girls, Olivia and
Sophia, and the two sons, George and Moses, they
all seem equally generous, credulous and good. We
feel that the author is living up to an announcement
in the opening chapter which of itself is a sort of
promise of the idealized treatment of poor human

nature.   But into this pretty and perfect scene of
domestic felicity come trouble and disgrace: the ser-
pent creeps into the unsullied nest, the villain, Thorn-
hill, ruins Olivia, their house burns, and the soft-
hearted, honorable father is haled to prison.   There
is no blinking the darker side of mortal experience.
And the prison scenes, with their noble teaching with
regard to penal punishment, showing Goldsmith far
in advance of his age, add still further to the shadows.   Yet the idealization is there, like an atmosphere, and through it all, shining and serene, is Dr.
Primrose to draw the eye to the eternal good.   We
smile mayhap at his simplicity but note at the same
time that his psychology is sound: the influence of
his sermonizing upon the jailbirds is true to experience often since tested.   Nor are satiric side-
strokes in the realistic vein wanting—as in the drawing of such a high lady of quality as Miss Carolina
Wilhelmina Amelia Skeggs—the very name sending
our thoughts forward to Thackeray.   In the final
analysis it will be found that what makes the work
a romance is its power to quicken the sense of the
attraction, the beauty of simple goodness through
the portrait of a noble man whose environment is
such as best to bring out his qualities.   Dr. Primrose is humanity, if not actual, potential: he *can* be,
if he never was.   A helpful comparison might be
instituted between Goldsmith's country clergyman
and Balzac's country doctor in the novel of that

name; another notable attempt at the idealization of a typical man of one of the professions.   It would bring out the difference between the late eighteenth and the middle nineteenth centuries, as well as that between a great novelist, Balzac, and a great English writer, Goldsmith, who yet is not a novelist at all. It should detract no whit from one's delight in such a work as " The Vicar of Wakefield " to acknowledge that its aim is not to depict society as it then existed, but to give a pleasurable abstract of human nature for the purpose of reconciling us through art with life, when lived so sanely, simply and sweetly as by Primrose of gentle memory.   Seldom has the divine quality of the forgiveness of sins been portrayed with more salutary effect than in the scene where the erring and errant Olivia is taken back to the heart of her father—just as the hard-headed landlady would drive her forth with the words: " ' Out I say! Pack out this moment! tramp, thou impudent strumpet, or I'll give thee a mark that won't be better for this three months.   What! you trumpery, to come and take up an honest house without cross or coin to bless yourself with!   Come along, I say.' "

" I flew to her rescue while the woman was dragging her along by her hair, and I caught the dear forlorn wretch in my arms.   ' Welcome, anyway welcome, my dearest lost one, my treasure, to your poor old father's bosom.   Though the vicious forsake thee, there is yet one in the world who will never forsake thee; though thou hadst ten thousand crimes to answer for, he will forget them all!'"

Set beside this father the fathers of Clarissa and Sophia Western, and you have the difference between the romance and realism that express opposite moods; the mood that shows the average and the mood that shows the best. For portraiture, then, rather than plot, for felicity of manner and sweetness of interpretation we praise such a work;—qualities no less precious though not so distinctively appertaining to the Novel.

It may be added, for a minor point, that the Novel type as already developed had assumed a conventional length which would preclude " The Vicar of Wakefield " from its category, making it a sketch or novelette. The fiction-makers rapidly came to realize that for their particular purpose—to portray a complicated piece of contemporary life—more leisurely movement and hence greater space are necessary to the best result. To-day any fiction under fifty thousand words would hardly be called a novel in the proper sense,—except in publishers' advertisements. Goldsmith's story does not exceed such limits.

Therefore, although we may like it all the more because it is a romantic sketch rather than a novel proper, we must grant that its share in the eighteenth century shaping of the form is but ancillary. The fact that the book upon its appearance awakened no such interest as waited upon the fiction of Rich-

ardson or Fielding a few years before, may be taken
to mean that the taste was still towards the more
photographic portrayals of average contemporary
humanity. Several editions, to be sure, were issued
the year of its publication, but without much finan-
cial success, and contemporary criticism found little
remarkable in this permanent contribution to English
literature. Later, it was beloved both of the elect
and the general. Goethe's testimony to the strong
and wholesome effect of the book upon him in his
formative period, is remembered. Dear old Dr.
Johnson too believed in the story, for, summoned to
Goldsmith's lodging by his friend's piteous appeal
for help, he sends a guinea in advance and on arrival
there, finds his colleague in high choler because, forsooth, his landlady has arrested him for his rent:
whereupon Goldsmith (who had already expended
part of the guinea in a bottle of Madeira) displays a
manuscript,—" a novel ready for the press," as we
read in Boswell; and Johnson—" I looked into it and
saw its merit," says he—goes out and sells it for sixty
pounds, whereupon Goldsmith paid off his obligation,
and with his mercurial Irish nature had a happy evening, no doubt, with his chosen cronies! It is a sordid,
humorous-tragic Grub Street beginning for one of
the little immortals of letters—so many of which,
alack! have a similar birth.

Certain other authors less distinguished than these,
produced fiction of various kinds which also had some

influence in the development, and further illustrate the tendency of the Novel to become a pliable medium for literary expression; a sort of net wherein divers fish might be caught. Dr. Johnson, essayist, critic, coffee-house dictator, published the same year that Sterne's "Tristram Shandy" began to appear, his "Rasselas, Prince of Abyssinia"; a stately elegiac on the vanity of human pleasures, in which the Prince leaves his idyllic home and goes into the world to test its shams, only to return to his kingdom with the sad knowledge that it is the better part of wisdom in this vale of tears to prepare for heaven. Of course this is fiction only in seeming and by courtesy, almost as far removed from the Novel as the same author's mammoth dictionary or Lives of the Poets. It has Richardson's method of moralizing, while lacking that writer's power of studying humanity in its social relations. The sturdy genius of Dr. Johnson lay in quite other directions.

Richardson's sentimentality, too, was carried on by MacKenzie in his "Man of Feeling" already mentioned as the favorite tear-begetter of its time, the novel which made the most prolonged attack upon the lachrymosal gland. But it is only fair to this author to add that there was a welcome note of philanthropy in his story—in spite of its mawkishness; his appeal for the under dog in great cities is a forecast of the humanitarianism to become rampant in later fiction.

Again, the seriousness which has always, in one guise or the other, underlain English fiction, soon crystalized in the contemporary eighteenth century novelists into an attempt to preach this or that by propaganda in story-form. William Godwin, whose relations as father-in-law to Shelley gives him a not altogether agreeable place in our memory, was a leader in this tendency with several fictions, the best known and most readable being " Caleb Williams ": radical ideas, social, political and religious, were mooted by half a dozen earnest-souled authors whose works are now regarded as links in the chain of development—missing links for most readers of fiction, since their literary quality is small. In later days, this kind of production was to be called purpose fiction and condemned or applauded according to individual taste and the esthetic and vital value of the book. When the moralizing overpowered all else, we get a book like that friend of childhood, " Sanford and Merton," which Thomas Day perpetrated in the year of grace 1783. Few properly reared boys of a generation ago escaped this literary indiscretion: its Sunday School solemnity, its distribution of life's prizes according to the strictest moral tests, had a sort of bogey fascination; it was much in vogue long after Day's time, indeed down to within our own memories. Perhaps it is still read and relished in innocent corners of the earth. In any case it is one of the outcomes of the movement just touched upon.

At present, being more *ennuyé* in our tastes for fiction than were our forefathers, and the pretence of piety being less a convention, we incline to insist more firmly that the pill at least be sugar-coated,—if indeed we submit to physic at all.

There was also a tendency during the second half of the eighteenth century—very likely only half serious and hardly more than a literary fad—toward the romance of mystery and horror. Horace Walpole, the last man on earth from whom one would expect the romantic and sentimental, produced in his " Castle of Otranto " such a book; and Mrs. Radcliffe's " The Mystery of Udolpho " (standing for numerous others) manipulated the stage machinery of this pseudo-romantic revival and reaction; moonlit castles, medieval accessories, weird sounds and lights at the dread midnight hour,—an attack upon the reader's nerves rather than his sensibilities, much the sort of paraphernalia employed with a more spiritual purpose and effect in our own day by the dramatist, Maeterlinck. Beckford's " Vathek " and Lewis' " The Monk " are variations upon this theme, which for a while was very popular and is decidedly to be seen in the work of the first novelist upon American soil, Charles Brockden Brown, whose somber " Wieland," read with the Radcliffe school in mind, will reveal its probable parentage. We have seen how the movement was happily satirized by its natural enemy, Jane Austen. Few more enjoyable things can be quoted than this conversation from "Northanger Abbey" between two typical young ladies of the time:—

"'But, my dearest Catherine, what have you been doing with yourself all this morning? Have you gone on with Udolpho?'

"'Yes, I have been reading it ever since I woke; and I am got to the black veil.'

"'Are you, indeed? How delightful! Oh! I would not tell you what is behind the black veil for the world! Are you not wild to know?'

"'Oh! yes, quite; what can it be? But do not tell me; I would not be told upon any account. I know it must be a skeleton; I am sure it is Laurentina's skeleton. Oh! I am delighted with the book! I should like to spend my whole life in reading it, I assure you; if it had not been to meet you, I would not have come away from it for all the world.'

"'Dear creature! how much I am obliged to you; and when you have finished Udolpho, we will read the Italian together; and I have made out a list of ten or twelve more of the same kind for you.'

"'Have you, indeed! How glad I am! What are they all?'

"'I will read you their names directly; here they are in my pocket-book. "Castle of Wolfenbach," "Clermont," "Mysterious Warnings," "Necromancer of the Black Forest," "Midnight Bell,"

" Orphan of the Rhine," and " Horrid Mysteries." Those will last us some time.'

" ' Yes; pretty well; but are they all horrid? Are you sure they are all horrid? '

" ' Yes, quite sure; for a particular friend of mine, a Miss Andrews, a sweet girl, one of the sweetest creatures in the world, has read every one of them.' "

After all, human nature is constant, independent of time; and fashions social, mental, literary, return like fashions in feminine headgear! Two club women were coming from a city play house after hearing a particularly lugubrious drama of Ibsen's, and one was overheard exclaiming to the other: " O isn't Ibsen just *lovely!* He does so take the hope out of life! "

Yet the tendency of eighteenth century fiction, with its handling of the bizarre and sensational, its use of occult effects of the Past and Present, was but an eddy in a current which was setting strong and steadily toward the realistic portrayal of contemporary society.

One other tendency, expressive of a lighter mood, an attempt to represent society *a la mode*, is also to be noted during this half century so crowded with interesting manifestations of a new spirit; and they who wrote it were mostly women. It is a remarkable fact that for the fifty years between Sterne and Scott, the leading novelists were of that sex, four of whom at least, Burney, Radcliffe, Edgeworth and

Austen, were of importance. Of this group the lively
Fanny Burney is the prophet; she is the first woman
novelist of rank. Her " Evelina," with its somewhat
starched gentility and simpering sensibility, was once
a book to conjure with; it fluttered the literary dove-
cotes in a way not so easy to comprehend to-day.
Yet Dr. Johnson loved his " little Burney " and
greatly admired her work, and there are entertaining
and without question accurate pictures of the fashionable London at the time of the American Revolution drawn by an observer of the inner circle, in her
" Evelina " and " Cecilia "; one treasures them for
their fresh spirit and lively humor, nor looks in them
for the more serious elements of good fiction. She
contributes, modestly, to that fiction to which we go
for human documents. No one who has been admitted to the privileges of Miss Burney's Diary can
fail to feel that a woman who commands such idiom
is easily an adept in the realistic dialogue of the
novel. Here, even more than in her own novels or
those of Richardson and Fielding, we hear the exact
syllable and intonation of contemporary speech.
" Mr. Cholmondeley is a clergyman," she writes,
" nothing shining either in person or manners but
rather somewhat grim in the first and glum in the
last." And again: " Our confab was interrupted
by the entrance of Mr. King," or yet again: " The
joke is, the people speak as if they were afraid of
me, instead of my being afraid of them. . . .

Next morning, Mrs. Thrale asked me if I did not want to see Mrs. Montagu? I truly said I should be the most insensible of animals not to like to see our sex's glory." It is hard to realize that this was penned in the neighborhood of one hundred and fifty years ago, so modern is its sound.

A great writer, with a wider scope and a more incisive satire, is Maria Edgeworth, whose books take us over into the nineteenth century. The lighter, more frivolous aspects of English high society are admirably portrayed in her " Belinda " and eight or ten other tales: and she makes a still stronger claim to permanent remembrance in such studies of Irish types, whether in England or on the native soil, as " The Absentee " and " Castle Rackrent." I venture the statement that even the jaded novel reader of to-day will find on a perusal of either of these capital stories that Miss Edgeworth makes literature, and that a pleasure not a penance is in store. She first in English fiction exploited the better-class Irishman at home and her scenes have historic value. Some years later, Susan Ferrier, who enjoyed the friendship of Scott, wrote under the stimulus of Maria Edgeworth's example a series of clever studies of Scotch life, dashed with decided humor and done with true observation.

These women, with their quick eye and facile ability to report what they saw, and also their ease of manner which of itself seems like a social gift, were but the prelude to the work so varied, gifted and vastly influential, which the sex was to do in the modern Novel; so that, at present, in an open field and no favors given, they are honorable rivals of men, securing their full share of public favor. And the English Novel, written by so many tentatively during these fifty years when the form was a-shaping, culminates at the turn of the century in two contrasted authors compared with whom all that went before seems but preparatory; one a man, the other a woman, who together express and illustrate most conveniently for this study the main movements of modern fiction,—romance and realism,—the instinct for truth and the instinct for beauty; not necessarily an antagonism, as we shall have ample occasion to see, since truth, rightly defined, is only "beauty seen from another side." It hardly needs to add that these two novelists are Jane Austen and Walter Scott.

CHAPTER V

REALISM: JANE AUSTEN

It has been said that Miss Austen came nearer
to showing life as it is,—the life she knew and
chose to depict,—than any other novelist of English race. In other words, she is a princess among
the truth-tellers. Whether or not this claim can
be substantiated, it is sure that, writing practically
half a century after Richardson and Fielding, she
far surpassed those pioneers in the exquisite and easy
verisimilitude of her art. Nay, we can go further
and say that nobody has reproduced life with a
more faithful accuracy, that yet was not photography
because it gave the pleasure proper to art, than this
same Jane Austen, spinster, well-born and well-bred:
in her own phrase, an " elegant female " of the English past. Scott's famous remark can not be too
often quoted: " That young lady had a talent for
describing the movements and feelings of characters
of ordinary life, which is to me the most wonderful
I ever met with."

If you look on the map at the small Southern
county of Hampshire, you will see that the town
of Steventon lies hard by Selborne, another name

which the naturalist White has made pleasant to the ear. Throughout her forty-two years of life—she was born the year of American revolution and died shortly after Scott had begun his Waverley series—she was a country-woman in the best sense: a clergyman's daughter identified with her neighborhood, dignified and private in her manner of existence, her one sensational outing being a four years' residence in the fashionable watering-place of Bath, where Beau Nash once reigned supreme and in our day, Beaucaire has been made to rebuke Lady Mary Carlisle for her cold patrician pride. Quiet she lived and died, nor was she reckoned great in letters by her contemporaries. She wrote on her lap with others in the room, refused to take herself seriously and in no respect was like the authoress who is kodaked at the writing-desk and chronicled in her movements by land and sea. She was not the least bit "literary." Fanny Burney, who had talent to Jane Austen's genius, was in a blaze of social recognition, a petted darling of the town, where the other walked in rural ways and unnoted of the world, wrote novels that were to make literary history. Such are the revenges of the whirligig, Time.

Austen's indestructible reputation is founded on half a dozen pieces of fiction: the best, and best known, " Sense and Sensibility " and " Pride and Prejudice," although " Mansfield Park," " Emma," " Northanger Abbey " and " Persuasion " (in order of publication but not of actual composition) are all of importance to the understanding and enjoyment of her, and her evenness of performance, on the whole, is remarkable. The earlier three of these books were written by Miss Austen when a young woman in the twenties, but published much later, and were anonymous—an indication of her tendency to take her authorship as an aside. Two of them appeared posthumously. Curiously, " Northanger Abbey," that capital hit at the Radcliffe romanticism, and first written of her stories, was disposed of to a publisher when the writer was but three and twenty, yet was not printed until she had passed away nearly twenty years later,—a sufficient proof of her unpopularity from the mercantile point of view.

Here is one of the paradoxes of literature: this gentlewoman dabbling in a seemingly amateur fashion in letters, turns out to be the ablest novelist of her sex and race, one of the very few great craftsmen, one may say, since art is no respector of sex. Jane Austen is the best example in the whole range of English literature of the wisdom of knowing your limitations and cultivating your own special plot of ground. She offers a permanent rebuke to those who (because of youth or a failure to grasp the meaning of life) fancy that the only thing worth while lies on the other side of the Pyrenees; when all the while at one's own back-door blooms the miracle. She had a clear-eyed comprehension of her own restrictions; and possessed that power of self-criticism which some truly great authors lack. She has herself given us the aptest comment ever made on her books: speaking of the " little bit of ivory two inches wide on which she worked with a brush so fine as to produce little effect after much labor ";— a judgment hardly fair as to the interest she arouses, but nevertheless absolutely descriptive of the plus and minus of her gift.

Miss Austen knew the genteel life of the upper middle class Hampshire folk, " the Squirearchy and the upper professional class," as Professor Saintsbury expresses it, down to the ground—knew it as a sympathetic onlooker slightly detached (she never married), yet not coldly aloof but a part of it as devoted sister and maiden aunt, and friend-in-general to the community. She could do two things which John Ruskin so often lauded as both rare and difficult: see straight and then report accurately; a literary Pre-Raphaelite, be it noted, before the term was coined. It not only came natural to her to tell the truth about average humanity as she saw it; she could not be deflected from her calling. Winning no general recognition during her life-time, she was not subjected to the temptations of the popular novelist; but she had her chance to go wrong, for it is recorded how that the Librarian to King George the Third, an absurd creature yclept Clark, informed the authoress that his Highness admired her works, and suggested that in view of the fact that Prince Leonard was to marry the Princess Charlotte, Miss Austen should indite " An historical romance illustrative of the august house of Coburg " To which, Miss Jane, with a humor and good-sense quite in character (and, it may be feared, not appreciated by the recipient): " I could not sit down to write a serious romance under any other motive than amusement to save my life; and if it were indispensable for me to keep it up, and never relax into laughter at myself and other people, I am sure I should be hung before I had finished the first chapter. No, I must keep to my own style and go on in my own way."

There is scarce a clearer proof of genius than this ability to strike out a path and keep to it: in striking contrast with the weak wobbling so often shown in the desire to follow literary fashion or be complaisant before the suggestion of the merchants of letters.

All her novels are prophetic of what was long to rule, in their slight framework of fable; the handling of the scenes by the way, the characterization, the natural dialogue, the vraisemblance of setting, the witty irony of observation, these are the elements of interest. Jane Austen's plots are mere tempests in tea-pots; yet she does not go to the extreme of the plotless fiction of the present. She has a story to tell, as Trollope would say, and knows how to tell it in such a way as to subtract from it every ounce of value. There is a clear kernel of idea in each

and every one of her tales. Thus, in " Sense and
Sensibility," we meet two sisters who stand for the
characteristics contrasted in the title, and in the
fortunes of Mariane, whose flighty romanticism is
cured so that she makes a sensible marriage after
learning the villainy of her earlier lover and finding
that foolish sentimentalism may well give way to the
informing experiences of life,—the thesis, satirically
conveyed though with more subtlety than in the
earlier " Northanger Abbey," proclaims the folly of
young-girl sentimentality and hysteria. In " Pride
and Prejudice," ranked by many as her masterpiece,
Darcy, with his foolish hauteur, his self-consciousness
of superior birth, is temporarily blind to the worth
of Elizabeth, who, on her part, does not see the good
in him through her sensitiveness to his patronizing
attitude; as the course of development brings them
together in a happy union, the lesson of toleration,
of mutual comprehension, sinks into the mind. The
reader realizes the pettiness of the worldly wisdom
which blocks the way of joy. As we have said,
" Northanger Abbey " speaks a wise word against the
abuse of emotionalism; it tells of the experiences of
a flighty Miss, bred on the " Mysteries of Udolpho "
style of literature, during a visit to a country house
where she imagined all the medieval romanticism
incident to that school of fiction,—aided and abetted
by such innocuous helps as a storm without and a
lonesome chamber within doors. Of the later

stories, " Mansfield Park " asks us to remember what it is to be poor and reared among rich relations; " Emma " displays a reverse misery: the rich young woman whose character is exposed to the adulations and shams incident upon her position; while in " Persuasion," there is yet another idea expressed by and through another type of girl; she who has fallen into the habit of allowing herself to be over-ridden and used by friends and family.—There is something all but Shaksperian in that story's illustration of " the uncertainty of all human events and calculations," as she herself expresses it: Anne Eliot's radical victory is a moral triumph yet a warning withal. And in each book, the lesson has been conveyed with the unobtrusive indirection of fine art; the story is ever first, we are getting fiction not lectures. These novels adorn truth; they show what literature can effect by the method of much-in-little.

There is nothing sensational in incident or complication: as with Richardson, an elopement is the highest stretch of external excitement Miss Austen vouchsafes. Yet all is drawn so beautifully to scale, as in such a scene as that of the quarrel and estrangement of Elizabeth and Darcy in " Pride and Prejudice," that the effect is greater than in the case of many a misused opportunity where the events are earth-shaking in import. The situation means so much to the participants, that the reader becomes sympathetically involved. After all, importance in

fiction is exactly like importance in life; important
to whom? the philosopher asks. The relativity of
things human is a wholesome theory for the artist
to bear in mind. Even as the most terrific cataclysm
on this third planet from the sun in a minor system,
makes not a ripple upon Mars, so the most infini-
tesimal occurrence in eighteenth century Hampshire
may seem of account,—if only a master draws the
picture.

Not alone by making her characters thoroughly
alive and interesting does Miss Austen effect this
result: but by her way of telling the tale as well;
by a preponderance of dialogue along with clear
portraiture she actually gets an effect that is dramatic. Scenes from her books are staged even to
the present day. She found this manner of dialogue with comparative parsimony of description and
narration, to be her true method as she grew as a
fiction-maker: the early unpublished story " Susan,"
and the first draught of " Sense and Sensibility,"
had the epistolary form of Richardson, the more
undramatic nature of which is self-evident. As for
characterization itself, she is with the few: she has
added famous specimens—men and women both—to
the natural history of fiction. To think of but one
book, " Pride and Prejudice," what an inimitable
study of a foolish woman is Mrs. Bennett! Who
has drawn the insufferable patroness more vividly
than in a Lady Catherine de Bourgh! And is not

the sycophant clergyman hit off to the life in Mr. Collins! Looking to the stories as a group, are not her heroines, with Anne Eliot perhaps at their head, wonderful for quiet attraction and truth, for distinctness, charm and variety? Her personages are all observed; she had the admirable good sense not to go beyond her last. She had every opportunity to see the county squire, the baronet puffed up with a sense of his own importance, the rattle and rake of her day, the tuft hunter, the gentleman scholar, and the retired admiral (her two brothers had that rank)—and she wisely decided to exhibit these and other types familiar to her locality and class, instead of drawing on her imagination or trying to extend by guess-work her social purview. Her women in general, whether satiric and unpleasant like Mrs. Norris in " Mansfield Park " or full of winning qualities like Catherine Moreland and Anne Eliot, are drawn with a sureness of hand, an insight, a complete comprehension that cannot be over-praised. Jane Austen's heroines are not only superior to her heroes (some of whom do not get off scot-free from the charge of priggishness) but they excel the female characterization of all English novelists save only two or three,—one of them being Hardy. Her characters were so real to herself, that she made statements about them to her family as if they were actual, —a habit which reminds of Balzac.

The particular angle from which she looked on

life was the satirical: therefore, her danger is exaggeration, caricature. Yet she yielded surprisingly
little, and her reputation for faithful transcripts
from reality, can not now be assailed. Her detached,
whimsical attitude of scrutinizing the little cross-
section of life she has in hand, is of the very essence
of her charm: hers is that wit which is the humor
of the mind: something for inward smiling, though
the features may not change. Her comedy has in
this way the unerring thrust and the amused tolerance
of a Molière whom her admirer Macaulay should
have named rather than Shakspere when wishing
to compliment her by a comparison; with her manner
of representation and her view of life in mind, one
reverts to Meredith's acute description of the spirit
that inheres in true comedy. " That slim, feasting
smile, shaped like the longbow, was once a big round
satyr's laugh, that flung up the brows like a fortress
lifted by gunpowder. The laugh will come again,
but it will be of the order of the smile, finely tempered,
showing sunlight of the mind, mental richness rather
than noisy enormity. Its common aspect is one of
unsolicitous observation, as if surveying a full field
and having leisure to dart on its chosen morsels,
without any flattering eagerness. Men's future upon
earth does not attract it; their honesty and shapeli-
ness in the present does; and whenever they were out
of proportion, overthrown, affected, pretentious,
bombastical, hypocritical, pedantic, fantastically del-

ANNIE HALENBAKE ROSS LIBRARY
LOCK HAVEN, PENNSYLVANIA

icate; whenever it sees them self-deceived or hood-
winked, given to run riot in idolatries, drifting into
vanities, congregating in absurdities, planning short-
sightedly, plotting dementedly; whenever they are at
variance with their professions, and violate the unwritten but perceptible laws binding them in consideration one to another; whenever they offend
sound reason, fair justice; are false in humility or
mined with conceit, individually or in the bulk—the
Spirit overhead will look humanely malign and cast
an oblique light on them, followed by volleys of
silvery laughter. That is the Comic Spirit."

If the " silvery laughter " betimes sounds a bit
sharp and thinly feminine, what would you have?
Even genius must be subject to the defect of its
quality. Still, it must be confessed that this attitude
of the artist observer is broken in upon a little in
the later novels, beginning with " Mansfield Park,"
by a growing tendency to moral on the time, a
tendency that points ominously to didacticism.
There is something of the difference in Jane Austen
between early and late, that we shall afterwards
meet in that other great woman novelist, George
Eliot. One might push the point too far, but it is
fair to make it.

We may also inquire—trying to see the thing
freshly, with independence, and to get away from
the mere handing-on of a traditional opinion—if
Jane Austen's character-drawing, so far-famed for

its truth, does not at times o'erstep the modesty of
Nature.   Goldwin Smith, in his biography of her,
is quite right in pointing out that she unquestionably
overdraws her types: Mr. Collins is at moments almost
a reminder of Uriah Heap for oily submissiveness: Sir
Walter Eliot's conceit goes so far he seems a theory
more than a man, a "humor" in the Ben Jonson
sense.   So, too, the valetudinarianism of Mr. Wood-
house, like that of Smollett's Bramble, is something
strained; so is Lady de Bourgh's pride and General
Tilney's tyranny.   Critics are fond of violent contrasts and to set over against one another authors
so unlike, for example, as Miss Austen and Dickens
is a favorite occupation.   Also is it convenient to
put a tag on every author: a mask reading *realist,
romanticist, psychologue, sensation-monger*, or some
such designation, and then hold him to the name.
Thus, in the case of Austen it is a temptation to
call her the greatest truth-teller among novelists, and
so leave her.   But, as a matter of fact, great as
realist and artist as she was, she does not hesitate
at that heightening of effect which insures clearer
seeing, longer remembering and a keener pleasure.
Perhaps she is in the broad view all the better artist
because of this: a thought sadly forgotten by the
extreme veritists of our day.   It is the business of
art to improve upon Nature.
     Again the reader of Jane Austen must expect to
find her with the limitation of her time and place:

it is, frankly, a dreadfully contracted view of the
world she represents, just for the reason that it is
the view of her Hampshire gentry in the day of the
third George.   The ideals seem low, narrow; they
lack air and light.   Woman's only rôle is marriage;
female propriety chokes originality; money talks,
family places individuals, and the estimate of sex-
relations is intricately involved with these *eidola*.
There is little sense of the higher and broader issues:
the spiritual restrictions are as definite as the social
and geographical: the insularity is magnificent.   It
all makes you think of Tennyson's lines:

> "They take the rustic cackle of their burg
>   For the great wave that echoes round the world!"

Hence, one of the bye-products of Miss Austen's
books is their revelation of hide-bound class-distinc-
tion, the not seldom ugly parochialism—the utilitarian aims of a circle of highly respectable English
country folk during the closing years of the eighteenth century.   The opening sentence of her masterpiece reads: " It is a truth universally acknowledged
that a single man in possession of a good fortune
must be in want of a wife."   Needless to say that
" universally " here is applicable to a tiny area of
earth observed by a most charming spinster, at a
certain period of society now fast fading into a
dim past.   But the sentence might serve fairly well
as a motto for all her work: every plot she con-

ceived is firm-based upon this as a major premise, and the particular feminine deduction from those words may be found in the following taken from another work, " Mansfield Park ": " Being now in her twenty-first year, Maria Bertram was beginning to think marriage a duty; and as a marriage with Mr. Rushford would give her the enjoyment of a larger income than her father's, as well as insure her the house in town, which was now a prime object, it became by the same rule of moral obligation, her evident duty to marry Mr. Rushford if she could." The egocentric worldliness of this is superb. The author, it may be granted, has a certain playful satire in her manner here and elsewhere, when setting forth such views: yet it seems to be fair to her to say that, taking her fiction as a whole, she contentedly accepts this order of things and builds upon it. She and her world exhibit not only worldliness but that " other-worldliness " which is equally self-centered and materialistic. Jane Austen is a highly enjoyable *mondaine*. To compare her gamut with that of George Eliot or George Meredith is to appreciate how much has happened since in social and individual evolution. The wide social sympathy that throbs in modern fiction is hardly born.

In spite, too, of the thorough good breeding of this woman writer, the primness even of her outlook upon the world, there is plain speaking in her books, even touches of coarseness that are but the echo of the rankness which abounds in the Fielding-Smollett school. Happily, it is a faint one.

Granting the slightness of her plots and their family likeness, warm praise is due for the skill with which they are conducted; they are neatly articulated, the climactic effect is, as a rule, beautifully graduated and sure in its final force: the multitude of littles which go to make up the story are, upon examination, seen to be not irrelevant but members of the one body, working together towards a common end. It is a puzzling question how this firm art was secured: since technique does not mean so much a gift from heaven as the taking of forethought, the self-conscious skill of a practitioner. Miss Austen, setting down her thoughts of an evening in a copy-book in her lap, interrupted by conversations and at the beck and call of household duties, does not seem as one who was acquiring the mastery of a difficult art-form. But the wind bloweth where it listeth—and the evidences of skill are there; we can but chronicle the fact, and welcome the result.

She was old-fashioned in her adherence to the "pleasant ending"; realist though she was, she could not go to the lengths either of theme or interpretation in the portrayal of life which later novelists have so sturdily ventured. It is easy to understand that with her avowed dislike of tragedy, living in a time when it was regarded as the business of fiction to be amusing—when, in short, it was not

fashionable to be disagreeable, as it has since become
—Jane Austen should have preferred to round out
her stories with a " curtain " that sends the audience
home content. She treats this desire in herself with
a gentle cynicism which, read to-day, detracts somewhat perhaps from the verity of her pictures. She
steps out from the picture at the close of her book
to say a word in proper person. Thus, in " Mansfield Park," in bringing Fanny Price into the arms
of her early lover, Edmund, she says: " I purposely
abstain from dates on this occasion, that every one
may be at liberty to fix their own, aware that the
cure of unconquerable passions and the transfer of
unchanging attachments must vary much as to time
in different people. I only entreat everybody to
believe that exactly at the time when it was quite
natural that it should be so, and not a week earlier,
Edmund did cease to care about Miss Crawford and
became as anxious to marry Fanny as Fanny herself
could desire."

But it cannot be urged against her that it was her
habit to effect these agreeable conclusions to her
social histories by tampering with probability or
violently wresting events from their proper sequence.
Life is neither comedy nor tragedy—it is tragi-com-
edy, or, if you prefer the graver emphasis, comi-
tragedy. Miss Austen, truth-lover, has as good a
right to leave her lovers at the juncture when we
see them happily mated, as at those more grievous

junctures so much affected by later fiction. Both representations may be true or false in effect, according as the fictionist throws emphasis and manages light-and-shade. A final page whereon all is *couleur de rose* has, no doubt, an artificial look to us now: a writer of Miss Austen's school or her kind of genius for reporting fact, could not have finished her fictions in just the same way. There is no blame properly, since the phenomenon has to do with the growth of human thought, the change of ideals reflected in literature.

For one more point: Miss Austen only knew, or anyhow, only cared to write, one sort of Novel—the love story. With her, a young man and woman (or two couples having similar relations) are interested in each other and after various complications arising from their personal characteristics, from family interference or other criss-cross of events, misplacement of affection being a trump card, are united in the end. The formula is of primitive simplicity. The wonder is that so much of involvement and genuine human interest can be got out of such scant use of the possible permutations of plot. It is all in the way it is done.

Love stories are still written in profusion, and we imagine that so compelling a motive for fiction will still be vital (in some one of its innumerable phases) in the twenty-fifth century. Yet it is true that novelists now point with pride to the work of the last generation of their art, in that it has so often made sex love subsidiary to other appeals, or even eliminated it altogether from their books. Some even boast of the fact that not a woman is to be found in the pages of their latest creation. Nearly one hundred years ago, Defoe showed the possibility (if you happen to have genius) of making a powerful story without the introduction of the eternal feminine: Crusoe could not declare with Cyrano de Bergerac:

"Je vous dois d'avoir eu tout au moins, une amie;
Grace à vous, une robe a passé dans ma vie."

It is but natural that, immensely powerful as it is, such a motive should have been over-worked: the gamut of variations has been run from love licit to love illicit, and love degenerate and abnormal to no-love-at-all. But any publisher will assure you that still "love conquers all"; and in the early nineteenth century any novelist who did not write tales of amatory interest was a fool: the time was not ripe to consider an extension of the theme nor a shifted point of view. For the earlier story-tellers, in the language of Browning's lyric,

"Love is best."

Jane Austen's diction—or better, her style, which is more than diction—in writing her series of social studies, affords a fine example of the adaptation of means to end. Given the work to be accomplished,

the tools are perfect instruments for the purpose.
The student of English style in its evolution must
marvel at the idiom of Austen, so strangely modern
is it, so little has time been able to make it *passé*.
From her first book, her manner seems to be easy,
adequate, unforced, with nothing about it self-conscious or gauche.   In the development of some great
writers the change from unsureness and vulgarity
to the mastery of mature years can be traced: Dickens is one such.   But nothing of the sort can be
found in Austen.   She has in " Northanger Abbey "
and " Pride and Prejudice "—early works—a power
in idiomatic English which enables her reader to see
her thought through its limpid medium of language,
giving, it may be, as little attention to the form of
expression as a man uninstructed in the niceties of
a woman's dress gives to those details which none
the less in their totality produce on him a most
formidable effect.   Miss Austen's is not the style of
startling tricks: nor has she the flashing felicities of
a Stevenson which lead one to return to a passage
for re-gustation.   Her manner rarely if ever takes
the attention from her matter.   But her words and
their marshaling (always bearing in her mind her un-
ambitious purpose) make as fit a garment for her
thought as was ever devised upon English looms.
If this is style, then Jane Austen possesses it, as
have very few of the race.   There is just a touch
of the archaic in it, enough to give a quaintness that

has charm without being precious in the French
sense; hers are breeding and dignity without distance
or stiffness.   Now and again the life-likeness is ac-
centuated by a sort of undress which goes to the
verge of the slip-shod—as if a gentlewoman should
not be too particular, lest she seem professional;
the sort of liberty with the starched proprieties of
English which Thackeray later took with such delightful results.   Of her style as a whole, then, we
may say that it is good literature for the very reason
that it is not literary; neither mannered nor mincing
nor affectedly plain.   The style is the woman—and
the woman wrote as a lady should who is portraying
genteel society; very much as she would talk—with
the difference the artist will always make between
life and its expression in letters.

Miss Austen's place was won slowly but surely,
unlike those authors whose works spring into instantaneous popularity, to be forgotten with equal
promptness, or others who like Mrs. Stowe write a
book which, for historical reasons, gains immediate
vogue and yet retains a certain reputation.   The
author of "Pride and Prejudice" gains in position
with the passing of the years.   She is one of the
select company of English writers who after a century are really read, really of more than historical
significance.   New and attractive editions of her
books are frequent: she not only holds critical regard
(and to criticism her importance is permanent) but

is read by an appreciable number of the lovers of
sound literature; read far more generally, we feel
sure, than Disraeli or Bulwer or Charles Kingsley,
who are so much nearer our own day and who filled so
large a place in their respective times.   Compared
with them, Jane Austen appears a serene classic.
When all is said, the test, the supreme test, is to
be read: that means that an author is vitally alive,
not dead on the shelves of a library where he has
been placed out of deference to the literary Mrs.
Grundy.   Lessing felt this when he wrote his brilliant quatrain:

> Wer wird nicht einen Klopstock loben,
> Doch wird ihn jeder lesen? Nein!
> Wir wollen weniger erhoben
> Und fleissiger gelesen sein.

So was the century which was to be conspicuous
for its development of fiction that should portray
the social relations of contemporary life with fine
and ever-increasing truth, most happily inaugurated
by a woman who founded its traditions and was a
wonderful example of its method.   She is the literary godmother of Trollope and Howells, and of
all other novelists since who prefer to the most spectacular uses of the imagination the unsensational
chronicling of life.

CHAPTER VI

MODERN ROMANTICISM: SCOTT

THE year after the appearance of " Pride and
Prejudice " there began to be published in England
a series of anonymous historical stories to which the
name of Waverley Novels came to be affixed, the title
of the first volume.   It was not until the writer had
produced for more than a decade a splendid list of
fictions familiar to all lovers of literature, that his
name—by that time guessed by many and admitted
to some—was publicly announced as that of Walter
Scott—a man who, before he had printed a single
romance, had won more than national importance by
a succession of narrative poems beginning with " The
Lay of the Last Minstrel."

Few careers, personal and professional, in letters,
are more stimulating and attractive than that of
Scott.   His life was winsome, his work of that large
and noble order that implies a worthy personality
behind it.   Scott, the man, as he is portrayed in
Lockhart's Life and the ever-delightful Letters, is
as suitable an object of admiration as Scott the
author of " Guy Mannering " and " Old Mortality."
And when we reflect that by the might of his genius

he set his seal on the historical romance, that the
modern romance derives from Scott, and that, moreover, in spite of the remarkable achievements in this
order of fiction during almost a century, he remains
not only its founder but its chief ornament, his contribution to modern fiction begins to be appreciated.

The characteristics of the Novel proper as a specific kind of fiction have been already indicated and
illustrated in this study: we have seen that it is a
picture of real life in a setting of to-day: the romance, which is Scott's business, is distinguished
from this in its use of past time and historic personages, its heightening of effect by the introducing
of the exceptional in scene and character, its general
higher color in the conductment of the narrative: and
above all, its emphasis upon the larger, nobler, more
inspiring aspects of humanity. This, be it understood, is the romance of modern times, not the elder
romance which was irresponsible in its picture of
life, falsely idealistic. When Sir Walter began his
fiction, the trend of the English Novel inheriting the
method and purpose of Richardson, was away from
the romantic in this sense. The analysis given has,
it may be hoped, made this plain. It was by the
sheer force of his creative gift, therefore, that Scott
set the fashion for the romance in fiction: aided
though he doubtless was by the general romanticism
introduced by the greater English poets and expressive of the movement in literature towards free-

dom, which followed the French Revolution.   That
Scott at this time gave the fiction an impulse not
in the central flow of development is shown in the
fact of its rapid decadence after he passed away.
While the romance is thus a different thing from the
Novel, modern fiction is close woven of the two
strands of realism and romance, and a comprehensive
study must have both in mind.   Even authors like
Dickens, Thackeray and Eliot, who are to be regarded as stalwart realists, could not avoid a single
sally each into romance, with " A Tale of Two
Cities," " Henry Esmond " and " Romola "; and on
the other hand, romanticists like Hawthorne and
Stevenson have used the methods and manner of the
realist, giving their loftiest flights the most solid
groundwork of psychologic reality.   It must always
be borne in mind that there is a romantic way of
dealing with fact: that a novel of contemporary society which implies its more exceptional possibilities
and gives due regard to the symbol behind every
so-called fact, can be, in a good sense, romantic.
Surely, that is a more acceptable use of the realistic
formula which, by the exercise of an imaginative
grasp of history, makes alive and veritable for us
some hitherto unrealized person or by-gone epoch.
Scott is thus a romanticist because he gave the romantic implications of reality: and is a novelist in
that broader, better definition of the word which ad-
mits it to be the novelist's business to portray social

humanity, past or present, by means of a unified, progressive prose narrative. Scott, although he takes advantage of the romancer's privilege of a free use of the historic past, the presentation of its heroic episodes and spectacular events, is a novelist, after all, because he deals with the recognizably human, not with the grotesque, supernatural, impossible. He imparts a vivid sense of the social interrelations, for the most part in a medieval environment, but in any case in an environment which one recognizes as controlled by human laws; not the brain-freak of a pseudo-idealist. Scott's Novels, judged broadly, make an impression of unity, movement and climax. To put it tersely: he painted manners, interpreted character in an historic setting and furnished story for story's sake. Nor was his genius helpless without the historic prop. Certain of his major successes are hardly historical narratives at all; the scene of " Guy Mannering," for example, and of " The Antiquary," is laid in a time but little before that which was known personally to the romancer in his young manhood.

It will be seen in this theory of realism and romance that so far from antagonists are the story of truth and the story of poetry, they merely stand for diverging preferences in handling material. Nobody has stated this distinction better than America's greatest romancer, Nathaniel Hawthorne. Having " The House of the Seven Gables " in mind, he says:

" When a writer calls his work a romance, it need hardly be observed that he wishes to claim a certain latitude both as to its fashion and material, which he would not have felt himself entitled to assume, had he professed to be writing a novel.   The latter form of composition is presumed to aim at a very minute fidelity, not only to the possible, but to the probable and ordinary course of man's experience. The former, while as a work of art it must rigidly subject itself to laws and while it sins unpardonably so far as it may swerve aside from the truth of the human heart, has fairly a right to present that truth under circumstances to a great extent of the author's own choosing or creation.   If he think fit, also, he may so manage his atmospherical medium as to bring out or mellow the lights and deepen and enrich the shadows of the picture.   He will be wise, no doubt, to make a very moderate use of the privileges here stated, and, especially, to mingle the marvelous rather as a slight, delicate and evanescent flavor than as any portion of the actual substance of the dish offered to the public.   The point of view in which this tale comes under the romantic definition lies in the attempt to connect a by-gone time with the very present that is flitting away from us.   It is a legend, prolonging itself from an epoch now gray in the distance, down into our own broad daylight, and bringing along with it some of its legendary mist, which the reader may either dis-

regard or allow it to float almost imperceptibly about
the characters and events for the sake of a picturesque effect.   The narrative, it may be, is woven
of so humble a texture, as to require this advantage
and at the same time to render it the more difficult
of attainment."   These words may be taken as the
modern announcement of Romance, as distinguished
from that of elder times.

The many romantic Novels written by Scott can
be separated into two groups, marked by a cleavage
of time: the year being 1819, the date of the publication of " Ivanhoe."   In the earlier group, containing the fiction which appeared during the five
years from 1814 to 1819, we find world-welcomed
masterpieces which are an expression of the unforced
first fruits of his genius: the three series of " Tales
of My Landlord," " Guy Mannering," " Rob Roy,"
" The Heart of Midlothian " and " Old Mortality,"
to mention the most conspicuous.   To the second
division belong stories equally well known, many of
them impressive: " The Monastery," " Kenilworth,"
" Quentin Durward," and " Red Gauntlet " among
them, but as a whole marking a falling off of power
as increasing years and killing cares made what was
at first hardly more than a sportive effort, a burden
under which a man, at last broken, staggered toward
the desired goal.   There is no manlier, more gallant
spectacle offered in the annals of literature than this
of Walter Scott, silent partner in a publishing house

and ruined by its failure after he has set up country
gentleman and gratified his expensive taste for ba-
ronial life, as he buckles to, and for weary years
strives to pay off by the product of his pen the
obligations incurred; his executors were able to clear
his estate of debt.   It was an immense drudgery
(with all allowance for its moments of creative joy)
accomplished with high spirits and a kind of French
gayety.   Nor, though the best quality of the work
was injured towards the end of the long task, and
Scott died too soon at sixty-one, was the born *raconteur* in him choked by this grim necessity of grind.
There have been in modern fiction a few masters,
and but a few, who were natural *improvvisatori:* conspicuous among them are Dumas the elder and Walter Scott.   Such writers pour forth from a very
spring of effortless power invention after invention,
born of the impulse of a rich imagination, a mind
stored with bountiful material for such shaping, and
a nature soaked with the humanities.   They are
great lovers of life, great personalities, gifted, resourceful, unstinted in their giving, ever with something of the boy in them, the careless prodigals of
literature.   Often it seems as if they toiled not to
acquire the craft of the writer, nor do they lose time
over the labor of the file.   To the end, they seem in
a way like glorious amateurs.   They are at the
antipodes of those careful craftsmen with whom all
is forethought, plan and revision.   Scott, fired by

a period, a character or scene, commonly sat down without seeing his way through and wrote *currente calamo*, letting creation take care of its own. The description of him by a contemporary is familiar where he was observed at a window, reeling off the manuscript sheets of his first romance.

" Since we sat down I have been watching that confounded hand—it fascinates my eye. It never stops—page after page is finished and thrown on the heap of manuscript, and still it goes on unwearied —and so it will be until candles are brought in, and God knows how long after that. It is the same every night."

The great merits of such a nature and the method that is its outcome should not blind us to its dangers, some of which Scott did not escape. Schoolboys to-day are able to point out defects in his style, glibly talking of loosely-built sentences, redundancies, diffuseness, or what not. He seems long-winded to the rising generation, and it may be said in their defense that there are Novels of Scott which if cut down one-third would be improved. Critics, too, speak of his anachronisms, his huddled endings, the stiffness of his young gentleman heroes, his apparent indifference to the laws of good construction; as well as of his Tory limitations, the ponderosity of his manner and the unmodernness of his outlook on the world along with the simple superficiality of his psychology. All this may cheerfully be granted, and yet the Scott lover will stoutly maintain that the spirit and the truth are here, that the Waverley books possess the great elements of fiction-making: not without reason did they charm Europe as well as the English-speaking lands for twenty years. The Scott romances will always be mentioned, with the work of Burns, Carlyle and Stevenson, when Scotland's contribution to English letters is under discussion; his position is fortified as he recedes into the past, which so soon engulfs lesser men. And it is because he was one of the world's natural story-tellers: his career is an impressive object-lesson for those who would elevate technique above all else.

He produced romances which dealt with English history centuries before his own day, or with periods near his time: Scotch romances of like kind which had to do with the historic past of his native land: romances of humbler life and less stately *entourage*, the scenes of which were laid nearer, sometimes almost within his own day. He was, in instances, notably successful in all these kinds, but perhaps most of all in the stories falling in the two categories last-named: which, like "Old Mortality," have the full flavor of Scotch soil.

The nature of the Novels he was to produce became evident with the first of them all, "Waverley." Here is a border tale which narrates the adventures of a scion of that house among the loyal Highlanders temporarily a rebel to the reigning English sovereign and a recruit in the interests of the young pretender: his fortunes, in love and war, and his eventual reinstatement in the King's service and happiness with the woman of his choice. While it might be too sweeping to say that there was in this first romance (which has never ranked with his best) the whole secret of the Scott historical story, it is true that the book is typical, that here as in the long line of brilliantly envisaged chronicle histories that followed, some of them far superior to this initial attempt, are to be found the characteristic method and charm of Sir Walter. Here, as elsewhere, the reader is offered picturesque color, ever varied scenes, striking situations, salient characters and a certain nobility both of theme and manner that comes from the accustomed representation of life in which large issues of family and state are involved—the whole merged in a mood of fealty and love. You constantly feel in Scott that life " means intensely and means good." A certain amount of lovable partisanship and prejudice goes with the view, not unwelcomely; there is also some carelessness as to the minute details of fact. But the effect of truth, both in character and setting, is overwhelming. Scott has vivified English and Scotch history more than all the history books: he saw it himself—so we see it. One of the reasons his work rings true—whereas Mrs. Radcliffe's adventure tales seem fictitious as well as feeble—is because it is the natural outcome of his life: all his interest, his liking, his belief went into the Novels. When he sat down at the mature age of forty-three to make fiction, there was behind him the large part of a lifetime of unconscious preparation for what he had to do: for years he had been steeped in the folk-lore and legend of his native country; its local history had been his hobby; he had not only read its humbler literature but wandered widely among its people, absorbed its language and its life, felt " the very pulse of the machine." Hence he differed *toto cælo* from an archeologist turned romancer like the German Ebers: being rather a genial traveler who, after telling tales of his experiences by word of mouth at the tavern hearth, sets them down upon paper for better preservation. He had been no less student than pedestrian in the field; lame as he was, he had footed his way to many a tall memorial of a hoary past, and when still hardly more than a boy, burrowed among the manuscripts of the Advocates' Library in Edinburgh, making himself an able antiquary at a time when most youth are idling or philandering. Moreover, he was himself the son of a border chief and knew minstrelsy almost at his nurse's knee: and the lilt of a ballad was always like wine to his heart. It makes you think of Sir Philip Sidney's splendid testimony to such an influence: " I never heard the old song of Percy and Douglas that I found not my heart moved more than with a trumpet."

All this could not but tell; the incidents in a book like " Waverley " are unforced: the advance of the story closely imitates Life in its ever-shifting succession of events: the reader soon learns to trust the author's faculty of invention.   Plot, story-interest, is it not the backbone of romantic fiction? And Scott, though perchance he may not conduct it so swiftly as pleases the modern taste, may be relied on to furnish it.

In the earlier period up to " Ivanhoe," that famous sortie into English history, belong such masterpieces as " Guy Mannering," " Old Mortality," " Heart of Midlothian," " The Bride of Lammermoor," and " Rob Roy "; a list which, had he produced nothing else would have sufficed to place him high among the makers of romance.   It is not the intention to analyze these great books one by one— a task more fit for a volume than a chapter; but to bring out those qualities of his work which are responsible for his place in fiction and influence in the Novel of the nineteenth century.

No story of this group—nor of his career as a writer—has won more plaudits than " The Heart of Midlothian."   Indeed, were the reader forced to the unpleasant necessity of choosing out of the thirty stories which Scott left the world the one most deserving of the prize, possibly the choice would fall on that superb portrayal of Scotch life—although other fine Novels of the quintet named would have

their loyal friends.   To study the peerlessly pathetic
tale of Effie and Jeanie Deans is to see Scott at
his representative best and note the headmarks of
his genius: it is safe to say that he who finds nothing
in it can never care for its author.

The first thing to notice in this novel of the ancient
Edinburgh Tolbooth, this romance of faithful sister-
hood, is its essential Scotch fiber.   The fact affects
the whole work.   It becomes thereby simpler, home-
lier, more vernacular: it is a story that is a native
emanation.   The groundwork of plot too is simple,
vital: and moreover, founded on a true incident.
Effie, the younger of two sisters, is betrayed; concerning her betrayer there is mystery: she is supposed to commit child-murder to hide her shame:
a crime then punishable by death.   The story deals
with her trial, condemnation and final pardon and
happy marriage with her lover through the noble
mediation of Jeanie, her elder sister.

In the presentation of an earlier period in Scotland, the opening of the eighteenth century, when
all punitive measures were primitive and the lawless
social elements seethed with restless discontent, Scott
had a fine chance: and at the very opening, in describing the violent putting to death of Captain
Porteous, he skilfully prepares the way for the general picture to be given. Then, as the story progresses,
to the supreme sacrificial effort of Jeanie in behalf
of her erring sister's life, gradually, stroke upon

stroke, the period with its religious schisms, its political passions and strong family ties, is so illuminated that while the interest is centered upon the Deans and their homely yet tragic history, Scotch life in an earlier century is envisaged broadly, truthfully, in a way never to grow pale in memory. Cameronian or King's man, God-fearing peasant, lawless ruffian or Tory gentleman, the characters are so marshaled that without sides being taken by the writer, one feels the complexity of the period: and its uncivil wildness is dramatically conveyed as a central fact in the Tolbooth with its grim concomitants of gallows and gaping crowd of sightseers and malcontents.

Scott's feeling for dramatic situation is illustrated in several scenes that stand out in high relief after a hundred details have been forgotten: one such is the trial scene in which Effie implores her sister to save her by a lie, and Jeanie in agony refuses; the whole management of it is impressively pictorial. Another is that where Jeanie, on the road to London, is detained by the little band of gypsy-thieves and passes the night with Madge Wildfire in the barn: it is a scene Scott much relishes and makes his reader enjoy. And yet another, and greater, is that meeting with Queen Caroline and Lady Suffolk when the humble Scotch girl is conducted by the Duke of Argyll to the country house and in the garden beseeches pardon for her sister Effie. It is intensely picturesque, real with many homely touches which add to the truth without cheapening the effect of royalty.   The gradual working out of the excellent plot of this romance to a conclusion pleasing to the reader is a favorable specimen of this romancer's method in story-telling.   There is disproportion in the movement: it is slow in the first part, drawing together in texture and gaining in speed during its closing portion.   Scott does not hesitate here, as so often, to interrupt the story in order to interpolate historical information, instead of interweaving it atmospherically with the tale itself.   When Jeanie is to have her interview with the Duke of Argyll, certain preliminary pages must be devoted to a sketch of his career.   A master of plot and construction to-day would have made the same story, so telling in motive, so vibrant with human interest, more effective, so far as its conductment is concerned.   Scott in his fiction felt it as part of his duty to furnish chronicle-history, very much as Shakspere seems to have done in his so-called chronicle-history plays; whereas at present the skilled artist feels no such responsibility.   It may be questioned if the book's famous scenes—the attempted breaking into the Tolbooth, or the visit of Jeanie to the Queen—would not have gained greatly from a dramatic point of view had they been more condensed; they are badly languaged, looking to this result, not swift enough for the best effects of drama, whereas conception and framework are highly dramatic.   In a word, if more carefully written, fuller justice would have been done the superb theme.

The characters that crowd the novel (as, in truth, they teem throughout the great romances) testify to his range and grasp: the Dean family, naturally, in the center.   The pious, sturdy Cameronian father and the two clearly contrasted sisters: Butler, the clergyman lover; the saddle-maker, Saddletree, for an amusing, long-winded bore; the quaint Laird Dumbiedikes; the soldiers of fortune, George Wilson and his mate; that other soldier, Porteous; the gang of evildoers with Madge in the van—a wonderful creation, she, only surpassed by the better known Meg— the high personages clustered about the Queen: loquacious Mrs. Glass, the Dean's kinswoman—one has to go back to Chaucer or Shakspere for a companion picture so firmly painted in and composed on such a generous scale.

Contention arises in a discussion of a mortal so good as Jeanie: it would hardly be in the artistic temper of our time to draw a peasant girl so well-nigh superhuman in her traits; Balzac's " Eugénie Grandet " (the book appeared only fifteen years later), is much nearer our time in its conception of the possibilities of human nature: Eugénie does not strain credence, while Jeanie's pious tone at times seems out of character, if not out of humanity.   The

striking contrast with Effie is in a way to her advantage: the weaker damsel appears more natural,
more like flesh and blood. But the final scene when,
after fleeing with her high-born lover, she returns
to her simple sister as a wife in a higher grade of
society and the sister agrees that their ways hence-
forth must be apart—that scene for truth and
power is one of the master-strokes. The reader finds
that Jeanie Deans somehow grows steadily in his
belief and affection: quietly but surely, a sense of
her comeliness, her truthful love, her quaint touch of
Scotch canniness, her daughterly duteousness and
her stanch principle intensifies until it is a pang to
bid her farewell, and the mind harks back to her
with a fond recollection. Take her for all in all,
Jeanie Deans ranks high in Scott's female portraiture: with Meg Merillies in her own station, and with
Lucy Ashton and Di Vernon among those of higher
social place. In her class she is perhaps unparal-
leled in all his fiction. The whole treatment of Effie's
irregular love is a fine example of Scott's kindly
tolerance (tempered to a certain extent by the social
convention of his time) in dealing with the sins of
human beings. He is plainly glad to leave Effie
an honestly married woman with the right to look
forward to happy, useful years. The story breeds
generous thoughts on the theme of young womanhood: it handled the problem neither from the superior altitude of the conventional moralist nor the

cold aloofness of the latter-day realist—Flaubert's attitude in " Madame Bovary."

" A big, imperfect, noble Novel," the thoughtful reader concludes as he closes it, and thinking back to an earlier impression, finds that time has not loosened its hold.

And to repeat the previous statement: what is true of this is true of all Scott's romances. The theme varies, the setting with its wealth of local color may change, the period or party differ with the demands of fact. Scotch and English history are widely invoked: now it is the time of the Georges, now of the Stuarts, now Elizabethan, again back to the Crusades. Scott, in fact, ranges from Rufus the Red to the year 1800, and many are the complications he considers within that ample sweep. It would be untrue to say that his plots imitate each other or lack in invention: we have seen that invention is one of his virtues. Nevertheless, the motives are few when disencumbered of their stately historical trappings: hunger, ambition, love, hate, patriotism, religion, the primary passions and bosom interests of mankind are those he depicts, because they are universal. It is his gift for giving them a particular dress in romance after romance which makes the result so often satisfactory, even splendid. Yet, despite the range of time and grasp of Life's essentials, there is in Scott's interpretation of humanity a certain lack which one feels in comparing

him with the finest modern masters: with a Meredith, a Turgeneff or a Balzac. It is a difference
not only of viewpoint but of synthetic comprehension
and philosophic penetration. It means that he mirrored a day less complex, less subtle and thoughtful.
This may be dwelt upon and illustrated a little in
some further considerations on his main qualities.

Scott, like the earlier novelists in general, was content to depict character from without rather than
from within: to display it through act and scene
instead of by the probing analysis so characteristically modern. This meant inevitable limitations in
dealing with an historical character or time. A high-church Tory himself, a frank Jacobite in his leanings—Taine declared he had a feudal mind—he naturally so composed a picture as to reflect this predilection, making effects of picturesqueness accordingly. The idea given of Mary Queen of Scots
from " The Abbot " is one example of what is meant;
that of Prince Charley in " Waverley " is another.
In a sense, however, the stories are all the better for
this obvious bias. Where a masculine imagination
moved by warm affection seizes on an historic figure
the result is sure to be vivid, at least; and let it be
repeated that Scott has in this way re-created history
for the many. He shows a sound artistic instinct in
his handling of historic personages relative to those
imaginary: rarely letting them occupy the center
of interest, but giving that place to the creatures of

his fancy, thereby avoiding the hampering restriction of a too close following of fact. The manipulation of Richard Cœur de Lion in "Ivanhoe" is instructive with this in mind.

While the lights and shadows of human life are duly blended in his romances, Scott had a preference for the delineation of the gentle, the grand (or grandiose), the noble and the beautiful: loving the medieval, desiring to reproduce the age of chivalry, he was naturally aristocratic in taste, as in intellect, though democratic by the dictates of a thoroughly good heart. He liked a pleasant ending —or, at least, believed in mitigating tragedy by a checker of sunlight at the close. He had little use for the degenerate types of mankind: certainly none for degeneracy for its own sake, or because of a kind of scientific interest in its workings. Nor did he conceive of the mission of fiction as being primarily instructional: nor set too high a value on a novel as a lesson in life—although at times (read the moral tag to "The Heart of Midlothian") he speaks in quite the preacher's tone of the improvement to be got from the teaching of the tale. Critics to-day are, I think, inclined to place undue emphasis upon what they regard as Scott's failure to take the moral obligations of fiction seriously: they confuse his preaching and his practice. Whatever he declared in his letters or Journal, the novels themselves, read in the light of current methods, certainly leave an old-fashioned taste on the palate, because of their moralizings and avowments of didactic purpose. The advantages and disadvantages of this general attitude can be easily understood: the loss in philosophic grasp is made up in healthiness of tone and pleasantness of appeal.   One recognizes such an author as, above all, human and hearty.   The reserves and delicacies of Anglo-Saxon fiction are here, of course, in full force: and a doctored view of the Middle Ages is the result, as it is in Tennyson's " Idylls of the King."   A sufficient answer is that it is not Scott's business to set us right as to medievalism, but rather to use it for the imaginative purposes of pleasure.   The frank intrusion of the author himself into the body of the page or in the way of footnotes is also disturbing, judged by our later standards: but was carried on with much charm by Thackeray in the mid-century, to reappear at its end in the pages of Du Maurier.

In the more technical qualifications of the story-maker's art, Scott compensated in the more masculine virtues for what he lacked in the feminine.   Possessing less of finesse, subtlety and painstaking than some who were to come, he excelled in sweep, movement and variety, as well as in a kind of largeness of effect: " the big bow-wow business," to use his own humorously descriptive phrase when he was comparing himself with Jane Austen, to his own disadvantage.   And it is these very qualities that endear

him to the general and keep his memories green:
making " Ivanhoe " and " Kenilworth " still useful
for school texts—unhappy fate! Still, this means
that he always had a story to tell and told it with
the flow and fervor and the instinctive coherence of
the story-teller born, not made.

When the fortunes of his fictive folk were settled,
this novelist, always more interested in characters
than in the plot which must conduct them, often
loses interest and his books end more or less lamely,
or with obvious conventionality. Anything to close
it up, you feel. But of action and incident, scenes
that live and situations with stage value, one of
Scott's typical fictions has enough to furnish the
stock in trade for life of many later-day romanticists
who feebly follow in his wake. He has a special
skill in connecting the comparatively small private
involvement, which is the kernel of a story, with important public matters, so that they seem part of
the larger movements or historic occurrences of the
world. Dignity and body are gained for the tale
thereby.

In the all-important matter of characterization,
Scott yields the palm to very few modern masters.
Merely to think of the range, variety and actuality
of his creations is to feel the blood move quicker.
From figures of historic and regal importance—Richard, Elizabeth, Mary—to the pure coinage of imagination—Dandy Dinmont, Dugald Dalgetty,

Dominie Sampson, Rebecca, Lucy, Di Vernon and Jeanie—how the names begin to throng and what a motley yet welcome company is assembled in the assizes where this romancer sits to mete out fate to those within the wide bailiwick of his imagination! This central gift he possessed with the princes of story-making.   It is also probable that of the imaginative writers of English speech, nobody but Shakspere and Dickens—and Dickens alone among fellow fiction-makers—has enriched the workaday world with so many people, men and women, whose speech, doings and fates are familiar and matter for common reference.   And this is the gift of gifts. It is sometimes said that Scott's heroes and heroines (especially, perhaps, the former) are lay figures, not convincing, vital creations.   There is a touch of truth in it.   His striking and successful figures are not walking gentlemen and leading ladies.   When, for example, you recall " Guy Mannering," you do not think of the young gentleman of that name, but of Meg Merillies as she stands in the night in high relief on a bank, weather-beaten of face and wild of dress, hurling her anathema: " Ride your ways, Ellangowan! " In characters rather of humble pathos like Jeanie Deans or of eccentric humor like Dominie Sampson, Scott is at his best.   He confessed to misliking his heroes and only warming up to full creative activity over his more unconventional types: border chiefs, buccaneers, freebooters and smugglers.   " My

rogue always, in spite of me, turns out my hero,"
is his whimsical complaint.

But this does not apply in full force to his women.
Di Vernon—who does not recall that scene where
from horseback in the moonlight she bends to her
lover, parting from him with the words: "Farewell,
Frank, forever! There is a gulf between us—a gulf
of absolute perdition. Where we go, you must not
follow; what we do, you must not share in—farewell,
be happy!" That is the very accent of Romance,
in its true and proper setting: not to be staled by
time nor custom.

Nor will it do to claim that he succeeds with his
Deans and fails with women of regal type: his Marys
and Elizabeth Tudors. In such portrayals it seems
to me he is pre-eminently fine: one cannot understand the critics who see in such creations mere stock
figures supplied by history not breathed upon with
the breath of life. Scott had a definite talent for
the stage-setting of royalty: that is one of the reasons for the popularity of "Kenilworth." It is,
however, a true discrimination which finds more of
life and variety in Scott's principal women than in
his men of like position. But his Rob Roys, Hat-
teraicks and Dalgettys justify all praise and help
to explain that title of Wizard of the North which
he won and wore.

In nothing is Scott stronger than in his environ-
ments, his devices for atmosphere. This he largely

secures by means of description and with his wealth
of material, does not hesitate to take his time in
building up his effects.   Perhaps the most common
criticism of him heard to-day refers to his slow movement.   Superabundance of matter is accompanied
by prolixity of style, with a result of breeding im-
patience in the reader, particularly the young.   Boys
and girls at present do not offer Scott the unreserved
affection once his own, because he now seems an
author upon whom to exercise the gentle art of skip-
ping.   Enough has been said as to Scott's lack of
modern economy of means.   It is not necessary to
declare that this juvenile reluctance to his leisurely
manner stands for total depravity.   The young
reader of the present time (to say nothing of the
reader more mature) is trained to swifter methods,
and demands them.   At the same time, it needs to
be asserted that much of the impressiveness of Scott
would be lost were his method and manner other than
they are: nor will it do harm to remind ourselves
that we all are in danger of losing our power of
sustained and consecutive attention in relation to
literature, because of the scrap-book tendency of so
much modern reading.   On the center-table, cheap
magazines; on the stage, vaudeville—these are habits
that sap the ability for slow, ruminative pleasure in
the arts.   Luckily, they are not the only modern
manifestation, else were we in a parlous state, indeed!   The trouble with Scott, then, may be re-

solved in part into a trouble with the modern folk who read him.

When one undertakes the thankless task of analyzing coldly and critically the style of Scott, the faults are plain enough. He constantly uses two adjectives or three in parallel construction where one would do the work better. The construction of his sentences loses largely the pleasing variation of a richly articulated system by careless punctuation and a tendency to make parallel clauses where subordinate relations should be expressed. The unnecessary copula stars his pages. Although his manner in narration rises with his subject and he may be justly called a picturesque and forceful writer, he is seldom a distinguished one. One does not turn to him for the inevitable word or phrase, or for those that startle by reason of felicity and fitness. These strictures apply to his descriptive and narrative parts, not to the dialogue: for there, albeit sins of diffuseness and verbosity are to be noted—and these are modified by the genial humanity they embody—he is one of the great masters. His use of the Scotch dialect adds indefinitely to his attraction and native smack: racy humor, sly wit, canny logic, heartful sympathy—all are conveyed by the folk medium. All subsequent users of the people-speech pay toll to Walter Scott. Small courtesy should be extended to those who complain that these idioms make hard reading. Never does

Scott give us dialect for its own sake, but always for the sake of a closer revelation of the human heart—dialect's one justification.

At its worst, Scott's style may fairly be called ponderous, loose, monotonous: at its finest, the adequate instrument of a natural story-teller who is most at home when, emerging from his *longueur,* he writes of grand things in the grand manner.

Thus, Sir Walter Scott defined the Romance for modern fiction, gave it the authority of his genius and extended the gamut of the Novel by showing that the method of the realist, the awakening of interest in the actualities of familiar character and life, could be more broadly applied. He opposed the realist in no true sense: but indicated how, without a lapse of art or return to outworn machinery, justice might yet be done to the more stirring, large, heroic aspects of the world of men: a world which exists and clamors to be expressed: a world which readers of healthy taste are perennially interested in, nay, sooner or later, demand to be shown. His fiction, whether we award it the somewhat grudging recognition of Carlyle or with Ruskin regard its maker as the one great novelist of English race, must be deemed a precious legacy, one of literature's most honorable ornaments—especially desirable in a day so apparently plain and utilitarian as our own, eschewing ornament and perchance for that reason needing it all the more.

CHAPTER VII

FRENCH INFLUENCE

In the first third of the nineteenth century English fiction stood at the parting of the ways. Should it follow Scott and the romance, or Jane Austen and the Novel of everyday life? Should it adopt that form of story-making which puts stress on action and plot and is objective in its method, roaming all lands and times for its material; or, dealing with the familiar average of contemporary society, should it emphasize character analysis and choose the subjective realm of psychology for its peculiar domain? The pen dropped from the stricken hand of Scott in 1832; in that year a young parliamentary reporter in London was already writing certain lively, closely observed sketches of the town, and four years later they were to be collected and published under the title of " Sketches by Boz," while the next year that incomparable extravaganza, " The Pickwick Papers," was to go to an eager public. English fiction had decided: the Novel was to conquer the romance for nearly a century. It was a victory which to the present day has been a dominant influence in story-making; establishing

150

a tendency which, until Stevenson a few years since, with the gaiety of the inveterate boy, cried up Romance once more, bade fair to sweep all before it.

Before tracing this vigorous development of the Novel of Reality with Dickens, Thackeray and Eliot (to name three great leaders), it is important to get an idea of the growth on French soil which was so deeply influential upon English as well as upon other modern fiction. Nothing is more certain in literary evolution than the fact that the French Novel in the nineteenth century has molded and defined modern fiction, thus repaying an earlier debt owed the English pioneers, Richardson and Fielding. English fiction of our own generation may be described as a native variation on a French model: in fact, the fictionists of Europe and the English-speaking lands, with whatever divergencies personal or national, have derived in large measure from the Gaul the technique, the point of view and the choice of theme which characterizes the French Novel from Stendhal to Balzac, from Zola to Guy de Maupassant.

I

The name of Henri Beyle, known to literature under the sobriquet of Stendhal, has a meaning in the development of the modern type of fiction out of proportion to the intrinsic value of his stories.

He was, of course, far surpassed by mightier followers like Balzac, Flaubert and Zola; yet his significance lies in the very fact that they were followers. His is all the merit pertaining to the feat
of introducing the Novel of psychic analysis: of that
persistent and increasingly unpleasant bearing-down
upon the darker facts of personality. Hence his
"Rouge et Noir," dated 1830 and typical of his
aim and method, is in a sense an epoch-making
book.

Balzac was at the same time producing the earlier
studies to culminate in that Human Comedy which
was to stand as the chief accomplishment of his
nation in the literature of fiction. But Stendhal,
sixteen years older, began to print first and to him
falls the glory of innovation. Balzac gives full
praise to his predecessor in his essay on Beyle, and
his letters contain frequent references to the debt
he owed that curious bundle of fatuities, inconsist-
encies and brilliancies, the author of "The Char-
treuse de Parme." Later, Zola calls him "the father
of us all," meaning of the naturalistic school of
which Zola himself was High Priest. Beyle's business was the analysis of soul states: an occupation
familiar enough in these times of Hardy, Meredith
and Henry James. He held several posts of importance under Napoleon, worshiped that leader,
loved Italy as his birthplace, loved England too, and
tried to show in his novels the result of the inactive

Restoration upon a generation trained by Napoleon to action, violence, ambition and passion.

Read to-day, " Le Rouge et Noir," which it is sufficient to consider for our purposes, seems somewhat slow in movement, struggling in construction, meticulous in manner.   At times, its interminability recalls " Clarissa Harlowe," but it possesses the traits which were to mark the coming school of novel-writing in France and hence in the modern world: to wit, freedom in dealing with love in its irregular relation, the tendency towards tragedy, and that subtlety of handling which makes the main interest to depend upon motive and thought rather than upon the external action itself.   " Thus conscience doth make cowards of us all,"—that might be the motto.   The young quasi-hero is Julian, an ambitious worldling of no family, and his use of the Church as a means of promotion, his amours with several women and his death because of his love for one of them, are traced with a kind of tortuous revelation of the inner workings of the human heart which in its way declares genius in the writer: and which certainly makes a work disillusioning of human nature.   Its more external aspect of a study of the politic Church and State, of the rivalry between the reds and the blacks of the state religion, is entirely secondary to this greater purpose and result: here, for the first time at full length, a writer shows the possibility of that realistic portrayal

sternly carried through, no matter how destructive
of romantic preconceptions of men and women. It
is the method of Richardson flowering in a time of
greater freedom and more cynical questioning of the
gods.

II

But giving Stendhal his full mint and cummin
of praise, he yet was but the forerunner of a mightier
man. Undoubtedly, he prepared the soil and was
a necessary link in the chain of development wherewith fiction was to forge itself an unbreakable sequence of strength. Balzac was to put out his lesser
light, as indeed the refulgence of his genius was to
overshine all French fiction, before and since. It
would be an exaggeration to say that the major
English novelists of the middle nineteenth century
were consciously disciples of Balzac—for something
greater even than he moved them; the spirit of the
Time. But it is quite within bounds to say that
of all modern fiction he is the leader and shaper.
Without him, his greatest native follower, Zola, is
inconceivable. He gathers up into himself and expresses at its fullest all that was latent in the striking modern growth whose banner-cry was Truth,
and whose method was that of the social scientist.
Here was a man who, early in his career, for the
first time in the history of the Novel, deliberately
planned to constitute himself the social historian of

his epoch and race: and who, in upwards of a hundred remarkable pieces of fiction in Novel form executed that plan in such fulness that his completed work stands not only as a monument of industry, but as perhaps the most inspiring example of literary synthesis in the history of letters.   In bigness of conception and of construction—let alone the way in which the work was performed—the Human Comedy is awe-begetting; it drives one to Shakspere for like largeness of scale.   Such a performance, ordered and directed to a foreseen end, is unique in literature.

As Balzac thus gave birth, with a fiery fecundity of invention, to book after book of the long list of Novels that make up his story of life, there took shape in his mind a definite intention: to become the Secretary of an Age of which he declared society to be the historian.   He wished to exhibit man in his species as he was to be seen in the France of the novelist's era, just as a naturalist aims to study beast-kind, segregating them into classes for zoological investigation.   Later, Balzac's great successor (as we shall see) applied this analogy with more rigid insistence upon the scientific method which should obtain in all literary study.   The survey proposed covered a period of about half a century and included the Republic, the Empire and the Restoration: it ranged through all classes and conditions of men with no appearance of prejudice, preference or parti-pris (this is one of the marvels of Balzac), thus gaining the immense advantage of an apparently complete and catholic comprehension of the human show. Of all modern novelists, Balzac is the one whose work seems like life instead of an opinion of life; he has the objectivity of Shakspere. Even a Tolstoy set beside him seems limited.

This idea of a plan was not crystallized into the famous title given to his collective works—La Comédie Humaine—until 1842, when but eight years of life remained to him. But four years earlier it had been mentioned in a letter, and when Balzac was only a little over thirty, at a time when his better-known books were just beginning to appear, he had signified his sense of an inclusive scheme by giving such a running title to a group of his stories as the familiar "Scenes from Private Life"—to which, in due course, were added other designations for the various parts of the great plan. The encyclopedic survey was never fully completed, but enough was done to justify all the laudation that belongs to a Herculean task and the exploitation of an almost incredible amount of human data. As for finishing the work, the failure hardly detracts from its value or affects its place in literature. Neither Spenser's " Faëry Queen " nor Wordsworth's " The Excursion " was completed, and, per contra, it were as well for Browning if " The Ring and the Book " had not been. In all such cases of so-

called incompletion, one recognizes Hercules from
the feet. Had this mighty story-teller and student
of humanity carried out his full intention there would
have been nearly 150 pieces of fiction; of the plan-
on-paper he actually completed ninety-seven, two-
thirds of the whole, and enough to illustrate the conception. And it must be remembered that Balzac
died at fifty. One result of the incompletion, as
Brunetière has pointed out, is to give disproportion-
ate treatment to certain phases of life, to the military, for instance, for which Balzac has twenty-four
stories on his list, whereas only two, " The Chouans "
and " A Passion in the Desert," were executed. But
surely, sufficient was done, looking to the comedy
as a whole, to force us to describe the execution as
well as the conception as gigantic. Had the work
been more mechanically pushed to its end for the
exact plan's sake, the perfection of scheme might
have been attained at the expense of vitality and
inspiration. Ninety-seven pieces of fiction, the majority of them elaborate novels, the whole involving
several thousand characters, would be impressive in
any case, but when they come from an author who
marvelously reproduces his time and country, creating his scenes in a way to afford us a sense of the
complexity of life—its depth and height, its beauty,
terror and mystery—we can but hail him as Master.

And in spite of the range and variety in Balzac's
unique product, it has an effect of unity based upon

a sense of social solidarity. He conceives it his duty to present the unity of society in his day, whatever its apparent class and other divergencies. He would show that men and women are members of the one body social, interacting upon each other in manifold relations and so producing the dramas of earth; each story plays its part in this general aim, illustrating the social laws and reactions, even as the human beings themselves play their parts in the world. In this way Balzac's Human Comedy is an organism, however much it may fall short of symmetry and completion.

In the outline of the plan we find him separating his studies into three groups or classes: The Studies of Manners, the Philosophical Studies, and the Analytic Studies. In the first division were placed the related groups of scenes of Private life, Provincial life, Parisian life, Political life, Military life and Country life. It was his desire, as he says in a letter to Madame Hanska, to have the group of studies of Manners " represent all social effects "; in the philosophic studies the causes of those effects: the one exhibits individualities typified, the other, types individualized: and in the Analytic Studies he searches for the principles. " Manners are the performance; the causes are the wings and the machinery. The principles—they are the author. . . . Thus man, society and humanity will be described, judged, analyzed without repetition and in a work which will be, as it were, 'The Thousand and One Nights' of the west."

The scheme thus categorically laid down sounds rather dry and formal, nor is it too easy to understand.   But all trouble vanishes when once the Human Comedy itself, in any example of it, is taken up; you launch upon the great swollen tide of life and are carried irresistibly along.

It is plain that with an author of Balzac's productive powers, any attempt to convey an idea of his quality must perforce confine itself to a few representative specimens.   A few of them, rightly chosen, give a fair notion of his general interpretation.   What then are some illustrative creations?

In the case of most novelists, although of first rank, it is not as a rule difficult to define their class and name their tendency: their temperaments and beliefs are so-and-so, and they readily fall under the designation of realist or romanticist, pessimist, or optimist, student of character or maker of plots. This is, in a sense, impossible with Balzac.   The more he be read, the harder to detect his bias: he seems, one is almost tempted to say, more like a natural force than a human mind.   Persons read two or three—perhaps half a dozen of his books— and then prate glibly of his dark view, his predilection for the base in mankind; when fifty fictions have been assimilated, it will be realized that but a phase of Balzac had been seen.

When the passion of creation, the birth-throes of a novel were on him, he became so immersed in the aspect of life he was depicting that he saw, felt, knew naught else: externally this obsession was expressed by his way of life and work while the story was growing under his hand: his recluse habits, his monkish abstention from worldly indulgences, the abnormal night hours of activity, the loss of flesh, so that the robust man who went into the guarded chamber came out at the end of six weeks the shadow of himself.

As a consequence of the consecration to the particular task (as if it embraced the one view of existence), the reader perhaps experiences a shock of surprise in passing from " The Country Doctor " to "Père Goriot." But the former is just as truly part of his interpretation as the latter. A dozen fictions can be drawn from the body of his production which portray humanity in its more beautiful, idealistic manifestations. Books like " The Country Doctor" and " Eugénie Grandet " are not alone in the list. And how beautiful both are! " The Country Doctor " has all the idyllic charm of setting which a poetic interpretation of life in a rural community can give. Not alone Nature, but human nature is hymned. The kindly old physician, whose model is the great Physician himself, is like Chaucer's good parson, an unforgettable vision of the higher potentialities of the race. Such a novel de-

serves to be called quite as truly romance and prose
poem, save that Balzac's vraisemblance, his gift for
photographic detail and the contemporaneousness of
the setting, make it modern.   And thus with " Eugénie Grandet " the same method applied in " The
Country Doctor " to the study of a noble profession
in a rural atmosphere, is here used for the portrait
of a good woman whose *entourage* is again that of
simple, natural conditions.   There is more of light
and shade in the revelation of character because
Eugénie's father, the miser—a masterly sketch—
furnishes a dark background for her radiant personality.   But the same effect is produced, that of
throwing into bold relief the sweet, noble, high and
pure in our common humanity.   And in this case it
is a girl of humble station far removed from the
shams and shameful passions of the town.   The
conventional contrast would be to present in another
novel some woman of the city as foul as this daughter
of Grandet is fair.   Not so Balzac.   He is too broad
an observer of humanity, and as artist too much the
master for such cheap effects of *chiaroscuro*.   In
" The Duchess De Langeais " he sets his central character amidst the frivolities of fashion and behold,
yet another beautiful type of the sex!   As Richardson drew his Pamela and Clarissa, so Balzac his
Eugénie and the Duchess: and let us not refrain
from carrying out the comparison, and add, how
feeble   seems   the   Englishman   in   creation   when

one thinks of the half a hundred other female figures, good and bad, high and low, distinctly etched upon the memory by the mordant pen of the Frenchman!

Then if we turn to that great tragedy of family, " Père Goriot," the change is complete. Now are we plunged into an atmosphere of greed, jealousy, uncleanliness and hate, all steeped in the bourgeois street air of Paris. In this tale of thankless daughters and their piteous old father, all the hideousness possible to the ties of kin is uncovered to our frightened yet fascinated eye. The plot holds us in a vise; to recall Madame Vautrin's boarding house is to shudder at the sights and smells! Compare it with Dickens' Mrs. Todgers, and once and for all you have the difference between the Anglo-Saxon and Celtic genius.

Suppose, now, the purpose be to reveal not a group or community, but one human soul, a woman's this time: read " A Woman of Thirty " and see how the novelist,—for the first time—and one is inclined to add, for all time,—has pierced through the integuments and reached the very quick of psychologic exposure. It is often said that he has created the type of young-old, or old-young woman: meaning that before him, novelists overlooked the fact that a woman of this age, maturer in experience and still ripe in physical charms, is really of intense social attraction, richly worth study. But this is because

Balzac knows that all souls are interesting, if only
we go beneath the surface.   The only work of modern
fiction which seems to me so nakedly to lay open the
recesses of the human spirit as does " A Woman of
Thirty " is Meredith's " The Egoist " ; and, of course,
master against master, Balzac is easily the superior,
since the English author's wonderful book is so mannered and grotesque.   Utter sympathy is shown in
these studies of femininity, whether the subject
be a harlot, a saint or a patrician of the *Grande
Monde.*

If the quest be for the handling of mankind *en
masse,* with big effects of dark and light : broad brush-
work on a canvas suited to heroical, even epic, themes,
—a sort of fiction the later Zola was to excel in—
Balzac will not fail us.   His work here is as noteworthy as it is in the fine detailed manner of his most
realistical modern studies—or in the searching analysis of the human spirit.   " The Chouans " may stand
for this class : it has all the fire, the color, the élan
that emanate from the army and the call of country.
We have flashed before us one of those reactionary
movements, after the French Revolution, which take
on a magic romanticism because they culminate
in the name of Napoleon.   While one reads, one
thinks war, breathes war—it is the only life for
the moment.   Just ahead a step, one feels, is the
" imminent deadly breach " ; the social or business
or Bohemian doings of later Paris are as if they

did not exist.   And this particular novel will achieve
such a result with the reader, even although it is not
by any means one of Balzac's supreme achievements,
being in truth, a little aside from his metier, since it
is historical and suggests in spots the manner of
Scott.   But this power of envisaging war (which will
be farther realized if such slighter works as " A Dark
Affair " and " An Episode Under the Terror " be
also perused), is only a single manifestation of a
general gift.   Suppose there is desired a picture very
common in our present civilization—most common it
may be in America,—that of the country boy going
up to the city to become—what?   Perhaps a captain
of commerce, or a leader of fashion: perhaps a great
writer or artist: or a politician who shall rule the
capitol.   It is a venture packed full of realistic
experience but equally full of romance, drama, poetry
—of an epic suggestiveness.   In two such volumes
as " A Great Provincial Man in Paris " and " Lost
Illusions," all this, with its dire chances of evil as
well as its roseate promise of success, has been wonderfully expressed.   So cogently modern a motive
had never been so used before.

Sometimes in a brace of books Balzac shows us the
front and back-side of some certain section of life:
as in " Cousin Pons " and " Cousine Bette."—The
corner of Paris where artists, courtesans and poor
students most do congregate, where Art capitalized
is a sacred word, and the odd estrays of humanity,

picturesque, humorous, and tragic, display all the chances of mankind,—this he paints so that we do not so much look on as move amidst the throng. In the first-named novel, assuredly a very great book, the figure of the quaint old connoisseur is one of fiction's superlative successes: to know him is to love him in all his weakness. In the second book, Bette is a female vampire and the story around her as terrible as the other is heart-warming and sweet. And you know that both are true, true as they would not have been apart: "helpless each without the other."

Again, how much of the gambling activities of modern business are emblazoned in another of the acknowledged masterpieces, "Cæsar Birotteau." We can see in it the prototype of much that comes later in French fiction: Daudet's "Risler Ainè et Froment Jeune" and Zola's "L'Argent," to name but two. Such a story sums up the practical, material side of a reign or an epoch.

Nor should it be forgotten that this close student of human nature, whose work appears so often severely mundane, and most strong when its roots go down into the earth, sometimes seeming to prefer the rankness and slime of human growths,—can on occasion soar into the empyrean, into the mystic region of dreams and ideals and all manner of subtle imaginings. Witness such fiction as "The Magic Skin," "Seraphita," and "The Quest of the Absolute." It is hard to believe that the author of such creations is he of " Père Goriot " or " Cousine Bette." But it is Balzac's wisdom to see that such pictures are quite as truly part of the Human Comedy: because they represent man giving play to his soul— exercising his highest faculties. Nor does the realistic novelist in such efforts have the air of one who has left his true business in order to disport himself for once in an alien element. On the contrary, he seems absolutely at home: for the time, this is his only affair, his natural interest.

And so with illustrations practically inexhaustible, which the long list prodigally offers. But the scope and variety have been already suggested; the best rule with Balzac is, each one to his taste, always remembering that in a writer so catholic, there is a peculiar advantage in an extended study. Nor can from twenty to twenty-five of his best books be read without a growing conviction that here is a man of genius who has done a unique thing.

It is usual to refer to Balzac as the first great realist of the French, indeed, of modern fiction. Strictly, he is not the first in France, as we have seen, since Beyle preceded him; nor in modern fiction, for Jane Austen, so admirably an artist of verity, came a generation before. But, as always when a compelling literary force appears, Balzac without any question dominates in the first half of the nineteenth century: more than this, he sets the mold of the type which marks the second half. In fact, the modern Novel means Balzac's recipe. English fiction, along with that of Europe, shares this influence. We shall see in dealing with Dickens how definitely the English writer adopted the Balzac method as suited to the era and sympathetic to Dickens' own nature.

As to the accuracy with which he gave a representation of contemporary life—thus deserving the name realist—considerable may be said in the way of qualification. Much of it applies with similar force to Zola, later to be hailed as a king among modern realists in the naturalistic extreme to which he pushed the movement. Balzac, through his remarkable instinct for detail and particularity, did introduce into nineteenth century fiction an effect of greater truth in the depiction of life. Nobody perhaps had—nobody has since—presented *mis-en-scene* as did he. He builds up an impression by hundreds of strokes, each seemingly insignificant, but adding to a totality that becomes impressive. Moreover, again and again in his psychologic analysis there are home-thrusts which bring the blood to the face of any honest person. His detail is thus quite as much subjective as external. It were a great mistake to regard Balzac as merely a writer who photographed things outside in the world; he is intensely interested in the things within—and if objectivity meant realism exclusively, he would be no realist at all.

But farther than this; with all his care for minute touches and his broad and painstaking observation, it is not so much life, after all, as a vision of life which he gives. This contradicts what was said early in the present chapter: but the two statements stand for the change likely to come to any student of Balzac: his objective personality at last resolves itself into a vividly personal interpretation. His breadth blinds one for a while, that is all. Hence Balzac may be called an incurable romantic, an impressionist, as much as realist. Like all first-class art, his gives us the seeming-true for our better instruction. He said in the Preface to " Père Goriot " that the novelist should not only depict the world as it is, but " a possibly better world." He has done so. The most untrue thing in a novel may be the fact lifted over unchanged from life? Truth is not only stranger than fiction, but great fiction is truer than truth. Balzac understood this, remembered it in his heart. He is too big as man and artist to be confined within the narrow realistic formula. While, as we have seen, he does not take sides on moral issues, nor allow himself to be a special pleader for this or that view, his work strikes a moral balance in that it shows universal humanity—not humanity tranced in metaphysics, or pathologic in analysis, or enmeshed in sensualism. In this sense, Balzac is a great realist. There is no danger of any novelist —any painter of life—doing harm, if he but gives us the whole. It is the story-teller who rolls some prurient morsel under his tongue who has the taint in him: he who, to sell his books, panders to the degraded instincts of his audience. Had Balzac been asked point-blank what he deemed the moral duty of the novelist, he would probably have disclaimed any other responsibility than that of doing good work, of representing things as they are. But this matters not, if only a writer's nature be large and vigorous enough to report of humanity in a trustworthy way. Balzac was much too well endowed in mind and soul and had touched life far too widely, not to look forth upon it with full comprehension of its spiritual meaning.

In spite, too, of his alleged realism, he believed that the duty of the social historian was more than to give a statement of present conditions—the social documents of the moment,—variable as they might be for purposes of deduction. He insisted that the coming,—perhaps seemingly impossible things, should be prophesied;—those future ameliorations, whether individual or collective, which keep hope alive in the human breast. Let me again quote those words, extraordinary as coming from the man who is called arch-realist of his day: "The novelist should depict the world not alone as it is, but a possibly better world." In the very novel where he said it ("Père Goriot") he may seem to have violated the principle: but taking his fiction in its whole extent, he has acted upon it, the pronunciamento exemplifies his practice.

Balzac's work has a Shaksperian universality, because it is so distinctly French,—a familiar paradox in literature. He was French in his feeling for the social unit, in his keen receptivity to ideas, in his belief in Church and State as the social organisms through which man could best work out his salvation. We find him teaching that humanity, in terms of Gallic temperament, and in time limits between the Revolution and the Second Republic, is on the whole best served by living under a constitutional monarchy and in vital touch with Mother Church,—that form of religion which is a racial inheritance from the Past. In a sense, then, he was a man with the limitations of his place and time, as, in truth, was Shakspere. But the study of literature instructs us that it is exactly those who most vitally grasp and voice their own land and period, who are apt to give a comprehensive view of humanity at large; to present man *sub specie æternitatis*. This is so because, thoroughly to present any particular part of mankind, is to portray all mankind. It is all tarred by the same stick, after all. It is only in the superficials that unlikenesses lie.

Balzac was intensely modern. Had he lived today, he might have been foremost in championing the separation of Church and State and looked on serenely at the sequestration of the religious houses.

But writing his main fiction from 1830 to 1850, his attitude was an enlightened one, that of a thoughtful patriot.

His influence upon nineteenth century English fiction was both direct and indirect. It was direct in its effect upon several of the major novelists, as will be noted in studying them; the indirect influence is perhaps still more important, because it was so all-pervasive, like an emanation that expressed the Time. It became impossible, after Balzac had lived and wrought, for any artist who took his art seriously to write fiction as if the great Frenchman had not come first. He set his seal upon that form of literature, as Ibsen, a generation later, was to set his seal upon the drama, revolutionizing its technique. To the student therefore he is a factor of potent power in explaining the modern fictional development. Nor should he be a negligible quantity to the cultivated reader seeking to come genially into acquaintance with the best that European letters has accomplished. While upon the lover of the Novel as a form of literature—which means the mass of all readers to-day—Balzac cannot fail to exercise a personal fascination.—Life widens before us at his touch, and that glamour which is the imperishable gift of great art, returns again as one turns the pages of the little library of yellow books which contain the Human Comedy.

Balzac died in 1850, when in the prime of his powers. Seven years later was published the " Madame Bovary " of Flaubert, one of the most remarkable novels of the nineteenth century and the most unrelenting depiction of the devolution of a woman's soul in all fiction: certainly it deserved that description up to the hour of its appearance, if not now, when so much has been done in the realm of female pathology. Flaubert is the most noteworthy intermediate figure between Balzac and Zola. He seems personally of our own day, for, living to be an old man, he was friend and fellow-worker with the brothers Goncourt (whom we associate with Zola) and extended a fatherly hand to the young Maupassant at the beginning of the latter's career,—so brilliant, brief, tragic. The influence of this one novel (overlooking that of " Salambo," in its way also of influence in the modern growth) has been especially great upon a kind of fiction most characteristic of the present generation: in which, in fact, it has assumed a " bad preëminence." I mean the Novel of sexual relations in their irregular aspects. The stormy artist of the Goncourt dinners has much to answer for, if we regard him only as the creator of such a creature as Madame Bovary. Many later books were to surpass this in license, in coarseness, or in the effect of evoking a libidinous taste; but none in its unrelenting gloom, the cold detachment of the artist-scientist obsessed with the idea of truthfully reflecting certain sinister facets of the many-faced gem called life! It is hardly too much to say, in the light of the facts, that " Madame Bovary " was epochal. It paved the way for Zola. It justified a new aim for the modern fiction of so-called unflinching realism. The saddest thing about the book is its lack of pity, of love. Emma Bovary is a weak woman, not a bad woman; she goes downhill through the force of circumstances coupled with a want of backbone. And she is not responsible for her flabby moral muscles. Behind the story is an absolutely fatalistic philosophy; given a certain environment, any woman (especially if assisted a bit by her ancestors) will go to hell,—such seems the lesson. Now there is nothing just like this in Balzac. We hear in it a new note, the latter-day note of quiescence, and despair. And if we compare Flaubert's indifference to his heroine's fate with the tenderness of Dumas fils, or of Daudet, or the English Reade and Dickens—we shall realize that we have here a mixture of a personal and a coming general interpretation: Flaubert having by nature a kind of aloof determinism, yet feeling, like the first puffs of a cold chilling wind, the oncoming of an age of Doubt.

III.

These three French writers then, Stendhal, Balzac and Flaubert, molded the Novel before 1860 into such a shape as to make it plastic to the hand of Zola a decade later. Zola's influence upon our present generation of English fiction has been great, as it has upon all novel-making since 1870. Before explaining this further, it will be best to return to the study of the mid-century English novelists who were too early to be affected by him to any perceptible degree.

CHAPTER VIII

DICKENS

By the year 1850, in England, the so-called Novel of realism had conquered. Scott in an earlier generation had by his wonderful gift made the romance fashionable. But, as we said, it was the romance with a difference: the romance with its feet firmly planted on mother-earth, not ballooning in cloudland; the romance depicting men and women of the past but yet *men and women*, not creatures existing only in the fancy of the romance-maker. In short, Scott, romancer though he was, helped modern realism along, because he handled his material more truthfully than it had been handled before. And his great contemporary, Jane Austen, with her strict adherence to the present and to her own locale, threw all her influence in the same direction, justifying Mr. Howell's assertion that she leads all English novelists in that same truthful handling.

Moreover, that occult but imperative thing, the spirit of the Time, was on the side of Realism: and all bend to its dictation. Then, in the mid-century, Dickens and Thackeray, with George Eliot a little later on their heels, and Trollope too, came to give a deeper set to the current which was to flow in similar channels for the remainder of the period. In brief, this is the story, whatever modifications of the main current are to be noted: the work of Bulwer and Disraeli, of Reade, Kingsley and Collins.

A decade before Thackeray got a general hearing Dickens had fame and mighty influence. It was in the eighteen thirties that the self-made son of an impecunious navy clerk, who did not live in vain since he sat for a portrait of Micawber and the father of the Marshalsea, turned from journalism to that higher reporting which means the fiction of manners and humors. All the gods had prepared him for his destiny. Sympathy he had for the poor, the oppressed, the physically and morally unfit, for he had suffered in his own person, or in his imagination, for them all. His gift of observation had been sharpened in the grim school of necessity: he had learned to write by writing under the pressure of newspaper needs. And he had in his blood, while still hardly more than a lad, a feeling for idiomatic English which, so far as it was not a boon straight from heaven, had been fostered when the very young Charles had battened, as we saw, upon the eighteenth century worthies.

It is now generally acknowledged that Dickens is not a temporary phenomenon in Victorian letters, but a very solid major fact in the native literature, too large a creative force to be circumscribed by a generation. Looked back upon across the gap of time, he looms up all the more impressively because the years have removed the clutter about the base of the statue. The temporary loss of critical regard (a loss affecting his hold on the general reading public little, if any) has given way to an almost violent critical reaction in his favor. We are widening the esthetic canvas to admit of the test of life, and are coming to realize that, obsessed for a time by the attraction of that lower truth which makes so much of external realities, realism lost sight of the larger demands of art which include selection, adaptation, and that enlargement of effect marking the distinction between art and so-called reality. No critic is now timid about saying a good word for the author of " Pickwick " and " Copperfield." A few years ago it was otherwise. Present-day critics such as Henley, Lang, and Chesterton have assured the luke-warm that there is room in English literature for both Thackeray and Dickens.

That Dickens began to write fiction as a very young journalist was in some ways in his favor; in other ways, to the detriment of his work. It meant an early start on a career of over thirty years. It meant writing under pressure with the spontaneity and reality which usually result. It also meant the bold grappling with the technique of a great art, learning to make novels by making them. Again, one truly inspired to fiction is lucky to have a novitiate in youth. So far the advantages.

On the other hand, the faults due to inexperience, lack of education, uncertainty of aim, haste and carelessness and other foes of perfection, will probably be in evidence when a writer who has scarcely attained to man's estate essays fiction. Dickens' early work has thus the merits and demerits of his personal history. A popular and able parliamentary reporter, with sympathetic knowledge of London and the smaller towns where his duties took him, possessed of a marvelous memory which photographed for him the boyish impressions of places like Chatham and Rochester, he began with sketches of that life interspersed with more fanciful tales which drew upon his imagination and at times passed the melodramatic border-line. When these collected pieces were published under the familiar title " Sketches by Boz," it is not too much to say that the Dickens of the " Pickwick Papers " (which was to appear next year) was revealed. Certainly, the main qualities of a great master of the Comic were in these pages; so, in truth, was the master of both tears and smiles. But not at full-length: the writer had not yet found his occasion;—the man needs the occasion, even as it awaits the man. And so, hard upon the Boz book, followed, as it were by an accident, the world-famous " Adventures of Mr. Pickwick." By accident, I say, because the promising young author was asked to

furnish the letter-press for a series of comic sporting
pictures by the noted artist, Seymour; whereupon—
doubtless to the astonishment of all concerned, the
pictures became quite secondary to the reading matter
and the Wellers soon set all England talking and
laughing over their inimitable sayings.   Here in a
loosely connected series of sketches the main unity of
which was the personality of Mr. Pickwick and his
club, its method that of the episodic adventure story
of " Gil Blas " lineage, its purpose frankly to amuse
at all costs, a new creative power in English literature
gave the world over three hundred characters in some
sixty odd scenes: intensely English, intensely human,
and still, after the lapse of three quarters of a century, keenly enjoyable.

In a sense, all Dickens' qualities are to be found
in " The Pickwick Papers," as they have come to
be called for brevity's sake.   But the assertion is
misleading, if it be taken to mean that in the fifteen
books of fiction which Dickens was to produce, he
added nothing, failed to grow in his art or to widen
and deepen in his hold upon life.   So far is this
from the truth, that one who only knows Charles
Dickens in this first great book of fun, knows a phase
of him, not the whole man: more, hardly knows the
novelist at all.   He was to become, and to remain,
not only a great humorist, but a great novelist as
well: and " Pickwick " is not, by definition, a Novel
at all.   Hence, the next book the following year,

"Oliver Twist," was important as answering the question: Was the brilliant new writer to turn out very novelist, able to invent, handle and lead to due end a tangled representation of social life?

Before replying, one rather important matter may be adverted to, concerning the Dickens introduced to the world by "Pickwick": his astonishing power in the evocation of human beings, whom we affectionately remember, whose words are treasured, whose fates are followed with a sort of sense of personal responsibility. If the creation of differentiated types of humanity who persist in living in the imagination be the cardinal gift of the fiction writer, then this one is easily the leading novelist of the race. Putting aside for the moment the question of his caricaturing tendency, one fact confronts us, hardly to be explained away: we can close our eyes and see Micawber, Mrs. Gamp, Pegotty, Dick Swiveller, the Artful Dodger, Joe Gargery, Tootles, Captain Cutter, and a hundred more, and their sayings, quaint and dear, are like household companions. And this is true in equal measure of no other story-maker who has used English speech— it may be doubted if it is true to like degree of Shakspere himself.

In the quick-following stories, "Oliver Twist" and "Nicholas Nickleby," the author passed from episode and comic characterization to what were in some sort Novels: the fiction of organism, growth and climax.

His wealth of character creation was continued and
even broadened. But there was more here: an attempt to play the game of Novel-making. It may be
granted that when Dickens wrote these early books
(as a young man in the twenties), he had not yet
mastered many of the difficulties of the art of fiction.
There is loose construction in both: the melodrama
of " Oliver Twist " blends but imperfectly with the
serious and sentimental part of the narrative, which
is less attractive. So, too, in " Nickleby," there is
an effect at times of thin ice where the plot is secondary to the episodic scenes and characters by the
way. Yet in both Novels there is a story and a good
one: we get the spectacle of genius learning its lesson,
—experimenting in a form. And as those other
early books, differing totally from each other too,
" Old Curiosity Shop," and " Barnaby Rudge," were
produced, and in turn were succeeded by a series of
great novels representing the writer's young prime,—
I mean " Martin Chuzzlewit," " Dombey and Son "
and " David Copperfield,"—it was plain that the
hand of Dickens was becoming subdued to the element
it worked in. Not only was there a good fable, as
before, but it was managed with increasing mastery,
while the general adumbration of life gained in solid-
ity, truth and rich human quality. In brief, by
the time " Copperfield," the story most often referred to as his best work, was reached, Dickens was
an artist. He wrought in that fiction in such a

fashion as to make the most of the particular class of Novel it represented: to wit, the first-person autobiographic picture of life. Given its purpose, it could hardly have been better done. It surely bears favorable comparison, for architecture, with Thackeray's "Vanity Fair," a work in the same genre, though lacking the autobiographic method. This is quite aside from its remarkable range of character-portrayal, its humor, pathos and vraisemblance, its feeling for situation, its sonorous eloquence in massed effects.

By the time he had reached mid-career, then, Charles Dickens had made himself a skilled, resourceful story-teller, while his unique qualities of visualization and interpretation had strengthened. This point is worth emphasis, since there are those who contend that "The Pickwick Papers" is his most characteristic performance. Such a judgment is absurd, It overlooks the grave beauty of the picture of Chesney Wold in Bleak House; the splendid harmony of the Yarmouth storm in "Copperfield"; the fine melodrama of the chapter in "Chuzzlewit" where the guilty Jonas takes his haggard life; the magnificent portraiture of the Father of the Marshalsea in "Little Dorrit": the spiritual exaltation in vivid stage terms of Carton's death; the exquisite April-day blend of tenderness and fun in limning the young life of a Marchioness, a little Dombey and a tiny Tim. To call Dickens a comic writer and stop there, is

to try to pour a river into a pint pot; for a sort of
ebullient boy-like spirit of fun, the high jinks of
literature, we go to " Pickwick "; for the light and
shade of life to " Copperfield "; for the structural
excellencies of fiction to later masterpieces like " The
Tale of Two Cities " and " Great Expectations."

Just here a serious objection often brought against
Dickens may be considered: his alleged tendency
to caricature. Does Dickens make his characters
other than what life itself shows, and if so, is he
wrong in so doing?

His severest critics assume the second if the first
be but granted. Life—meaning the exact reproduction of reality—is their fetish. Now, it must be
granted that Dickens does make his creatures talk
as their prototypes do not in life. Nobody would for
a moment assert that Mrs. Gamp, Pecksniff and
Micawber could be literally duplicated from the
actual world. But is not Dickens within his rights
as artist in so changing the features of life as to
increase our pleasure? That is the nub of the
whole matter. The artist of fiction should not aim
at exact photography, for it is impossible; no fiction-
maker since time began has placed on the printed
pages half the irrelevance and foolishness or one-fifth
the filth which are in life itself. Reasons of art
and ethics forbid. The aim, therefore, should rather
be at an effect of life through selection and re-shap-
ing. And I believe Dickens is true to this require-

ment. We hear less now than formerly of his crazy
exaggerations: we are beginning to realize that perhaps he saw types that were there, which we would
overlook if they were under our very eyes: we feel
the wisdom of Chesterton's remarks that Dickens'
characters will live forever because they never lived
at all! We suffered from the myopia of realism.
Zola desired above all things to tell the truth by
representing humanity as porcine, since he saw it
that way: he failed in his own purpose, because
decency checked him: his art is not photographic
(according to his proud boast) but has an almost
Japanese convention of restraint in its suppression
of facts.   Had Sarah Gamp been allowed by Dickens
to speak as she would speak in life, she would have
been unspeakably repugnant, never cherished as a
permanently laughable, even lovable figure of fiction.
Dickens was a master of omissions as well as of those
enlargments which made him carry over the foot-
lights.   Mrs. Gamp is a monumental study of the
coarse woman rogue: her creator makes us hate the
sin and tolerate the sinner.   Nor is that other masterly portrait of the woman rascal—Thackeray's
Becky Sharp—an example of strict photography; she is great in seeming true, but she is not
life.

So much, then, for the charge of caricature: it
is all a matter of degree. It all depends upon the
definition of art, and upon the effect made upon the

world by the characters themselves. If they live in
loving memory, they must, in the large sense, be true.
Thus we come back to the previous statement:
Dickens' people live—are known by their words and
in their ways all over the civilized world. No collection of mere grotesques could ever bring this to
pass. Prick any typical creation of Dickens and it
runs blood, not sawdust. And just in proportion as
we travel, observe broadly and form the habit of a
more penetrating and sympathetic study of mankind, shall we believe in these emanations of genius.
Occasionally, under the urge and surplusage of his
comic force, he went too far and made a Quilp: but
the vast majority even of his drolls are as credible
as they are dear.

That he showed inequality as he wrought at the
many books which filled the years between " Pickwick " and the unfinished " Mystery of Edwin
Drood," may also be granted. Also may it be confessed that within the bounds of one book there are
the extremes of good and bad. It is peculiar to
Dickens that often in the very novel we perchance
feel called upon to condemn most, occurs a scene
or character as memorably great as anything he
left the world. Thus, we may regard " Old Curiosity
Shop," once so beloved, as a failure when viewed
as a whole; and yet find Dick Swiveller and the
Marchioness at their immortal game as unforgettable
as Mrs. Battle engaged in the same pleasant em-

ployment. Nor because other parts of "Little Dorrit" seem thin and artificial, would we forego the description of the debtor's prison. And our belief that the presentation of the labor-capital problem in "Hard Times" is hasty and shallow, does not prevent a recognition of the opening sketch of the circus troop as displaying its author at his happiest of humorous observation. There are thus always redeeming things in the stories of this most unequal man of genius. Seven books there are, novels in form, which are indubitable masterpieces: "Martin Chuzzlewit," "Dombey and Son," "David Copperfield," "Bleak House," "A Tale of Two Cities," "Great Expectations" and "Our Mutual Friend." These, were all the others withdrawn, would give ample evidence of creative power: they have the largeness, variety and inventive verve which only are to be found in the major novelists. Has indeed the same number of equal weight and quality been given forth by any other English writer?

Another proof that the power of Dickens was not dependent exclusively upon the comic, is his production of "A Tale of Two Cities." It is sometimes referred to as uncharacteristic because it lacks almost entirely his usual gallery of comics: but it is triumphantly a success in a different field. The author says he wished for the nonce to make a straight adventure tale with characters secondary. He did it in a manner which has always made the romance a favorite, and compels us to include this dramatic study of the French Revolution among the choicest of his creations. Its period and scene have never—save by Carlyle—been so brilliantly illuminated. Dickens was brooding on this story at a time when, wretchedly unhappy, he was approaching the crisis of a separation from his wife: the fact may help to explain its failure to draw on that seemingly inexhaustible fountain of bubbling fun so familiar in his work. But even subtract humor and Dickens exhibits the masterhand in a fiction markedly of another than his wonted kind. This Novel—or romance, as it should properly be called—reminds us of a quality in Dickens which has been spoken of in the way of derogation: his theatrical tendency. When one declares an author to be dramatic, a compliment is intended. But when he is called theatric, censure is implied. Dickens, always possessed of a strong sense of the dramatic and using it to immense advantage, now and again goes further and becomes theatric: that is, he suggests the manipulating of effects with artifice and the intention of providing sensational and scenic results at the expense of proportion and truth. A word on this is advisable.

Those familiar with the man and his works are aware how close he always stood to the playhouse and its product. He loved it from early youth, all but went on the stage professionally, knew its people as have few of the writing craft, was a fine amateur actor himself, wrote for the stage, helped to dramatize his novels and gave delightful studies of theatrical life in his books.   Shall we ever forget Mr. Crummles and his family?   He had an instinctive feeling for what was scenic and effective in the stage sense. When he appeared as a reader of his own works, he was an impersonator; and noticeably careful to have the stage accessories exactly right.   And when all this, natural and acquired, was applied to fiction, it could not but be of influence.   As a result, Dickens sometimes forced the note, favored the lurid, exaggerated his comic effects.   To put it in another way, this theater manner of his now and then injured the literature he made.   But that is only one side of the matter: it also helped him greatly and where he went too far, he was simply abusing a precious gift.   To speak of Dickens' violent theatricality as if it expressed his whole being, is like describing the wart on Cromwell's face as if it were his set of features. Remove from Dickens his dramatic power, and the memorable master would be no more: he would vanish into dim air.   We may be thankful—in view of what it produced—that he possessed even in excess this sense of the scenic value of character and situation: it is not a disqualification but a virtue, and not Dickens alone but Dumas, Hugo and Scott were great largely because of it.

In the praise naturally enough bestowed upon a great autobiographical Novel like " David Copperfield," the fine art of a late work like "Great Expectations" has been overlooked or at least minimized. If we are to consider skilful construction along with the other desirable qualities of the novelist, this noble work has hardly had justice done it: moreover, everything considered,—story value, construction, characters, atmosphere, adequacy of style, climactic interest, and impressive lesson, I should name "Great Expectations," published when the author was fifty, as his most perfect book, if not the greatest of Charles Dickens' novels. The opinion is unconventional: but as Dickens is studied more as artist progressively skilful in his craft, I cannot but believe this particular story will receive increasing recognition. In the matter of sheer manipulation of material, it is much superior to the book that followed it two years later, the last complete novel: "Our Mutual Friend." It is rather curious that this story, which was in his day and has steadily remained a favorite with readers, has with equal persistency been severely handled by the critics. What has insured its popularity? Probably its vigor and variety of characterization, its melodramatic tinge, the teeming world of dramatic contrasts it opens, its bait to our sense of mystery. It has a power very typical of the author and one of the reasons for Dickens' hold upon his audience. It is a power also exhibited markedly in such other fictions as "Dombey and Son," "Martin Chuzzlewit" and "Bleak House." I refer to the impression

conveyed by such stories that life is a vast, tumult-
uous, vari-colored play of counter-motives and
counter-characters, full of chance, surprise, change
and bitter sweet: a thing of mystery, terror, pity and
joy. It has its masks of respectability, its frauds of
place, its beauty blossoming in the mud, its high and
low of luck, its infinite possibilities betwixt heaven
and hell. The effect of this upon the sensitive reader
is to enlarge his sympathetic feeling for humanity:
life becomes a big, awful, dear phantasmagoria in
such hands. It seems not like a flat surface, but a
thing of length, breadth, height and depth, which it
has been a privilege to enter. Dickens' fine gift—
aside from that of character creation—is found in
this ability to convey an impression of puissant life.
He himself had this feeling and he got it into his
books: he had, in a happier sense, the joy of life
of Ibsen, the life force of Nietzsche. From only a
few of the world's great writers does one receive this
sense of life, the many-sided spectacle; Cervantes,
Hugo, Tolstoy, Sienkiewicz, it is men like they that
do this for us.

Another side of Dickens' literary activity is shown
in his Christmas stories, which it may be truly said
are as well beloved as anything he gave the world
in the Novel form. This is assuredly so of the
" Christmas Carol," " The Chimes " and " The
Cricket on the Hearth." This last is on a par with
the other two in view of its double life in a book

and on the boards of the theater. The fragrance
of Home, of the homely kindness and tenderness of
the human heart, is in them, especially in the Carol,
which is the best tale of its kind in the tongue and
likely to remain so. It permanently altered the
feeling of the race for Christmas. Irving preceded
him in the use of the Christmas motive, but Dickens
made it forever his own. By a master's magic evocation, the great festival shines brighter, beckons more
lovingly than it did of old. Thackeray felt this
when he declared that such a story was " a public
benefit." Such literature lies aside from our main
pursuit, that of the Novel, but is mentioned because
it is the best example possible, the most direct, simple
expression of that essential kindness, that practical
Christianity which is at the bottom of Dickens'
influence. It is *bonhomie* and something more. It
is not Dickens the reformer, as we get him when he
satirizes Dotheboys hall, or the Circumlocution
Office or the Chancery Court: but Dickens as Mr.
Greatheart, one with all that is good, tender, sweet
and true. Tiny Tim's thousand-times quoted saying
is the quintessence, the motto for it all and the
writer speaks in and through the lad when he says:
" God bless us, every one." When an author gets that
honest unction into his work, and also has the gift of
observation and can report what he sees, he is likely to
contribute to the literature of his land. With a sneer
of the cultivated intellect, we may call it elementary:

but to the heart, such a view of life is royally right.

This thought of Dickens' moral obligation in his work and his instinctive attitude towards his audience, leads to one more point: a main reason for this Victorian novelist's strong hold on the affections of mankind is to be found in the warm personal relation he establishes with the reader. The relationship implies obligation on the part of the author, a vital bond between the two, a recognition of a steady, not a chance, association. There goes with it, too, an assumption that the author believes in and cares much for his characters, and asks the reader for the same faith. This personal relation of author to reader and of both to the imagined characters, has gone out of fashion in fiction-making: in this respect, Dickens (and most of his contemporaries) seem now old-fashioned. The present realist creed would keep the novelist away and out of sight both of his fictive creations and his audience; it being his business to pull the strings to make his puppets dance—up to heaven or down to hell, whatever does it matter to the scientist-novelist? Tolstoy's novel " Resurrection " is as a subject much more disagreeable than Flaubert's " Madame Bovary "; but it is beautiful where the other is horrible, because it palpitates with a Christ-like sympathy for an erring woman, while the French author cares not a button whether his character is lost or not. The healthy-minded public (which can be trusted in heart, if not in head) will

instinctively choose that treatment of life in a piece
of fiction which shows the author kindly coöperative
with fate and brotherly in his position towards his
host of readers. That is the reason Dickens holds
his own and is extremely likely to gain in the future,
while spectacular reputations based on all the virtues
save love, continue to die the death. What M.
Anatole France once said of Zola, applies to the
whole school of the aloof and unloving: " There is
in man an infinite need of loving which renders him
divine. M. Zola does not know it. . . . The
holiness of tears is at the bottom of all religions.
Misfortune would suffice to render man august to
man. M. Zola does not know it."

Charles Dickens *does* know these truths and they
get into his work and that work, therefore, gets not
so much into the minds as into the souls of his
fellow-man. When we recite the sayings which iden-
tify his classic creations: when we express ourselves
in a Pickwickian sense, wait for something to turn up
with Mr. Micawber, drop into poetry with Silas
Wegg, move on with little Joe, feel 'umble after the
manner of Uriah Heap, are willin' with Barkis, make
a note of, in company with Captain Cuttle, or conclude with Mr. Weller, Senior, that it is the part of
wisdom to beware of " widders," we may observe that
what binds us to this motley crowd of creatures is
not their grotesquerie but their common humanity,
their likeness to ourselves, the mighty flood-tide of

tolerant human sympathy on which they are floated into the safe haven of our hearts. With delightful understanding, Charles Dudley Warner writes: "After all, there is something about a boy I like." Dickens, using the phrasing for a wider application, might have said: "After all, there is something about men and women I like!" It was thus no accident that he elected to write of the lower middle classes; choosing to depict the misery of the poor, their unfair treatment in institutions; to depict also the unease of criminals, the crushed state of all underlings —whether the child in education or that grown-up evil child, the malefactor in prison. He was a spokesman of the people, a democratic pleader for justice and sympathy. He drew the proletariat preferably, not because he was a proletariat but because he was a brother-man and the fact had been overlooked. He drew thousands of these suppressed humans, and they were of varied types and fortunes: but he loved them as though they were one, and made the world love them too: and love their maker. The deep significance of Dickens, perhaps his deepest, is in the social note that swells loud and insistent through his fiction. He was a pioneer in the democratic sympathy which was to become so marked a feature in the Novel in the late nineteenth century: and which, as we have already seen, is from the first a distinctive trait of the modern fiction, one of the explanations of its existence.

CHAPTER IX

THACKERAY

THE habit of those who appraise the relative worth of Dickens and Thackeray to fall into hostile camps, swearing by one, and at the other, has its amusing side but is to be deprecated as irrational. Why should it be necessary to miss appreciation of the creator of " Vanity Fair " because one happens to like " David Copperfield "? Surely, our literary tastes or standards should be broad enough to admit into pleasurable companionship both those great early Victorian novelists.

Yet, on second thought, there would appear to be some reason for the fact that ardent lovers of Thackeray are rarely devotees of the mighty Charles —or vice versa. There is something mutually exclusive in the attitude of the two, their different interpretation of life. Unlike in birth, environment, education and all that is summed up in the magic word personality, their reaction to life, as a scientist would say, was so opposite that a reader naturally drawn to one, is quite apt to be repelled by (or at least, cold to) the other. If you make a wide canvass among booklovers, it will be found that this is just what happens.   Rarely does a stanch supporter of Dickens show a more than Laodicean temper towards Thackeray; and for rabid Thackerians, Dickens too often spells disgust. It is a rare and enjoyable experience to meet with a mind so catholic as to welcome both.   The backbone of the trouble is personal, in the natures of the two authors.   But I think it is worth while to say that part of the explanation may be found in the fact that Thackeray began fiction ten years later than his rival and was in a deeper sense than was Dickens a voice of the later century.   This means much, because with each decade between 1830 and 1860, English thought was moving fast toward that scientific faith, that disillusionment and that spirit of grim truth which culminated in the work of the final quarter of the century.   Thackeray was impelled more than was Dickens by the spirit of the times to speak the truth in his delineations of contemporary mankind: and this operated to make him a satirist, at times a savage one. The modern thing in Dickens—and he had it—was the humanitarian sympathy for the submerged tenth; the modern thing in Thackeray, however, was his fearlessness in uncovering the conventional shams of polite society.   The idols that Dickens smashed (and never was a bolder iconoclast) were to be seen of all men: but Thackeray's were less tangible, more subtle, part and parcel of his own class.   In this sense, and I believe because he began his major novel-writing

about 1850, whereas the other began fifteen years
before, Thackeray is more modern, more of our own
time, than his great co-mate in fiction.   When we
consider the question of their respective interpreta-
tions of Life it is but fair to bear in mind this historical consideration, although it would be an error
to make too much of it.   Of course, in judging
Thackeray and trying to give him a place in English
fiction, he must stand or fall, like any other writer,
by two things: his art, and his message.   Was the
first fine, the other sane and valuable—those are the
twin tests.

A somewhat significant fact of their literary history may be mentioned, before an attempt is made
to appreciate Thackeray's novels.   For some years
after Dickens' death, which, it will be remembered,
occurred six years after Thackeray's, the latter
gained in critical recognition while Dickens slowly
lost.   There can be little question of this.   Lionized
and lauded as was the man of Gadshill, promptly
admitted to Westminster Abbey, it came to pass in
time that, in a course on modern English literature
offered at an old and famous New England college,
his name was not deemed worthy of even a reference.
Some critics of repute have scarce been able to take
Dickens seriously: for those who have steadily had
the temerity to care for him, their patronage has
been vocal.   This marks an astonishing shift of
opinion from that current in 1870.   Thackeray,

gaining in proportion, has been hailed as an exquisite artist, one of the few truly great and permanent English figures not only of fiction but of letters. But in the most recent years, again a change has come: the pendulum has swung back, as it always does when an excessive movement carries it too far beyond the plumb line. Dickens has found valiant, critical defenders; he has risen fast in thoughtful so well as popular estimation (although with the public he has scarcely fluctuated in favor) until he now enjoys a sort of resurrection of popularity. What is the cause of this to-and-fro of judgment? The main explanation is to be found in the changing literary ideals from 1850 to 1900. When Dickens was active, literature, broadly speaking, was estimated not exclusively as art, but as human product, an influence in the world. With the coming of the new canon, which it is convenient to dub by the catch-phrase, Art for Art's Sake, a man's production began to be tested more definitely by the technique he possessed, the skilled way in which he performed his task. Did he play the game well? That was the first question. Often it was the first and last. If he did, his subject-matter, and his particular vision of Life, were pretty much his own affair. And this modern touchstone, applied to the writings of our two authors, favored Thackeray. Simple, old-fashioned readers inclined to give Dickens the preference over him because the former's interpretation of humanity was, they averred, kindlier and more wholesome. Thackeray was cynical, said they; Dickens humanitarian; but the later critical mood rebounded from Dickens, since he preached, was frankly didactic, insisted on his mission of doing good—and so failed in his art. Now, however, that the *l'art pour art* shibboleth has been sadly overworked and is felt to be passing or obsolete, the world critical is reverting to that broader view which demands that the maker of literature shall be both man and artist: as a result, Dickens gains in proportion. This explanation makes it likely that, looking to the future, while Thackeray may not lose, Dickens is sure to be more and more appreciated. A return to a saner and truer criterion will be general and the confines of a too narrow estheticism be understood: or, better yet, the esthetic will be so defined as to admit of wider application. The Gissings and Chestertons of the time to come will insist even more strenuously than those of ours that while we may have improved upon Dickens' technique—and every schoolboy can tinker his faults—we shall do exceedingly well if we duplicate his genius once in a generation. And they will add that Thackeray, another man of genius, had also his *malaises* of art, was likewise a man with the mortal failings implied in the word. For it cannot now be denied that just as Dickens' faults have been exaggerated, Thackeray's have been overlooked.

Thackeray might lose sadly in the years to come could it be demonstrated that, as some would have it, he deserved the title of cynic. Here is the most mooted point in Thackeray appreciation: it interests thousands where the nice questions concerning the novelist's art claim the attention of students alone. What can be said with regard to it? It will help just here to think of the man behind the work. No sensible human being, it would appear, can become aware of the life and personality of Thackeray without concluding that he was an essentially kind-hearted, even soft-hearted man. He was keenly sensitive to praise and blame, most affectionate and constant with his friends, generous and impulsive in his instincts, loving in his family, simple and humble in his spiritual nature, however questioning in his intellect. That is a fair summary of Thackeray as revealed in his daily walk—in his letters, acts and thoughts. Nothing could be sweeter and more kindly than the mass of his writings in this regard, *pace* " The Book of Snobs "—even in such a mood the satire is for the most part unbitter. The reminiscential essays continually strike a tender note that vibrates with human feeling and such memorials as the paper he wrote on the deaths of Irving and Macaulay represent a frequent vein. Thackeray's friends are almost a unit in this testimony: Edward Fitzgerald, indeed—" dear old Fitz," as Tennyson loved to call him—declares in a letter to

somebody that he hears Thackeray is spoiled: meaning that his social success was too much for him.
It is true that after the fame of " Vanity Fair," its
author was a habitué of the best drawing-rooms,
much sought after, and enjoying it hugely.   But
to read his letter to Mrs. Brookfield after the return
home from such frivolities is to feel that the real
man is untouched.   Why Thackeray, with such a
nature, developed a satirical bent and became a critic
of the foibles of fashion and later of the social faults
of humanity, is not so easy perhaps to say—unless
we beg the question by declaring it to be his nature.
When he began his major fiction at the age of thirty-
seven he had seen much more of the seamy side of
existence than had Dickens when he set up for author.
Thackeray had lost a fortune, traveled, played Bohemian, tried various employments, failed in a business venture—in short, was an experienced man of
the world with eyes wide open to what is light, mean,
shifty and vague in the sublunary show.   " The
Book of Snobs " is the typical early document expressing the subacidulous tendency of his power:
" Vanity Fair " is the full-length statement of it
in maturity.   Yet judging his life by and large (in
contrast with his work) up to the day of his sudden
death, putting in evidence all the testimony from
many sources, it may be asserted with considerable
confidence that William Makepeace Thackeray, whatever we find him to be in his works, gave the general

impression personally of being a genial, kind and thoroughly sound-hearted man. We may, therefore, look at the work itself, to extract from it such evidence as it offers, remembering that, when all is said, the deepest part of a man, his true quality, is always to be discovered in his writings.

First a word on the books secondary to the four great novels. It is necessary at the start in studying him to realize that Thackeray for years before he wrote novels was an essayist, who, when he came to make fiction introduced into it the essay touch and point of view. The essay manner makes his larger fiction delightful, is one of its chief charms and characteristics. And contrariwise, the looseness of construction, the lack of careful architecture in Thackeray's stories, look to the same fact.

It can not justly be said of these earlier and minor writings that, taken as a whole, they reveal a cynic. They contain many thrusts at the foolishness and knavery of society, especially that genteel portion of it with which the writer, by birth, education and experience, was familiar. When Thackeray, in the thirties, turned to newspaper writing, he did so for practical reasons: he needed money, and he used such talents as were his as a writer, knowing that the chances were better than in art, which he had before pursued. It was natural that he should have turned to account his social experiences, which gave him a power not possessed by the run of literary hacks, and which had been to some extent disillusioning, but had by no means soured him. Broadly viewed, the tone of these first writings was genial, the light and shade of human nature—in its average, as it is seen in the world—was properly represented. In fact, often, as in " The Great Hoggarty Diamond," the style is almost that of burlesque, at moments, of horse-play: and there are too touches of beautiful young-man pathos. Such a work is anything rather than tart or worldly. There are scenes in that enjoyable story that read more like Dickens than the Thackeray of " Vanity Fair." The same remark applies, though in a different way, to the " Yellowplush Papers." An early work like " Barry Lyndon," unique among the productions of the young writer, expresses the deeper aspect of his tendency to depict the unpleasant with satiric force, to make clear-cut pictures of rascals, male and female. Yet in this historical study, the eighteenth century setting relieves the effect and one does not feel that the author is speaking with that direct earnestness one encounters in " Pendennis " and " The Newcomes." The many essays, of which the " Roundabout Papers " are a type, exhibit almost exclusively the sunnier and more attractive side of Thackeray's genius. Here and there, in the minor fiction of this experimental period, there are premonitions of the more drastic treatment of later years: but the dominant mood is quite other. One who read the essays alone, with no knowledge of the fiction, would be astonished at a charge of cynicism brought against the author.

And so we come to the major fiction: " Vanity Fair," " Pendennis," " The Newcomes," and " Esmond." Of " The Adventures of Philip " a later word may be said. " The Virginians " is a comparatively unimportant pendant to that great historical picture, " Henry Esmond." The quartet practically composes the fundamental contribution of Thackeray to the world of fiction, containing as it does all his characteristic traits. Some of them have been pointed out, time out of mind: others, often claimed, are either wanting or their virtue has been much exaggerated.

Of the merits incontestable, first and foremost may be mentioned the color and motion of Life which spread like an atmosphere over this fiction. By his inimitable idiom, his knowledge of the polite world, and his equal knowledge of the average human being irrespective of class or condition, Thackeray was able to make his chronicle appear the very truth. Moreover, for a second great merit, he was able, quite without meretricious appeals, to make that truth interesting. You follow the fortunes of the folk in a typical Thackeray novel as you would follow a similar group in actual life. They interest because they are real—or seem to be, which, for the purposes of art, is the same thing. To read is not so much to look from an outside place at a fictive representation of existence as to be participant in such a piece of life—to feel as if you were living the story. Only masters accomplish this, and it is, it may be added, the specialty of modern masters.

For another shining merit: much of wisdom assimilated by the author in the course of his days is given forth with pungent power and in piquant garb in the pages of these books: the reader relishes the happy statements of an experience profounder than his own, yet tallying in essentials: Thackeray's remarks seem to gather up into final shape the scattered oracles of the years. Gratitude goes out to an author who can thus condense and refine one's own inarticulate conclusions. The mental palate is tickled by this, while the taste is titillated by the grace and fitness of the style.

Yet in connection with this quality is a habit which already makes Thackeray seem of an older time—a trifle archaic in technique. I refer to the intrusion of the author into the story in first-personal comment and criticism. This is tabooed by the present-day realist canons. It weakens the illusion, say the artists of our own day, this entrance of an actual personality upon the stage of the imagined scene. Thackeray is guilty of this lovable sin to a greater degree than is Dickens, and it may be added here that, while the latter has so often

been called preacher in contrast with Thackeray
the artist, as a matter of fact, Thackeray moralizes
in the fashion described fully as much: the difference being that he does it with lighter touch
and with less strenuosity and obvious seriousness:
is more consistently amusing in the act of instruction.

Thackeray again has less story to tell than his
greatest contemporary and never gained a sure hand
in construction, with the possible exception of
his one success in plot, " Henry Esmond." Nothing
is more apparent than the loose texture of " Vanity
Fair," where two stories centering in the antithetic
women, Becky and Amelia, are held together chronicle fashion, not in the nexus of an organism of
close weave. But this very looseness, where there
is such superlative power of characterization with
plenty of invention in incident, adds to the verisimilitude and attraction of the book. The impression
of life is all the more vivid, because of the lack of
proportioned progress to a climax. The story conducts itself and ends much as does life: people come
in and out and when Finis is written, we feel we
may see them again—as indeed often happens, for
Thackeray used the pleasant device of re-introducing
favorite characters such as Pendennis, Warrington
and the descendants thereof, and it adds distinctly
to the reality of the ensemble.

" Vanity Fair " has most often been given pre-

cedence over the other novels of contemporary life:
but for individual scenes and strength of character
drawing both " Pendennis " and " The Newcomes "
set up vigorous claims. If there be no single triumph
in female portraiture like Becky Sharp, Ethel Newcome (on the side of virtue) is a far finer woman
than the somewhat insipid Amelia: and no personage
in the Mayfair book is more successful and beloved
than Major Pendennis or Colonel Newcome. Also,
the atmosphere of these two pictures seems mellower,
less sharp, while as organic structures they are both
superior to " Vanity Fair." Perhaps the supremacy
of the last-named is due most of all to the fact that
a wonderfully drawn evil character has more fascination than a noble one of workmanship as fine. Or
is it that such a type calls forth the novelist's powers
to the full? If so, it were, in a manner, a reproach.
But it is more important to say that all three books
are delightfully authentic studies of upper-class society in England as Thackeray knew it: the social
range is comparatively restricted, for even the rascals are shabby-genteel. But the exposure of human nature (which depends upon keen observation
within a prescribed boundary) is wide and deep:
a story-teller can penetrate just as far into the
arcana of the human spirit if he confine himself to
a class as if he surveyed all mankind. But mental
limitations result: the point of view is that of the
gentleman-class: the ideas of the personal relation

to one's self, one's fellow men and one's Maker are
those natural to a person of that station.   The
charming poem which the author set as Finis to " Dr.
Birch and His Young Friends," with its concluding
lines, is an unconscious expression of the form in
which he conceived human duty.   The " And so,
please God, a gentleman," was the cardinal clause
in his creed and all his work proves it.   It is wiser
to be thankful that a man of genius was at hand
to voice the view, than to cavil at its narrow outlook.   In literature, in-look is quite as important.
Thackeray drew what he felt and saw, and like Jane
Austen, is to be understood within his limitations.
Nor did he ever forget that, because pleasure-giving
was the object of his art, it was his duty so to present
life as to make it somehow attractive, worth while.
The point is worth urging, for not a little nonsense
has been written concerning the absolute veracity of
Thackeray's pictures: as if he sacrificed all pleasur-
ableness to the modern Moloch, truth.   Neither he
nor any other great novelist reproduces Life *ver-
batim et literatim.*   Trollope, in his somewhat un-
satisfactory biography of his fellow fictionist, very
rightly puts his finger on a certain scene in " Vanity
Fair " in which Sir Pitt Crawley figures, which departs widely from reality.   The traditional comparison between the two novelists, which represents
Dickens as ever caricaturing, Thackeray as the pho-
tographer, is coming to be recognized as foolish.

It is all merely a question of degree, as has been said. It being the artist's business to show a few of the symbols of life out of the vast amount of raw material offered, he differs in the main from his brother artist in the symbols he selects. No one of them presents everything—if he did, he were no artist. Thackeray approaches nearer than Dickens, it is true, to the average appearances of life; but is no more a literal copyist than the creator of Mrs. Gamp. He was rather one of art's most capable exemplars in the arduous employment of seeming-true.

It must be added that his technique was more careless than an artist of anything like his caliber would have permitted himself to-day. The audience was less critical: not only has the art of fiction been evolved into a finer finish, but gradually the court of judgment made up of a select reading public, has come to decide with much more of professional knowledge. Thus, technique in fiction is expected and given. So much of gain there has been, in spite of all the vulgarization of taste which has followed in the wake of cheap magazines and newspapers. In "Vanity Fair," for example, there are blemishes which a careful revision would never have suffered to remain: the same is true of most of Thackeray's books. Like Dickens, Thackeray was exposed to all the danger of the Twenty Parts method of publication. He began his stories without seeing the end; in one of them he is humorously plaintive over the trouble of making this manner of fiction. While " Vanity Fair " is, of course, written in the impersonal third person, at least one passage is put into the mouth of a character in the book: an extraordinary slip for such a novelist.

But peccadilloes such as these, which it is well to realize in view of the absurd claims to artistic impeccability for Thackeray made by rash admirers, melt away into nothing when one recalls Rawdon Crawley's horsewhipping of the Marquis; George Osborn's departure for battle, Colonel Newcome's death, or the incomparable scene where Lady Castlewood welcomes home the wandering Esmond; that " rapture of reconciliation " ! It is by such things that great novelists live, and it may be doubted if their errors are ever counted against them, if only they can create in this fashion.

In speaking of Thackeray's unskilful construction the reference is to architectonics; in the power of particular scenes it is hard to name his superior. He has both the pictorial and the dramatic sense. The care with which " Esmond " was planned and executed suggests too that, had he taken his art more seriously and given needed time to each of the great books, he might have become one of the masters in that prime excellence of the craft, the excellence of proportion, progress and climax. He never quite brought himself to adopt the regular modern method of scenario. "Philip," his last full length fiction, may be cited as proof.

Yet it may be that he would have given increased attention to construction had he lived a long life. It is worth noting that when the unfinished " Denis Duval " dropt from a hand made inert by death, the general plan, wherefrom an idea of its architecture could be got, was among his effects.

To say a word now of Thackeray's style. There is practical unanimity of opinion as to this. Thackeray had the effect of writing like a cultivated gentleman not self-consciously making literature. He was tolerant of colloquial concessions that never lapsed into vulgarity; even his slips and slovenlinesses are those of the well-bred. To pass from him back to Richardson is to realize how stiffly correct is the latter. Thackeray has flexibility, music, vernacular felicity and a deceptive ease. He had, too, the flashing strokes, the inspirational sallies which characterize the style of writers like Lamb, Stevenson and Meredith. Fitness, balance, breeding and harmony are his chief qualities. To say that he never sinned or nodded would be to deny that he was human. He cut his cloth to fit the desired garment and is a modern English master of prose designed to reproduce the habit and accent of the polite society of his age. In his hortatory asides and didactic moralizings with their *thees* and *thous* and *yeas*, he is still the fine essayist, like Fielding in *his* eighteenth century prefatory exordiums. And here is undoubtedly one of his strongest appeals to the world of readers, whether or no it makes him less perfect a fictionist. The diction of a Thackeray is one of the honorable national assets of his race.

Thackeray's men and women talk as they might be expected to talk in life; each in his own idiom, class and idiosyncrasy. And in the descriptions which furnish atmosphere, in which his creatures may live and breathe and have their being, the hand of the artist of words is equally revealed. Both for dialogue and narration the gift is valid, at times superb. It would be going too far to say that if Thackeray had exercised the care in revision bestowed by later reputable authors, his style might not have been improved: beyond question it would have been, in the narrow sense. But the correction of trifling mistakes is one thing, a change in pattern another. The retouching, although satisfying grammar here and there, might have dimmed the vernacular value of his speech.

But what of Thackeray's view, his vision of things? Does he bear down unduly upon poor imperfect humanity? and what was his purpose in satire? If he is unfair in the representation his place among the great should suffer; since the truly great observer of life does general justice to humankind in his harmonious portrayal.

We have already spoken of Thackeray's sensitive nature as revealed through all available means: he conveys the impression of a suppressed sentimentalist, even in his satire.   And this establishes a presumption that the same man is to be discovered in the novels, the work being an unconscious revelation of the worker.   The characteristic books are of satirical bent, that must be granted: Thackeray's purpose, avowed and implicit in the stories, is that of a Juvenal castigating with a smiling mouth the evils of society.   With keen eye he sees the weaknesses incident to place and power, to the affectations of fashion or the corruptions of the world, the flesh and the devil.   Nobody of commonsense will deny that here is a welcome service if performed with skill and fair-mindedness in the interests of truth.   The only query would be: Is the picture undistorted? If Thackeray's studies leave a bad taste in the mouth, if their effect is depressing, if one feels as a result that there is neither virtue nor magnanimity in woman, and that man is incapable of honor, bravery, justice and tenderness—then the novelist may be called cynic. He is not a wholesome writer, however acceptable for art or admirable for genius.   Nor will the mass of mankind believe in and love him.

Naturally we are here on ground where the personal equation influences judgment.   There can never be complete agreement.   Some readers, and excellent people they are, will always be offended by what they never tire of calling the worldly tone of Thackeray; to others, he will be as lovable in his view of life as he is amusing. Speaking, then, merely for myself, it seems to me that for mature folk who have had some experience with humanity, Thackeray is a charming companion whose heart is as sound as his pen is incisive. The very young as a rule are not ready for him and (so far as my observation goes) do not much care for him. That his intention was to help the cause of kindness, truth and justice in the world is apparent. It is late in the day to defend his way of crying up the good by a frank exhibition of the evil. Good and bad are never confused by him, and Taine was right in calling him above all a moralist. But being by instinct a realist too, he gave vent to his passion for truth-telling so far as he dared, in a day when it was far less fashionable to do this than it now is. A remark in the preface to "Pendennis" is full of suggestion: "Since the author of 'Tom Jones' was buried, no writer of fiction among us has been permitted to depict to his utmost power a Man. We must drape him and give him a certain conventional simper. Society will not tolerate the Natural in our Art."

It will not do to say (as is often said) that Thackeray could not draw an admirable or perfect woman. If he did not leave us a perfect one, it was perhaps for the reason alleged to have been

given by Mr. Howells when he was charged with
the same misdemeanor: he was waiting for the Lord
to do it first! But Thackeray does no injustice to
the sex: if Amelia be stupid (which is matter of
debate), Helen Warrington is not, but rather a
very noble creature built on a large plan: whatever
the small blemishes of Lady Castlewood she is in-
delible in memory for character and charm. And
so with others not a few. Becky and Beatrix are
merely the reverse of the picture. And there is a
similar balance in the delineation of men: Colonel
Newcome over against Captain Costigan, and many
a couple more. Thackeray does not fall into the
mistake of making his spotted characters all-black.
Who does not find something likable in the Fotherin-
gay and in the Campaigner? Even a Barry Lyndon has the redeeming quality of courage. And
surely we adore Beatrix, with all her faults. Major
Pendennis is a thoroughgoing old worldling, but it
is impossible not to feel a species of fondness for
him. Jos. Sedley is very much an ass, but one's smile
at him is full of tolerance. Yes, the worst of them
all, the immortal Becky (who was so plainly liked
by her maker) awakens sympathy in the reader when
routed in her fortunes, black-leg though she be. She
cared for her husband, after her fashion, and she
plays the game of Bad Luck in a way far from despic-
able. Nor is that easy-going, commonplace scoundrel, Rawdon, with his dog-like devotion to the same

Becky, denied his touch of higher humanity. Behind all these is a large tolerance, an intellectual breadth, a spiritual comprehension that is merciful to the sinner, while never condoning the sin. Thackeray is therefore more than story-teller or fine writer: a sane observer of the Human Comedy; a satirist in the broad sense, devoting himself to revealing society to itself and for its instruction. It is easy to use negations: to say he did not know nor sympathize with the middle class nor the lower and outcast classes as did Dickens; that his interest was in peccadilloes and sins, not in courageous virtues: and that he judged the world from a club window. But this gets us nowhere and is aside from the critic's chief business: which is that of an appreciative explanation of his abiding power and charm. This has now been essayed. Thackeray was too great as man and artist not to know that it was his function to present life in such wise that while a pleasure of recognition should follow the delineation, another and higher pleasure should also result: the surprising pleasure of beauty. " Fiction," he declared, " has no business to exist, unless it be more beautiful than reality." And again: " The first quality of an artist is to have a large heart." With which revelatory utterances may be placed part of the noble sentence closing " The Book of Snobs ": " If fun is good, truth is better still, and love best of all." To read him with open mind is to feel assured that his works, taken in their entirety, reflect these humane sentiments. It is a pity, therefore, for any reader of the best fiction, through intense appreciation of Dickens or for any other reason, to cut himself off from such an enlightening student of humanity and master of imaginative literature.

CHAPTER X

GEORGE ELIOT

GEORGE ELIOT began fiction a decade later than Thackeray, but seems more than a decade nearer to us. With her the full pulse of modern realism is felt a-throbbing. There is no more of the *ye's* and *thous* with which, when he would make an exordium, Thackeray addressed the world—a fashion long since laid aside. Eliot drew much nearer to the truth, the quiet, homely verity of her scenes is a closer approximation to life, realizes life more vitally than the most veracious page of " Vanity Fair." Not that the great woman novelist made the mistake of a slavish imitation of the actual: that capital, lively scene in the early part of " The Mill on the Floss," where Mrs. Tulliver's connections make known to us their delightsome personalities, is not a mere transcript from life; and all the better for that. Nevertheless, the critic can easily discover a difference between Thackeray and Eliot in this regard, and the ten years between them (as we saw in the case of Dickens and Thackeray) are partly responsible: technique and ideal in literary art were changing fast. George Eliot was a truer realist. She took more seriously her aim of interpreting life, and had a higher conception of her artistic mission. Dickens in his beautiful tribute to Thackeray on the latter's death, speaks of the failure of the author of " Pendennis " to take his mission, his genius, seriously: there was justice in the remark. Yet we heard from the preface to " Pendennis " that Thackeray had the desire to depict a typical man of society with the faithful frankness of a Fielding, and since him, Thackeray states, never again used. But the novelist's hearers were not prepared, the time was not yet ripe, and the novelist himself lacked the courage, though he had the clear vision. With Eliot, we reach the psychologic moment: that deepest truth, the truth of character, exhibited in its mainsprings of impulse and thought, came with her into English fiction as it had never before appeared. It would hardly be overstatement to say that modern psychology in the complete sense as method and interest begins in the Novel with Eliot. For there is a radical difference, not only between the Novel which exploits plot and that which exploits character: but also between that which sees character in terms of life and that which sees it in terms of soul. Eliot's fiction does the latter: life to her means character building, and has its meaning only as an arena for spiritual struggle. Success or failure means but this: have I grown in my higher nature, has my existence shown on the whole an upward tendency?

If so, well and good. If not, whatever of place or power may be mine, I am among the world's failures, having missed the goal. This view, steadily to be encountered in all her fiction, gives it the grave quality, the deep undertone and, be it confessed, at times the almost Methodistic manner, which mark this woman's worth in its weakness and its notable strength. In her early days, long before she made fiction, she was morbidly religious; she became in the fulness of time one of the intellectually emancipated. Yet, emotionally, spiritually, she remained to the end an intensely religious person. Conduct, aspiration, communion of souls, these were to her always the realities. If Thackeray's motto was *Be good,* and Dickens', *Do good,* Eliot's might be expressed as: *Make me good!* Consider for a moment and you will see that these phrases stand successively for a convention, an action and an aspiration.

The life of Mary Ann Evans falls for critical purposes into three well-defined divisions: the early days of country life with home and family and school; her career as a savant; and the later years, when she performed her service as story-teller. Unquestionably, the first period was most important in influencing her genius. It was in the home days at Griff, the school days at Nuneaton nearby, that those deepest, most permanent impressions were absorbed which are given out in the finest of her fictions. Hence came the primal inspiration which produced

her best.   And it is because she drew most generously
upon her younger life in her earlier works that it
is they which are most likely to survive the shocks
of Time.

The experiences of Eliot's childhood, youth and
young womanhood were those which taught her the
bottom facts about middle-class country life in the
mid-century, and in a mid-county of England;
Shakspere's county of Warwick. Those experiences gave her such sympathetic comprehension
of the human case in that environment that she became its chronicler, as Dickens had become the chronicler of the lower middle-class of the cities.   Un-
erringly, she generalized from the microcosm of Warwickshire to the life of the world and guessed the
universal human heart.   With utmost sympathy,
joined with a nice power of scrutiny, she saw and
understood the character-types of the village, when
there was a village life which has since passed away:
the yeoman, the small farmer, the operative in the
mill, the peasant, the squire and the parson, the petty
tradesman, the man of the professions: the worker
with his hands at many crafts.

She matured through travel, books and social contact, her knowledge was greatly extended: she came
to be, in a sense, a cultured woman of the world,
a learned person.   Her later books reflected this:
they depict the so-called higher strata of English
society as in " Middlemarch," or, as in " Romola,"

give an historical picture of another time in a foreign land. The woman who was gracious hostess at those famous Sunday afternoons at the Priory seems to have little likeness to the frail, shy, country girl in Griff—seems, too, far more important; yet it may be doubted whether all this later work reveals such mastery of the human heart or comes from such an imperative source of expression as do the earlier novels, " Adam Bede " and " The Mill on the Floss." For human nature is one and the same in Griff or London or Florence, as all the amplitude of the sky is mirrored in the dewdrop. And although Eliot became in later life a more accurate reporter of the intellectual unrest of her day, and had probed deeper into the mystery and the burden of this unintelligible world, great novels are not necessarily made in that way and the majority of those who love her cleave to the less burdened, more unforced expression of her power.

In those early days, moreover, her attitude towards life was established: it meant a wish to improve the " complaining millions of men." Love went hand in hand with understanding. It may well be that the somberly grave view of humanity and of the universe at large which came to be hers, although strengthened by the positivistic trend of her mature studies, was generated in her sickly youth and a reaction from the narrow theologic thought with which she was then surrounded. Always frail—subject

through life to distressing illness—it would not be
fair to ask of this woman an optimism of the Mark
Tapley stripe.   In part, the grave outlook was
physical, temperamental: but also it was an expression of a swiftly approaching mood of the late
nineteenth century. And the beginning can be traced
back to the autumn evenings in the big farmhouse
at Griff when, as a mere child, she wrestled or prayed
with what she called her sick soul.   That stern,
upright farmer father of hers seems the dominant
factor in her make-up, although the iron of her blood
was tempered by the livelier, more mundane qualities
of her sprightly mother, towards whom we look for
the source of the daughter's superb gift of humor.
Whatever the component parts of father and mother
in her, and however large that personal variation
which is genius, of this we may be comfortably sure:
the deepest in the books, whether regarded as presentation of life or as interpretation, came from the
early Warwickshire years.

Gradually came that mental *éclaircissement* which
produced the editor, the magazinist, the translator
of Strauss. The friendship with the Brays more than
any one thing marks the external cause of this awakening: but it was latent, this response to the world
of thought and of scholarship, and certain to be
called out sooner or later.   Our chief interest in
it is due to the query how much it ministered to
her coming career as creative author of fiction.

George Eliot at this period looked perilously like a Blue Stocking. The range and variety of her reading and the severely intellectual nature of her pursuits justify the assertion. Was this well for the novelist?

The reply might be a paradox: *yes and no*. This learning imparted to Eliot's works a breadth of vision that is tonic and wins the respect of the judicious. It helps her to escape from that bane of the woman novelist—excessive sentiment without intellectual orientation. But, on the other hand, there are times when she appears to be writing a polemic, not a novel: when the tone becomes didactic, the movement heavy—when the work seems self-conscious and over-intellectualized. Nor can it be denied that this tendency grew on Eliot, to the injury of her latest work. There is a simple kind of exhortation in the "Clerical Scenes," but it disappears in the earliest novels, only to reappear in stories like "Daniel Deronda." Any and all culture that comes to a large, original nature (and such was Eliot's) should be for the good of the literary product: learning in the narrower, more technical sense, is perhaps likely to do harm. Here and there there is a reminder of the critic-reviewer in her fiction.

George Eliot's intellectual development during her last years widened her work and strengthened her comprehensive grasp of life. She gained in inter-

pretation thereby.   There will, however, always be
those who hold that it would have been better for
her reputation had she written nothing after " Middlemarch," or even after " Felix Holt."   Those who
object on principle to her agnosticism, would also
add that the negative nature of her philosophy, her
lack of what is called definite religious convictions,
had its share in injuring materially her maturest
fiction.   The vitality or charm of a novel, however,
is not necessarily impaired because the author holds
such views.   It is more pertinent to take the books
as they are, in chronologic order, to point out so far
as possible their particular merits.

And first, the " Scenes from Clerical Life."   It is
interesting to the student of this novelist that her
writing of fiction was suggested to her by Lewes,
and that she tried her hand at a tale when she was
not far from forty years old.   The question will
intrude: would a genuine fiction-maker need to be
thus prodded by a friend, and refrain from any independent attempt up to a period so late?   Yet it
will not do to answer glibly in the negative.   Too
many examples of late beginning and fine fiction as
a consequence are furnished by English literature to
make denial safe.   We have seen Defoe and Richardson and a number of later novelists breaking the
rules—if any such exist.   No one can now read the
" Clerical Scenes " without discovering in them qualities of head and heart which, when allowed an en-

larged canvas and backed by a sure technique, could
be counted on to make worthy fiction. The quiet
village life glows softly under the sympathetic touch
of a true painter.

A recent reading of this first book showed more
clearly than ever the unequalness of merit in the
three stories, their strong didactic bent, and the
charmingly faithful observation which for the present-day reader is their greatest attraction. The first
and simplest, " The Sad Fortunes of the Rev. Amos
Barton," is by far the best. The poorest is the
second, " Mr. Gilfil's Love Story," which has touches
of conventional melodrama in a framework reminis-
cent of earlier fictionists like Disraeli. " Janet's
Repentance," with its fine central character of the
unhappy wedded wife, is strong, sincere, appealing;
and much of the local color admirable. But—perhaps because there is more attempt at story-telling,
more plot—the narrative falls below the beautiful,
quiet chronicle of the days of Amos: an exquisite
portrayal of an average man who yet stands for
humanity's best. The tale is significant as a prelude to Eliot's coming work, containing, in the seed,
those qualities which were to make her noteworthy.
Perusing the volume to-day, we can hardly say that
it appears an epoch-making production in fiction,
the declaration of a new talent in modern literature.
But much has happened in fiction during the half
century since 1857, and we are not in a position to

judge the feeling of those who then began to follow
the fortunes of the Reverend Amos.

But it is not difficult for the twentieth century
reader, even if blasé, to understand that " Adam
Bede," published when its author was forty, aroused
a furore of admiration: it still holds general attention, and many whose opinion is worth having, regard it with respect, affection, even enthusiasm.

The broader canvas was exactly what the novelist
needed to show her power of characterization, her
ability to build up her picture by countless little
touches guided by the most unflinching faith in detail and given vibrancy by the sympathy which in
all George Eliot's fiction is like the air you breathe.
Then, too, as an appeal to the general, there is
more of story interest, although neither here nor
in any story to follow, does plot come first with a
writer whose chief interest is always character, and
its development.   The autobiographic note deepens
and gives at once verity and intensity to the novel;
here, as in " The Mill on the Floss " which was
to follow the next year, Eliot first gave free play
to that emotional seizure of her own past to which
reference has been made.   The homely material of
the first novel was but part of its strength.   Readers
who had been offered the flash-romantic fiction of
Disraeli and Bulwer, turned with refreshment to
the placid annals of a village where, none the less,
the human heart in its follies and frailties and no-

bilities, is laid bare. The skill with which the leisurely moving story rises to its vivid moments of
climactic interest—the duel in the wood, Hetty's
flight, the death of Adam's father—is marked and
points plainly to the advance, through study and
practice, of the novelist since the " Clerical Scenes ";
constructive excellencies do not come by instinct.
" Adam Bede " is preëminently a book of belief,
written not so much in ink as in red blood, and in
that psychic fluid that means the author's spiritual
nature. She herself declared, " I love it very much,"
and it reveals the fact on every page. Aside from
its indubitable worth as a picture of English middle-
class country life in an earlier nineteenth century
than we know—the easy-going days before electricity
—it has its highest claim to our regard as a reading
in life, not conveyed by word of mouth didactically,
but carried in scene and character. The author's
tenderness over Hetty, without even sentimentalizing
her as, for example, Dumas sentimentalizes his Ca-
mille, suggests the mood of the whole narrative: a
large-minded, large-hearted comprehension of humankind, an insistence on spiritual tests, yet with the
will to tell the truth and present impartially the
darkest shadows. It is because George Eliot's people are compounded with beautiful naturalness of
good and bad—not hopelessly bad with Hetty, nor
hopelessly good with Adam—that we understand
them and love them. Here is an element of her

effectiveness.   Even her Dinah walks with her feet
firmly planted upon the earth, though her mystic
vision may be skyward.

With " Adam Bede" she came into her own. The
" Clerical Scenes " had won critical plaudits: Dickens, in 1857 long settled in his seat of public idol-
atry, wrote the unknown author a letter of appreciation so warm-hearted, so generous, that it is hard
to resist the pleasure of quoting it: it is interesting
to remark that in despite the masculine pen-name,
he attributed the work to a woman.   But the public
had not responded.   With " Adam Bede " this was
changed; the book gained speedy popularity, the
author even meeting with that mixed compliment, a
bogus claimant to its authorship.   And so, greatly
encouraged, and stimulated to do her best, she produced " The Mill on the Floss," a novel, which, if
not her finest, will always be placed high on her list
of representative fiction.

This time the story as such was stronger, there
was more substance and variety because of the
greater number of characters and their freer interplay upon each other.   Most important of all, when
we look beyond the immediate reception by the public
to its more permanent position, the work is decidedly
more thoroughgoing in its psychology: it goes to
the very core of personality, where the earlier book
was in some instances satisfied with sketch-work.   In
" Adam Bede " the freshness comes from the treat-

ment rather than the theme. The framework, a
seduction story, is old enough—old as human nature
and pre-literary story-telling. But in " The Mill
on the Floss " we have the history of two inter-
twined lives, contrasted types from within the confines of family life, bound by kin-love yet separated
by temperament. It is the deepest, truest of tragedy and we see that just this particular study of
humanity had not been accomplished so exhaustively
before in all the annals of fiction. As it happened,
everything conspired to make the author at her best
when she was writing this novel: as her letters show,
her health was, for her, good: we have noted the
stimulus derived from the reception of " Adam Bede "
—which was as wine to her soul. Then—a fact
which should never be forgotten—the tale is carried
through logically and expresses, with neither palter-
ing nor evasion, George Eliot's sense of life's tragedy.
In the other book, on the contrary, a touch of the
fictitious was introduced by Lewes; Dinah and Adam
were united to make at the end a mitigation of the
painfulness of Hetty's downfall. Lewes may have
been right in looking to the contemporary audience,
but never again did Eliot yield to that form of the
literary lie, the pleasant ending. She certainly did
not in " The Mill on the Floss ": an element of its
strength is its truth. The book, broadly considered,
moves slow, with dramatic accelerando at cumulative moments; it is the kind of narrative where

this method is allowable without artistic sin. Another great excellence is the superb insight into the nature of childhood, boy and girl; if Maggie is drawn with the more penetrating sympathy, Tom is finely observed: if the author never rebukes his limitations, she states them and, as it were, lifts hands to heaven to cry like a Greek chorus: " See these mortals love yet clash!   Behold, how havoc comes!   Eheu! this mortal case! "

With humanity still pulling at her heart-strings, and conceiving fiction which offered more value of plot than before, George Eliot wrote the charming romance " Silas Marner," novelette in form, modern romance in its just mingling of truth and idealization: a work published the next year.   She interrupted " Romola " to do it, which is suggestive as indicating absorption by the theme.   This story offers a delightful blend of homely realism with poetic symbolism.   The miser is wooed from his sordid love of gold by the golden glint of a little girl's hair: as love creeps into his starved heart, heartless greed goes out forever: before a soulless machine, he becomes a man.   It is the world-old, still potent thought that the good can drive out the bad: a spiritual allegory in a series of vivid pictures carrying the wholesomest and highest of lessons.   The artistic and didactic are here in happy union.   And as nowhere else in her work (unless exception be made in the case of " Romola ") she sees a truth in terms of drama. To read the story is to feel its stage value: it is no surprise to know that several dramatizations of the book have been made. Aside from its central motive, the studies of homely village life, as well as of polite society, are in Eliot's best manner: the humor of Dolly Winthrop is of as excellent vintage as the humor of Mrs. Poyser in " Adam Bede," yet with the necessary differentiation. The typical deep sympathy for common humanity—just average folks—permeates the handling. Moreover, while the romance has a happy issue, as a romance should according to Stevenson, if it possibly can, it does not differ in its view of life from so fatalistic a book as " The Mill on the Floss "; for circumstances change Silas; if the child Eppie had not come he might have remained a miser. It was not his will alone that revolutionized his life; what some would call luck was at work there. In " Silas Marner " the teaching is of a piece with that of all her representative work.

But when we reach " Romola " there is a change, debatable ground is entered upon at once. Hitherto, the story-teller has mastered the preacher, although an ever more earnest soul has been expressing itself about Life. Now we enter the region of more self-conscious literary art, of planned work and study, and confront the possibility of flagging invention. Also, we leave the solid ground of contemporary themes and find the realist with her hang for truth, essaying an historical setting, an entirely new and foreign motive. Eliot had already proved her right to depict certain aspects of her own English life. To strive to exercise the same powers on a theme like " Romola " was a venturesome step. We have seen how Dickens and Thackeray essayed romance at least once with ringing success; now the third major mid-century novelist was to try the same thing.

It may be conceded at the start that in one important respect this Florentine story of Savonarola and his day is entirely typical: it puts clearly before us in a medieval romantic *mis-en scène*, the problem of a soul: the slow, subtle, awful degeneration of the man Tito, with its foil in the noble figure of the girl Romola. The central personality psychologically is that of the wily Greek-Italian, and Eliot never probed deeper into the labyrinths of the perturbed human spirit than in this remarkable analysis. The reader, too, remembers gratefully, with a catch of the breath, the great scenes, two of which are the execution of Savonarola, and the final confrontation of Tito by his adoptive father, with its Greek-like sense of tragic doom. The same reader stands aghast before the labor which must lie behind such a work and often comes to him a sudden, vital sense of fifteenth century Florence, then, as never since, the Lily of the Arno: so cunningly and with such felicity are innumerable details individualized, massed and blended.   And yet, somehow it all seems a splendid experiment, a worthy performance rather than a spontaneous and successful creative endeavor: this, in comparison with the fiction that came before.   The author seems a little over-burdened by the tremendousness of her material.   Whether it is because the Savonarola episode is not thoroughly synthetized with the Tito-Romola part: or that the central theme is of itself fundamentally unpleasant—or again, that from the nature of the romance, head-work had largely to supplant that genial draught upon the springs of childhood which gave us "Adam Bede" and "The Mill on the Floss";—or once more, whether the crowded canvas injures the unity of the design, be these as they may, "Romola" strikes one as great in spots and as conveying a noble though somber truth, but does not carry us off our feet. That is the blunt truth about it, major work as it is, with only half a dozen of its kind to equal it in all English literature.   It falls distinctly behind both "A Tale of Two Cities" and "Esmond." It is a book to admire, to praise in many particulars, to be impressed by: but not quite to treasure as one treasures the story of the Tullivers.   It was written by George Eliot, famous novelist, who with that anxious, morbid conscience of hers, had to live up to her reputation, and who received $50,000 for the work, even to-day a large sum for a piece of fiction. It was not written by a woman irresistibly impelled

to self-expression, seized with the passionate desire
to paint Life.   It is, in a sense, her first professional
feat and performance.

Meanwhile, she was getting on in life: we saw that
she was seven and thirty when she wrote the " Clerical Scenes ": it was almost a decade later when
"Felix Holt, Radical " appeared, and she was near-
ing fifty.   I believe it to be helpful to draw a line
between all her fiction before and after " Felix Holt,"
placing that book somewhat uncertainly on the dividing line.   The four earlier novels stand for a
period when there is a strong, or at least sufficient
story interest, the proper amount of objectification:
to the second division belong " Middlemarch " and
" Daniel Deronda," where we feel that problem comes
first and story second.   In the intermediate novel,
" Felix Holt," its excellent story places it with the
first books, but its increased didactic tendency with
the latest stories.   Why has " Felix Holt " been
treated by the critics, as a rule, as of comparatively
minor value?   It is very interesting, contains true
characterization, much of picturesque and dramatic
worth; it abounds in enjoyable first-hand observation
of a period by-gone yet near enough to have been
cognizant to the writer.   Her favorite types, too,
are in it.   Holt, a study of the advanced workman
of his day, is another Bede, *mutatis mutandis*, and
quite as truly realized.   Both Mr. Lyon and his
daughter are capitally drawn and the motive of the

novel—to teach Felix that he can be quite as true
to his cause if he be less rough and eccentric in dress
and deportment, is a good one handled with success.
To which may be added that the encircling theme
of Mrs. Transome's mystery, grips the attention
from the start and there is pleasure when it is seen
to involve Esther, leading her to make a choice which
reveals that she has awakened to a truer valuation
of life—and of Felix.   With all these things in its
favor, why has appreciation been so scant?

Is it not that continually in the narrative you
lose its broader human interest because of the narrower political and social questions that are raised?
They are vital questions, but still, more specific,
technical, of the time.   Nor is their weaving into
the more permanent theme altogether skilful: you
feel like exclaiming to the novelist: " O, let Kingsley
handle chartism, but do you stick to your last—
love and its criss-cross, family sin and its outcome,
character changed as life comes to be more vitally
realized."   George Eliot in this fine story falls into
this mistake, as does Mrs. Humphry Ward in her
well-remembered " Robert Elsmere," and as she has
again in the novel which happens to be her latest
as these words are written, " Marriage à la Mode."
The thesis has a way of sticking out obtrusively in
such efforts.

Many readers may not feel this in " Felix Holt,"
which, whatever its shortcomings, remains an ex-

tremely able and interesting novel, often underestimated. Still, I imagine a genuine distinction has been made with regard to it.

The difference is more definitely felt in " Middlemarch," not infrequently called Eliot's masterpiece. It appeared five years later and the author was over fifty when the book was published serially during 1871 and 1872. Nearly four years were spent in the work of composition: for it the sum of $60,000 was paid.

" Middlemarch," which resembles Thackeray's " Vanity Fair " in telling two stories not closely related, seems less a Novel than a chronicle-history of two families. It is important to remember that its two parts were conceived as independent; their welding, to call it such, was an afterthought. The tempo again, suiting the style of fiction, is leisurely: character study, character contrast, is the principal aim. More definitely, the marriage problem, illustrated by Dorothea's experience with Casaubon, and that of Lydgate with Rosamond, is what the writer places before us. Marriage is chosen simply because it is the modern spiritual battleground, a condition for the trying-out of souls. The greatness of the work lies in its breadth (subjective more than objective), its panoramic view of English country life of the refined type, its rich garner of wisdom concerning human motive and action. We have seen in earlier studies that its type, the chronicle of events as they affect character, is a legitimate one: a successful genus in English-speaking fiction in hands like those of Thackeray, Eliot and Howells. It is one accepted kind, a distinct, often able, sympathetic kind of fiction of our race: its worth as a social document (to use the convenient term once more) is likely to be high. It lacks the close-knit plot, the feeling for stage effect, the swift progression and the sense of completed action which another and more favored sort of Novel exhibits. Yet it may have as much chance of permanence in the hands of a master. The proper question, then, seems to be whether it most fitly expresses the genius of an author.

Perhaps there will never be general agreement as to this in the case of " Middlemarch." The book is drawn from wells of experience not so deep in Eliot's nature as those which went to the making of " Adam Bede " and " The Mill on the Floss," It is life with which the author became familiar in London and about the world during her later literary days. She knows it well, and paints it with her usual noble insistence upon truth. But she knows it with her brain; whereas, she knows " The Mill on the Floss " with her blood. There is surely that difference. Hence, the latter work has, it would seem, a better chance for long life; for, without losing the author's characteristic interpretation, it has more story-value, is richer in humor (that alleviating ingredient of all

fiction) and is a better work of art. It shows George
Eliot absorbed in story-telling: " Middlemarch " is
George Eliot using a slight framework of story for
the sake of talking about life and illustrating by
character. Those who call it her masterpiece are
not judging it primarily as art-work: any more
than those who call Whitman the greatest American
poet are judging him as artist. While it seems
necessary to make this distinction, it is quite as
necessary to bear down on the attraction of the
character-drawing. That is a truly wonderful portrait of the unconsciously selfish scholar in Casaubon.
Dorothea's noble naturalness, Will Ladislaw's fiery
truth, the verity of Rosamond's bovine mediocrity,
the fine reality of Lydgate's situation, so portentous
in its demand upon the moral nature—all this, and
more than this, is admirable and authoritative. The
predominant thought in closing such a study is that
of the tremendous complexity of human fate, influenced as it is by heredity, environment and the
personal equation, and not without melioristic hope,
if we but live up to our best. The tone is grave,
but not hopeless. The quiet, hesitant movement
helps the sense of this slow sureness in the working
of the social law:

> "Though the mills of God grind slowly,
> Yet they grind exceeding small."

In her final novel, " Daniel Deronda," between
which and " Middlemarch " there were six years,

so that it was published when the author was nearly sixty years old, we have another large canvas upon which, in great detail and with admirable variety, is displayed a composition that does not aim at complete unity—or at any rate, does not accomplish it, for the motive is double: to present the Jew so that *Judenhetze* may be diminished: and to exhibit the spiritual evolution through a succession of emotional experiences of the girl Gwendolen. This phase of the story offers an instructive parallel with Meredith's " Diana of the Crossways." If the Jew theme had been made secondary artistically to the Gwendolen study, the novel would have secured a greater degree of constructive success; but there's the rub. Now it seems the main issue; again, Gwendolen holds the center of the stage. The result is a suspicion of patchwork; nor is this changed by the fact that both parts are brilliantly done—to which consideration may be added the well-known antipathy of many Gentile readers to any treatment of the Jew in fiction, if an explanation be sought of the relative slighting of a very noble book.

For it has virtues, many and large. Its spirit is broad, tolerant, wide and loving. In no previous Eliot fiction are there finer single effects: no one is likely to forget the scene in which Gwendolen and Harcourt come to a rupture; or the scene of Deronda's dismissal. And in the way of character portrayal, nothing is keener and truer than the heroine of this book, whose unawakened, seemingly light, nature is chastened and deepened as she slowly learns the meaning of life. The lesson is sound and salutary: it is set forth so vividly as to be immensely impressive. Mordecai, against the background necessary to show him, is sketched with splendid power. And the percentage of quotable sayings, sword-thrusts, many of them, into the vitals of life, is as high perhaps as in any other of the Novels, unless it be " Middlemarch." Nevertheless those who point to " Deronda " as illustrating the novelist's decadence—although they use too harsh a word—have some right on their side. For, viewed as story, it is not so successful as the books of the first half of George Eliot's career. It all depends whether a vital problem Novel is given preference over a Novel which does not obtrude message, if it have any at all. And if fiction be a fine art, it must be confessed that this latter sort is superior. But we have perfect liberty to admire the elevation, earnestness and skill *en détail* that denote such a work. Nay, we may go further and say that the woman who wrote it is greater than she who wrote " The Mill on the Floss."

With a backward glance now at the list, it may be said in summary that the earlier fiction constitutes George Eliot's most authoritative contribution to English novel-making, since the thinking about life so characteristic of her is kept within the bounds

of good story-telling. And the compensation for
this artistic loss in her later fiction is found in its
wider intellectual outlook, its deeper sympathy, the
more profound humanity of the message.

But what of her philosophy? She was not a pessimist, since the pessimist is one who despairs of
human virtue and regards the world as paralyzing
the will nobly to achieve. She was, rather, a melio-
rist who hoped for better things, though tardy to
come; who believed, in her own pungent phrase, " in
the slow contagion of good." Of human happiness
she did in one of her latest moods despair: going
so far in a dark moment as to declare that the only
ideal left her was duty. In a way, she grew sadder
as she grew older. By intellect she was a positivist
who has given up any definite hope of personal im-
mortality—save that which by a metaphor is applied
to one's influence upon the life of the world here upon
earth. And in her own career, by her unconventional
union with Lewes, she made a questionable choice of
action, though from the highest motives; a choice
which I believe rasped her sensitive soul because of
the way it was regarded by many whom she respected
and whose good opinion she coveted. But she remained splendidly wholesome and inspiring in her
fiction, because she clung to her faith in spiritual
self-development, tested all life by the test of duty,
felt the pathos and the preciousness of inconspicuous
lives, and devoted herself through a most exceptional

career to loving service for others. She was therefore not only a novelist of genius, but a profoundly good woman. She had an ample practical credo for living and will always be, for those who read with their mind and soul as well as their eyes, anything but a depressing writer. For them, on the contrary, she will be a tonic force, a seer using fiction as a means to an end—and that end the betterment of mankind.

CHAPTER XI

TROLLOPE AND OTHERS

FIVE or six writers of fiction, none of whom has
attained a position like that of the three great Vic-
torians already considered, yet all of whom loomed
large in their day, have met with unequal treatment at the hands of time: Bulwer Lytton, Disraeli,
Reade, Trollope, Kingsley. And the Brontës might
well be added to the list. The men are mentioned
in the order of their birth; yet it seems more natural
to place Trollope last, not at all because he lived
to 1882, while Kingsley died seven years earlier.
Reade lived two years after Trollope, but seems
chronologically far before him as a novelist. In
the same way, Disraeli and Bulwer Lytton, as we
now look back upon them, appear to be figures of
another age; though the former lived to within a
few years of Trollope, and the latter died but two
years before Kingsley. Of course, the reason
that Disraeli impresses us as antiquated where Trollope looks thoroughly modern, is because the latter
is nearest our own day in method, temper and aim.
And this is the main reason why he has best survived
the shocks of time and is seen to be the most sig-

nificant figure of an able and interesting group. Before he is examined, something may be said of the others.

In a measure, the great reputation enjoyed by the remaining writers was secured in divisions of literature other than fiction; or derived from activities not literary at all. Thus Beaconsfield was Premier, Bulwer was noted as poet and dramatist, and eminent in diplomacy; Kingsley a leader in Church and State. They were men with many irons in the fire: naturally, it took some years to separate their literary importance pure and simple from the other accomplishments that swelled their fame. Reade stood somewhat more definitely for literature; and Trollope, although his living was gained for years as a public servant, set his all of reputation on the single throw of letters. He is Anthony Trollope, Novelist, or he is nothing.

I

Thinking of Disraeli as a maker of stories, one reads of his immense vogue about the middle of the last century and reflects sagely upon the change of literary fashions. The magic is gone for the reader now. Such claim as he can still make is most favorably estimated by " Coningsby," " Sybil " and " Tancred," all published within four years, and constituting a trilogy of books in which the follies

of polite society and the intimacies of politics are
portrayed with fertility and facility. The earlier
" Henrietta Temple " and " Venetia," however fervid
in feeling and valuable for the delineation of contemporary character, are not so characteristic. Nor
are the novels of his last years, " Lothair " and
" Endymion," in any way better than those of his
younger days. That the political trilogy have still
a certain value as studies of the time is beyond
argument. Also, they have wit, invention and a
richly pictorial sense for setting, together with flam-
boyant attraction of style and a solid substratum of
thought. One recognizes often that an athletic mind
is at play in them. But they do not now take hold,
whatever they once did; an air of the false-literary
is over them, it is not easy to read them as true
transcripts from life. To get a full sense of this,
turn to literally contemporaneous books like Dickens' " David Copperfield " and " Hard Times ";
compared with such, Disraeli and all his world seem
clever *pastiche*. Personal taste may modify this
statement: it can hardly reverse it. It would be
futile to explain the difference by saying that Disraeli was some eight years before Dickens or that
he dealt with another and higher class of society.
The difference goes deeper: it is due to the fact that
one writer was writing in the spirit of the age with
his face to the future and so giving a creative
representation of its life; whereas the other was

painting its manners and only half in earnest: playing with literature, in sooth.   A man like Dickens is married to his art; Disraeli indulges in a temporary liaison with letters.   There is, too, in the Lothair-Endymion kind of literature a fatal resemblance to the older sentimental and grandiose fiction of the eighteenth century: an effect of plush and padding, an atmosphere of patchouli and sachet powder.   It has the limitation that fashion ever sets; it is boudoir novel-writing: cabinet literature in both the social and political sense.   As Agnes Repplier has it: " Lothair is beloved by the female aristocracy of Great Britain; and mysterious ladies, whose lofty souls stoop to no conventionalities, die happy with his kisses on their lips."   It would be going too far perhaps to say that this type never existed in life, for Richardson seems to have had a model in mind in drawing Grandison; but it hardly survives in letters, unless we include " St. Elmo " and " Under Two Flags " in that denomination.

To sum it all up: For most of us Disraeli has become hard reading.   This is not to say that he cannot still be read with profit as one who gives us insight concerning his day; but his gorgeous pictures and personages have faded woefully, where Trollope's are as bright as ever; and the latter is right when he said that Lord Beaconsfield's creatures " have a flavor of paint and unreality."

II

Bulwer Lytton has likewise lost ground greatly: but read to-day he has much more to offer. In him, too, may be seen an imperfectly blent mixture of by-gone sentimentality and modern truth: yet whether in the romance of historic setting, "The Last Days of Pompeii," or in the satiric study of realism, like "My Novel," Bulwer is much nearer to us, and holds out vital literature for our appreciation. It is easy to name faults both in romance and realism of his making: but the important thing to acknowledge is that he still appeals, can be read with a certain pleasure. His most mature work, moreover, bears testimony to the coming creed of fiction, as Disraeli's never does. There are moments with Bulwer when he almost seems a fellow of Meredith's. I recall with amusement the classroom remark of a college professor to the effect that "My Novel" was the greatest fiction in English literature. While the freshmen to whom this was addressed did not appreciate the generous erraticism of the judgment, even now one of them sees that, coming as it did from a clergyman of genial culture, a true lover of literature and one to inspire that love in others— even in freshmen!—it could hardly have been spoken concerning a mere man-milliner of letters. Bulwer produced too much and in too many kinds to do his best in all—or in any one. But most of us sooner

or later have been in thrall to " Kenelm Chillingly "
or thrilled to that masterly horror story, " The
House and the Brain." There is pinchbeck with
the gold, but the shining true metal is there.

III

To pass to Kingsley, is like turning from the world
to the kingdom of God: all is religious fervor, humanitarian purpose.   Here again the activity is multiple
but the dominant spirit is that of militant Christianity. Outside of the Novel, Kingsley has left in
" Water Babies " a book deserving the name of
modern classic, unless the phrase be a contradiction
in terms. " Alton Locke," read to-day, is felt to
be too much the tract to bear favorable comparison
with Eliot's " Felix Holt "; but it has literary power
and noble sincerity. Kingsley is one of the first to
feel the ground-swell of social democracy which was
to sweep later fiction on its mighty tide. " West-
ward Ho! " is a sterling historical romance, one of
the more successful books in a select list which em-
braces " The Cloister and the Hearth," " Lorna
Doone," and " John Inglesant." " Hypatia," examined dispassionately, may be described as an historical romance with elements of greatness rather
than a great historical romance. But it shed its
glamour over our youth and there is affectionate
dread in the thought of a more critical re-reading.

In truth, Kingsley, viewed in all his literary work, stands out as an athlete of the intellect and the emotions, doing much and doing it remarkably well—a power for righteousness in his day and generation, but for this very reason less a professional novelist of assured standing. His gifted, erratic brother Henry, in the striking series of stories dealing prevailingly with the Australian life he so well knew, makes a stronger impression of singleness of power and may last longer, one suspects, than the better-known, more successful Charles, whose significance for the later generation is, as we have hinted, in his sensitiveness to the new spirit of social revolt,—an isolated voice where there is now full chorus.

IV

An even more virile figure and one to whom the attribution of genius need not be grudged, is the strong, pugnacious, eminently picturesque Charles Reade. It is a temptation to say that but for his use of a method and a technique hopelessly old-fashioned, he might claim close fellowship for gift and influence with Dickens. But he lacked art as it is now understood: balance, restraint, the impersonal view were not his. He is a glorious but imperfect phenomenon, back there in the middle century. He worked in a way deserving of the descriptive phrase once applied to Macaulay—" a steam engine in breeches; " he put

enough belief and heart into his fiction to float any
literary vessel upon the treacherous waters of fame.
He had, of the more specific qualities of a novelist,
racy idiom, power in creating character and a remarkable gift for plot and dramatic scene. His
frankly melodramatic novels like " A Terrible Temptation " are among the best of their kind, and in
" The Cloister and the Hearth" he performed the
major literary feat of reconstructing, with the large
imagination and humanity which obliterate any effect
of archeology and worked-up background, a period
long past. And what reader of English fiction does
not harbor more than kindly sentiments for those
very different yet equally lovable women, Christie
Johnstone and Peg Woffington? To run over his
contributions thus is to feel the heart grow warm
towards the sturdy story-teller. Reade also played
a part, as did Kingsley, in the movement for recognition of the socially unfit and those unfairly treated.
" Put Yourself in His Place," with its early word
on the readjustment of labor troubles, is typical of
much that he strove to do. Superb partisan that
he was, it is probable that had he cared less for
polemics and more for his art, he would have secured
a safer position in the annals of fiction. He can
always be taken up and enjoyed for his earnest conviction or his story for the story's sake, even if on
more critical evaluations he comes out not so well
as men of lesser caliber.

V

The writer of the group who has consistently gained ground and has come to be generally recognized as a great artist, a force in English fiction both for influence and pleasure-giving power, is Anthony Trollope. He is vital to-day and strengthening his hold upon the readers of fiction. The quiet, cultivated folk in whose good opinion lies the destiny of really worthy literature, are, as a rule, friendly to Trollope; not seldom they are devoted to him. Such people peruse him in an enjoyably ruminative way at their meals, or read him in the negligé of retirement. He is that cosy, enviable thing, a bedside author. He is above all a story-teller for the middle-aged and it is his good fortune to be able to sit and wait for us at that half-way house,—since we all arrive. Of course, to say this is to acknowledge his limitations. He does not appeal strongly to the young, though he never forgets to tell a love story; but he is too placid, matter-of-fact, unromantic for them. But if he do not shake us with lyric passion, he is always interesting and he wears uncommonly well. That his popularity is extending is testified to by new editions and publishers' hullabaloo over his work.

Such a fate is deserved by him, for Trollope is one of the most consummate masters of that commonplace which has become the modern fashion—and

fascination. He has a wonderful power in the realism
which means getting close to the fact and the average
without making them uninteresting. So, naturally,
as realism has gained he has gained. No one except
Jane Austen has surpassed him in this power of
truthful portrayal, and he has the advantage of being practically of our own day. He insisted that
fiction should be objective, and refused to intrude
himself into the story, showing himself in this respect
a better artist than Thackeray, whom he much admired but frankly criticized. He was unwilling to
pause and harangue his audience in rotund voice after
the manner of Dickens. First among modern novelists, Trollope stands invisible behind his characters,
and this, as we have seen, was to become one of the
articles of the modern creed of fiction. He affords
us that peculiar pleasure which is derived from seeing
in a book what we instantly recognize as familiar to
us in life. Just why the pleasure, may be left to the
psychologists; but it is of indisputable charm, and
Trollope possesses it. We may talk wisely and at
length of his commonplaceness, lack of spice, philistinism; he can be counted on to amuse us. He lived
valiantly up to his own injunction: " Of all the
needs a book has, the chief need is that it is
readable." A simple test, this, but a terrible one
that has slain its thousands. No nineteenth century maker of stories is safer in the matter of
keeping the attention. If the book can be easily

laid down, it is always agreeable to take it up again.

Trollope set out in the most systematic way to produce a series of novels illustrating certain sections of England, certain types of English society; steadily, for a life-time, with the artisan's skilful hand, he labored at the craft. He is the very antithesis of the erraticisms and irregularities of genius. He went to his daily stint of work, by night and day, on sea or land, exactly as the merchant goes to his office, the mechanic to his shop. He wrote with a watch before him, two hundred and fifty words to fifteen minutes. But he had the most unusual faculty of direct, unprejudiced, clear observation; he trained himself to set down what he saw and to remember it. And he also had the constructive ability to shape and carry on his story so as to create the effect of growth, along with an equally valuable power of sympathetic characterization, so that you know and understand his folk. Add to this a style perfectly accordant with the unobtrusive harmony of the picture, and the main elements of Trollope's appeal have been enumerated. Yet has he not been entirely explained. His art—meaning the skilled handling of his material —can hardly be praised too much; it is so easy to underestimate because it is so unshowy. Few had a nicer sense of scale and tone; he gets his effects often because of this harmony of adjustment. For one example, "The Warden" is a relatively short piece of fiction which opens the famous Chronicles of Barset series. Its interest culminates in the going of the Reverend Septimus Harding to London from his quiet country home, in order to prevent a young couple from marrying. The whole situation is tiny, a mere corner flurry. But so admirably has the climax been prepared, so organic is it to all that went before in the way of preparation, that the result is positively thrilling: a wonderful example of the principle of key and relation.

Or again, in that scene which is a favorite with all Trollope's readers, where the arrogant Mrs. Proudie is rebuked by the gaunt Mr. Crawley, the effect of his famous "Peace, woman!" is tremendous only because it is a dash of vivid red in a composition where the general color scheme is low and subdued.

In view of this faculty, it will not do to regard Trollope as a kind of mechanic who began one novel the day he finished another and often carried on two or three at the same time, like a juggler with his balls, with no conception of them as artistic wholes. He says himself that he began a piece of fiction with no full plan. But, with his very obvious skill prodigally proved from his work, we may beg leave to take all such statements in a qualified sense: for the kind of fiction he aimed at he surely developed a technique not only adequate but of very unusual excellence.

Trollope was a voluminous writer: he gives in his

delightful autobiography the list of his own works and it numbers upwards of sixty titles, of which over forty are fiction. His capacity for writing, judged by mere bulk, appears to have been inherited; for his mother, turning authoress at fifty years of age, produced no less than one hundred and fourteen volumes! There is inferior work, and plenty of it, among the sum-total of his activity, but two series, amounting to about twenty books, include the fiction upon which his fame so solidly rests: the Cathedral series and the Parliamentary series. In the former, choosing the southern-western counties of Wiltshire and Hants as Hardy chose Wessex for his peculiar venue, he described the clerical life of his land as it had never been described before, showing the type as made up of men like unto other men, unromantic, often this-worldly and smug, yet varying the type, making room for such an idealist as Crawley as well as for sleek bishops and ecclesiastical wire-pullers. Neither his young women nor his holy men are over-drawn a jot: they have the continence of Nature. But they are not cynically presented. You like them and take pleasure in their society; they are so beautifully true! The inspiration of these studies came to him as he walked under the shadow of Salisbury Cathedral; and one is never far away from the influence of the cathedral class. The life is the worldy-godly life of that microcosm, a small, genteel, conventional urban society; in sharp contrast with the

life depicted by Hardy in the same part of the land,—
but like another world, because his portraiture finds
its subjects among peasant-folk and yeoman—the
true primitive types whose speech is slow and their
roots deep down in the soil.

The realism of Trollope was not confined to the
mere reproduction of externals; he gave the illusion
of character, without departing from what can be
verified by what men know.   His photographs were
largely imaginary, as all artistic work must be; he
constructed his stories out of his own mind.   But
all is based on what may be called a splendidly
reasoned and reasonable experience with Life.   His
especial service was thus to instruct us about English
society, without tedium, within a domain which was
voluntarily selected for his own.   In this he was
also a pioneer in that local fiction which is a geographical effect of realism.   And to help him in this
setting down of what he believed to be true of humanity, was a style so lucid and simple as perfectly to
serve his purpose.   For unobtrusive ease, idiomatic
naturalness and that familiarity which escapes vulgarity and retains a quiet distinction, no one has
excelled him.   It is one reason why we feel an
intimate knowledge of his characters.   Mr. Howells
declares it is Trollope who is most like Austen " in
simple honesty and instinctive truth, as unphiloso-
phized as the light of common day "—though he goes
on to deplore that he too often preferred to be " like

the caricaturist Thackeray "—a somewhat hard saying. It is a particular comfort to read such a writer when intensely personal psychology is the order of the day and neither style nor interpretation in fiction is simple.

If Trollope can be said to be derivative at all, it is Thackeray who most influenced him. He avows his admiration, wrote the other's life, and deemed him one who advanced truth-telling in the Novel. Yet, as was stated, he did not altogether approve of the Master, thinking his satire too steady a view instead of an occasional weapon. Indeed his strictures in the biography have at times a cool, almost hostile sound. He may or may not have taken a hint from Thackeray on the re-introduction of characters in other books—a pleasant device long antedating the nineteenth century, since one finds it in Lyly's " Euphues." Trollope also disliked Dickens' habit of exaggeration (as he thought it) even when it was used in the interests of reform, and satirized the tendency in the person of Mr. Popular Sentiment in " The Warden."

The more one studies Trollope and the farther he recedes into the past, the firmer grows the conviction that he is a very distinctive figure of Victorian fiction, a pioneer who led the way and was to be followed by a horde of secondary realistic novelists who could imitate his methods but not reproduce his pleasant effect.

VI

The Brontës, coming when they did, before 1850, are a curious study. Realism was growing daily and destined to be the fashion of the literary to-morrow. But "Jane Eyre" is the product of Charlotte Brontë's isolation, her morbidly introspective nature, her painful sense of personal duty, the inextinguishable romance that was hers as the leal descendant of a race of Irish story-tellers. She looked up to and worshipped Thackeray, but produced fiction that was like something from another world. She and her sisters, especially Emily, whose vivid "Wuthering Heights" has all the effect of a visitant from a remote planet, are strangely unrelated to the general course of the nineteenth century. They seem born out of time; they would have left a more lasting impress upon English fiction had they come before— or after. There are unquestionable qualities of realism in "Jane Eyre," but it is romantic to the core, sentimental, melodramatic. Rochester is an elder St. Elmo—hardly truer as a human being; Jane's sacrificial worship goes back to the eighteenth century; and that famous mad-woman's shriek in the night is a moment to be boasted of on the Bowery. And this was her most typical book, that which gave her fame. The others, "Villette" and the rest, are more truly representative of the realistic trend of the day, but withal though interesting, less char-

acteristic, less liked. In proportion as she is romantic is she remembered. The streak of genius in
these gifted women must not blind us to the isolation,
the unrelated nature of their work to the main course
of the Novel. They are exceptions to the rule.

VII

This group then of novelists, sinking all individual
differences, marks the progress of the method of
realism over the romance. Scarcely one is conspicuous for achievement in the latter, while almost all
of them did yeoman service in the former. In some
cases—those of Disraeli and Bulwer—the transition
is seen where their earlier and later work is contrasted; with a writer like Trollope, the newer method
completely triumphs. Even in so confirmed a romance-maker as Wilkie Collins, to whom plot was
everything and whose cunning of hand in this is
notorious, there is a concession to the new ideal of
Truth. He was touched by his time in the matter
of naturalness of dialogue, though not of event.
Wildly improbable and wooden as his themes may
now seem, their manner is realistic, realism of speech,
in fact, being an element in his effectivism. Even
the author of " The Moonstone " is scotched by the
spirit of the age, and in the preface to " Armsdale "
declares for a greater freedom of theme—one of the
first announcements of that desire for an extension

of the subject-matter which was in the next generation to bring such a change.

It seems just to represent all these secondary novelists as subsidiary to Dickens, Thackeray and Eliot.
Fascinating isolated figures like Borrow, who will
always be cherished by the few, are perforce passed
by. We are trying to keep both quality and influence in mind, with the desire to show the writers
not by themselves alone but as part of a stream of
tendency which has made the English Novel the distinct form it is to-day. Even a resounding genius,
in this view, may have less meaning than an apparent
plodder like Trollope, who, as time goes by, is seen
more clearly to be one of the shaping forces in the
development of a literary form.

CHAPTER XII

HARDY AND MEREDITH

WE have seen in chapter seventh, how the influence of Balzac introduced to modern fiction that extension of subject and that preference for the external fact widely productive of change in the novel-making of the continent and of English-speaking lands. As the year 1830 was given significance by him, so, a generation later, the year 1870 was given significance by Zola. England, like other lands cultivating the Novel, felt the influence. Balzac brought to fiction a greater franchise of theme: Zola taught it to regard a human being—individual or collectively social—as primarily animal: that is, he explains action on this hypothesis. And as an inevitable consequence, realism passed to the so-called naturalism. Zola believed in this view as a theory and his practice, not always consistent with it, was sufficiently so in the famous Rougon-Macquart series of novels begun the year of the Franco-Prussian war, to establish it as a method, and a school of fiction. Naturalism, linking hands with *l'art pour art*—" a fine phrase is a moral action —there is no other morality in literature," cried Zola —became a banner-cry, with " the flesh is all " its

chief article of belief. No study of the growth of
English fiction can ignore this typical modern movement, however unpleasant it may be to follow it.
The baser and more brutal phases of the Novel con-
tinental and insular look to this derivation. Zola's
remarkable   pronunciamento   " The   Experimental
Novel," proves how honestly he espoused the doctrine
of the realist, how blind he is to its partial view.
His attempt to subject the art of fiction to the exact
laws of science, is an illustration of the influence
of scientific thought upon a mind not broadly cultured, though of unusual native quality. Realism
of the modern kind—the kind for which Zola stands
—is the result in a form of literature of the necessary
intellectual unrest following on the abandonment of
older religious ideals. Science had forced men to
give up certain theological conceptions; death, im-
mortality, God, Man,—these were all differently understood, and a period of readjustment, doubt and
negation, of misery and despair, was the natural
issue.   Man, being naturally religious, was sure
sooner or later to secure a new and more hopeful
faith: it was a matter of spiritual self-preservation.
But realism in letters, for the moment, before a new
theory had been formulated, was a kind of *pis aller*
by which literature could be produced and attention
given to the tangible things of this earth, many of
them not before thoroughly exploited; the things of
the mind, of the Spirit, were certain to be exploited

later, when a broader creed should come. The new
romanticism and idealism of our day marks this
return. Zola's theory is now seen to be wrong, and
there has followed a violent reaction from the realistic
tenets, even in Paris, its citadel. But for some years,
it held tyrannous sway and its leader was a man of
genius, his work distinctive, remarkable; at its best,
great,—in spite of, rather than because of, his
principles. It was in the later Trilogy of the cities
that, using a broader formula, he came into full expression of what was in him; during the last years
of his life he was moving, both as man and artist,
in the right direction. Yet naturally it was novels
like " Nana " and " L'Assomoir " that gave him his
vogue; and their obsession with the fleshly gave them
for the moment a strange distinction: for years their
author was regarded as the founder of a school and
its most formidable exponent. He wielded an influence that rarely falls to a maker of stories. And
although realism in its extreme manifestations no
longer holds exclusive sway, Zola's impulse is still
at work in the modern Novel. Historically, his name
will always be of interest.

I

Thomas Hardy is a realist in a sense true of no
English novelist of anything like equal rank pre-
ceding him: his literary genealogy is French, for his
" Jude The Obscure " has no English prototype,

except the earlier work of George Moore, whose inspiration is even more definitely Paris. To study Hardy's development for a period of about twenty-five years from " Under the Greenwood Tree " to " Jude," is to review, as they are expressed in the work of one great English novelist, the literary ideals before and after Zola. Few will cavil at the inclusion in our study of a living author like Hardy. His work ranks with the most influential of our time; so much may be seen already. His writing of fiction, moreover, or at least of Novels, seems to be finished. And like Meredith, he is a man of genius and, strictly speaking, a finer artist than the elder author. For quality, then, and significance of accomplishment, Hardy may well be examined with the masters whose record is rounded out by death. He offers a fine example of the logic of modern realism, as it has been applied by a first-class mind to the art of fiction. In Meredith, on the contrary, is shown a sort of synthesis of the realistic and poetic-philosophic interpretation. Hardy is for this reason easier to understand and explain; Meredith refuses classification.

The elements of strength in Thomas Hardy can be made out clearly; they are not elusive. Wisely, he has chosen to do a very definite thing and, with rare perseverance and skill, he has done it. He selected as setting the south-western part of England —Wessex, is the ancient name he gave it—that em-

braces Somersetshire and contiguous counties, because he felt that the types of humanity and the
view of life he wished to show could best be thrown
out against the primitive background.   Certain ele-
mental truths about men and women, he believed, lost
sight of in the kaleidoscopic attritions of the town,
might there be clearly seen.   The choice of locale was
thus part of an attitude toward life.   That attitude
or view may be described fairly well as one of
philosophic fatalism.

It has not the cold removedness of the stoic: it
has pity in it, even love.   But it is deeply sad, sometimes bitter.   In Hardy's presentation of Nature
(a remark applying to some extent to a younger novelist who shows his influence, Phillpotts), she is displayed as an ironic expression, with even malignant
moods, of a supreme cosmic indifference to the
petty fate of that animalcule, man.   And this, in
spite of a curious power she possesses of consoling
him and of charming him by blandishments that cheat
the loneliness of his soul.   There is no purer example
of tragedy in modern literature than Mr. Hardy's
strongest, most mature stories.   A mind deeply serious and honest, interprets the human case in this
wise and conceives that the underlying pitilessness
can most graphically be conveyed in a setting like
that of Egdon Heath, where the great silent forces
of Nature somberly interblend with the forces set
in motion by the human will, both futile to produce

happiness. Even the attempt to be virtuous fails
in "Jude": as the attempt to be happy does in
"Tess." That sardonic, final thought in the last-
named book will not out of our ears: Fate had
played its last little jest with poor Tess.

But there are mitigations, many and welcome.
Hardy has the most delightful humor. His peasants
and simple middle-class folk are as distinctive and
enjoyable as anything since Shakspere. He also
has a more sophisticated, cutting humor—tipped with
irony and tart to the taste—which he uses in those
stories or scenes where urbanites mingle with his
country folk. But his humorous triumphs are
bucolic. And for another source of keenest pleasure,
there is his style, ennobling all his work. Whether
for the plastic manipulation of dialogue or the elo-
quencies and exactitudes of description, he is em-
phatically a master. His mind, pagan in its bent,
is splendidly broad in its comprehension of
the arcana of Nature and that of a poet sensitive
to all the witchery of a world which at core is
inscrutably dark and mysterious. He knows, none
better, of the comfort to be got even from the sad
when its beauty is made palpitating. No one before
him, not Meredith himself, has so interfused Nature
with man as to bring out the thought of man's
ancient origin in the earth, his birth-ties, and her
claims on his allegiance. This gives a rare savor
to his handling of what with most novelists is often

mere background. Egdon Heath was mentioned;
the setting in " The Return of the Native " is not
background in the usual sense; that mighty stretch
of moorland is almost like the central actor of the
drama, so potent is its influence upon the fate of the
other characters. So with " The Woodlanders " and
still other stories. Take away this subtle and vital
relation of man to Nature, and the whole organism
collapses. Environment with Hardy is atmosphere,
influence, often fate itself. Being a scientist in the
cast of his intellect, although by temperament a poet,
he believes in environment as the shaping power conceived of by Taine and Zola.   It is this use of
Nature as a power upon people of deep, strong,
simple character, showing the sweep of forces far
more potent than the conventions of the polite world,
which distinguishes Hardy's fiction. Fate with him
being so largely that impersonal thing, environment;
allied with temperament (for which he is not responsible), and with opportunity—another element
of luck—it follows logically that man is the sport of
the gods. Hardy is unable, like other determinists,
to escape the dilemma of free-will versus predestina-
tion, and that other crux, the imputation of personality to the workings of so-called natural laws.
Indeed curiously, in his gigantic poem-cycle, " the
Dynasts," the culmination of his life-work, he seems
to hint at a plan of the universe which may be bene-
ficial.

To name another quality that gives distinction
to Hardy's work: his fiction is notably well-built, and
he is a resourceful technician. Often, the way he
seizes a plot and gives it proportionate progress to
an end that is inevitable, exhibits a well-nigh perfect
art. Hardy's novels, for architectural excellence,
are really wonderful and will richly repay careful
study in this respect. It has been suggested that
because his original profession was that of an arch-
itect, his constructive ability may have been carried
over to another craft. This may be fantastic; but
the fact remains that for the handling of material in
such a manner as to eliminate the unnecessary, and
move steadily toward the climax, while ever imitating
though not reproducing, the unartificial gait of life,
Hardy has no superior in English fiction and very
few beyond it. These ameliorations of humor and
pity, these virtues of style and architectural handling make the reading of Thomas Hardy a literary
experience, and very far from an undiluted course
in Pessimism. A sane, vigorous, masculine mind is
at work in all his fiction up to its very latest. Yet
it were idle to deny the main trend of his teaching.
It will be well to trace with some care the change
which has crept gradually over his view of the world.
As his development of thought is studied in the successive novels he produced between 1871 and 1898,
it may appear that there is little fundamental change
in outlook: the tragic note, and the dark theory of

existence, explicit in " Tess " and " Jude," is more
or less implicit in " Desperate Remedies." But
change there is, to be found in the deepening of the
feeling, the pushing of a theory to its logical extreme. This opening tale, read in the light of what
he was to do, strikes one as un-Hardy-like in its
rather complex plot, with its melodramatic tinge of
incident.

The second book, " Under the Greenwood Tree,"
is a blithe, bright woodland comedy and it would
have been convenient for a cut-and-dried theory of
Hardy's growth from lightness to gravity, had it
come first. It is, rather, a happy interlude, hardly
representative of his main interest, save for its clear-
cut characterizations of country life and its idyllic
flavor. The novel that trod on its heels, " A Pair
of Blue Eyes," maugre its innocently Della Cruscan
title,—it sounds like a typical effort of " The
Duchess,"—has the tragic end which light-minded
readers have come to dread in this author. He
showed his hand thus comparatively early and hence-
forth was to have the courage of his convictions in
depicting human fate as he saw it—not as the reader
wished it.

In considering the books that subsequently appeared, to strengthen Hardy's place with those who
know fine fiction, they are seen to have his genuine
hall-mark, just in proportion as they are Wessex
through and through: in the interplay of character

and environment there, we get his deepest expression as artist and interpreter. The really great novels are " Far From the Madding Crowd," " The Return of the Native," " The Mayor of Casterbridge " and " Tess of the D'Urbervilles ": when he shifts the scene to London, as in " The Hand of Ethelberta " or introduces sophisticated types as in the dull " Laodicean," it means comparative failure. Mother soil (he is by birth a Dorchester man and lives there still) gives him idiosyncrasy, flavor, strength. That the best, most representative work of Hardy is to be seen in two novels of his middle career, " Far From the Madding Crowd " and " The Return of the Native " rather than in the later stories, " Tess " and " Jude," can be established, I think, purely on the ground of art, without dragging cheap charges of immorality into the discussion. In the last analysis, questions of art always become a question of ethics: the separation is arbitrary and unnatural. That " Tess " is the book into which the author has most intensely put his mature belief, may be true: it is quiveringly alive, vital as only that is which comes from the deeps of a man's being. But Hardy is so much a special pleader for Tess, that the argument suffers and a grave fault is apparent when the story's climax is studied. There is an intrusion of what seems like factitious melodrama instead of that tissue of events which one expects from a stern necessitarian. Tess *need* not be a mur-

272 MASTERS OF THE ENGLISH NOVEL

deress; therefore, the work should not so conclude, for this is an author whose merit is that his effects of character are causal. He is fatalistic, yes; but in general he royally disdains the cheap tricks of plot whereby excitment is furnished at the expense of credulity and verisimilitude. In Tess's end, there is a suspicion of sensation for its own sake—a suggestion of savage joy in shocking sensibilities. Of course, the result is most powerful; but the superior power of the novel is not here so much as in its splendid sympathy and truth. He has made this woman's life-history deeply affecting and is right in claiming that she is a pure soul, judged by intention. The heart feels that she is sinned against rather than sinning and in the spectacle of her fall finds food for thought "too deep for tears." At the same time, it should not be forgotten that Tess's piteous plight,—the fact that fate has proved too strong for a soul so high in its capacity for unselfish and noble love,—is based upon Hardy's assumption that she could not help it. Here, as elsewhere in his philosophy, you must accept his premise, or call Tess (whom you may still love) morally weak. It is this reservation which will lead many to place the book, as a work of art, and notwithstanding its noble proportions and compelling power, below such a masterpiece as "The Return of the Native." That it is on the whole a sane and wholesome work, however, may be affirmed by one who finds Hardy's last novel "Jude

the Obscure " neither.   For there is a profound difference between two such creations.   In the former,
there is a piquant sense of the pathos and the awe-
someness of life, but not of its unrelieved ugliness
and disgust; an impression which is received from
the latter.   Not only is " Jude " " a tragedy of un-
fulfilled aim " as the author calls it; so is " Tess ";
but it fills the reader with a kind of sullen rage
to be an eye-witness of the foul and brutal: he is
asked to see a drama develop beside a pig-sty.   It is
therefore, intensely unesthetic which, if true, is a
word of condemnation for any work of art.   It is
deficient in poetry, in the broad sense; that, rather
than frankness of treatment, is the trouble with it.

And intellectually, it would seem to be the result
of a bad quarter of an hour of the author: a megrim
of the soul.   Elements of greatness it has; a fine
motive, too; to display the impossibilities for evolution on the part of an aspiring soul hampered by
circumstances and weak where most humanity is
weak, in the exercise of sex-passion.   A not dissimilar
theme as it is worked out by Daudet in " Le Petite
Chose " is beautiful in its pathos; in " Jude " there
is something shuddering about the arbitrary piling-up
of horror; the modesty of nature is overstept; it
is not a truly proportioned view of life, one feels;
if life were really so bad as that, no one would be
willing to live it, much less exhibit the cheerfulness
which is characteristic of the majority of human

beings. It is a fair guess that in the end it will be called the artistic mistake of a novelist of genius. Its harsh reception by critics in England and America was referred to by the author privately as an example of the " crass Philistinism " of criticism in those lands: Mr. Hardy felt that on the continent alone was the book understood, appreciated. I imagine, however, that whatever the limitations of the Anglo-Saxon view, it comes close to the ultimate decision to be passed upon this work.

One of the striking things about these Novels is the sense that they convey of the largeness of life. The action moves on a narrow stage set with the austere simplicity of the Elizabethans; the personages are extremely commonplace, the incidents in the main small and unexciting. Yet the tremendousness of human fate is constantly implied and brought home in the most impressive way. This is because all have spiritual value; if the survey be not wide, it sinks deep to the psychic center; and what matters vision that circles the globe, if it lacks grasp, penetration, uplift? These, Hardy has. When one calls his peasants Shaksperian, one is trying to express the strength and savor, the rich earthy quality like fresh loam that pertains to these quaint figures, so evidently observed on the ground, and lovingly lifted over into literature. Their speech bewrays them and is an index of their slow, shrewd minds.

Nor is his serious characterization less fine and

representative than his humorous; especially his
women. It is puzzling to say whether Hardy's comic
men, or his subtly drawn, sympathetically visualized
women are to be named first in his praise: for power
in both, and for the handling of nature, he will be
long remembered. Bathsheba, Eustacia, Tess and
the rest, they take hold on the very heart-strings and
are known as we know our very own. It is not that
they are good or bad,—generally they are both; it
is that they are beautifully, terribly human. They
mostly lack the pettiness that so often fatally limits
their sex and quite as much, they lack the veneer
that obscures the broad lines of character. And it
is natural to add, while thinking of Hardy's women,
that, unlike almost all the Victorian novelists, he has
insisted frankly, but in the main without offense,
on woman's involvement with sex-passion; he finds
that love, in a Wessex setting, has wider range than
has been awarded it in previous study of sex relations. And he has not hesitated to depict its rootage
in the flesh; not overlooking its rise in the spirit to
noblest heights. And it is this un-Anglo-Saxon-like
comprehension of feminine humanity that makes him
so fair to the sinning woman who trusts to her ruin
or proves what is called weak because of the generous
movement of her blood. No one can despise faithful-
hearted Fannie Robin, dragging herself to the poor-
house along Casterbridge highway; that scene, which
bites itself upon the memory, is fairly bathed in an

immense, understanding pity. Although Hardy has
thus used the freedom of France in treatment, he has,
unlike so much of the Gallic realism, remained an
idealist in never denying the soul of love while speaking more truthfully concerning its body than the
fiction-makers before him. There is no finer handling
of sex-love with due regard to its dual nature,—love
that grows in earth yet flowers until it looks into
heaven—than Marty's oft-quoted beautiful speech
at her lover's grave; and Hardy's belief rings again
in the defense of that good fellowship—that camera-
derie—which can grow into " the only love which is
as strong as death—beside which the passion usually
so-called by the name is evanescent as steam." A
glimpse like that of Hardy's mind separates him at
once from Maupassant's view of the world. The
traditions of English fiction, which he has insisted
on disturbing, have, after all, been strong to direct
his work, as they have that of all the writers born
into the speech and nourished on its racial ideals.

Another reason for giving the stories of the middle
period, such as " The Return of the Native," preference over those that are later, lies in the fact that
the former have no definite, aggressive theme; whereas
" Tess " announces an intention on the title page,
" Jude," in a foreword. Whatever view of life may
be expressed in " The Mayor of Casterbridge," for
example, is imbedded, as it should be, in the course
of the story. This tendency towards didacticism

is a common thing in the cases of modern writers
of fiction; it spoiled a great novelist in the case of
Tolstoy, with compensatory gains in another direction; of those of English stock, one thinks of Eliot,
Howells, Mrs. Ward and many another.   But however natural this may be in an age like ours, the art
of the literary product is, as a rule, injured by the
habit of using fiction as a jumping-board for theory.
In some instances, dullness has resulted.   Eliot has
not escaped scot-free.   With Hardy, he is, to my
taste, never dull.   Repellent as " Jude " may be, it
is never that.   But a hardness of manner and an
unpleasant bias are more than likely to follow this
aim, to the fiction's detriment.

It is a great temptation to deflect from the purpose of this work in order to discuss Hardy's short
stories, for a master in this kind he is.   A sketch like
" The Three Strangers " is as truly a masterpiece as
Stevenson's " A Lodging for The Night."   It must
suffice to say of his work in the tale that it enables
the author to give further assurance of his power of
atmospheric handling, his stippling in of a character
by a few strokes, his skill in dramatic scene, his
knowledge of Wessex types, and especially, his subdued but permeating pessimism.   There is nothing
in his writings more quietly, deeply hopeless than
most of the tales in the collection " Life's Little
Ironies."   One shrinks away from the truth and
terror of them while lured by their charm.   The short

stories increase one's admiration for the artist, but the full, more virile message comes from the Novels. It is matter for regret that "Jude the Obscure," unless the signs fail, is to be his last testament in fiction. For such a man to cease from fiction at scarce sixty can but be deplored. The remark takes on added pertinency because the novelist has essayed in lieu of fiction the poetic drama, a form in which he has less ease and authority.

Coming when he did and feeling in its full measure the tidal wave from France, Hardy was compelled both by inward and outward pressure to see life unromantically, so far as the human fate is concerned: but always a poet at heart (he began with verse), he found a vent for that side of his being in Nature, in great cosmic realities, in the stormy, passionate heart of humanity, so infinite in its aspirations, so doughty in its heroisms, so pathetic in its doom. There is something noble always in the tragic largeness of Hardy's best fiction. His grim determinism is softened by lyric airs; and even when man is most lonesome, he is consoled by contact with " the pure, eternal course of things "; whose august flow comforts Arnold. Because of his art, the representative character of his thought, reflecting in prose, as does Matthew Arnold in verse, the deeper thought-currents of the time; and because too of the personal quality which for lack of a better word one still must call genius, Thomas Hardy is sure to hold his place in

the English fiction of the closing years of the nineteenth century and is to-day the most distinguished
living novelist using that speech and one of the few
to be recognized and honored abroad. No writer of
fiction between 1875 and 1900 has more definitely
had a strong influence upon the English Novel as to
content, scope and choice of subject. If his convictions have led him to excess, they will be forgiven and
forgotten in the light of the serene mastery shed by
the half dozen great works he has contributed to
English literature.

II

Once in a while—a century or so, maybe,—comes
an artist who refuses to be classified. Rules fail to
explain him: he makes new rules in the end. He
seems too big for any formula. He impresses by
the might of his personality, teaching the world what
it should have known before, that the personal is the
life-blood of all and any art. Some such effect is
made upon the critic by George Meredith, who so
recently has closed his eyes to the shows of earth.
One can find in him almost all the tendencies of English fiction. He is realist and romanticist, frank
lover of the flesh, lofty idealist, impressionist and
judge, philosopher, dramatist, essayist, master of the
comic and above all, Poet. Eloquence, finesse,
strength and sweetness, the limpid and the cryptic,
are his in turn: he puts on when he will, like a defen-

sive armor, a style to frighten all but the elect. And they who persist and discover the secret, swear that it is more than worth the pains. Perhaps the lesson of it all is that a first-class writer, creative and distinctive, is a phenomenon transcending school, movement or period. George Meredith is not, if we weigh words, the greatest English novelist to-day—for both Hardy and Stevenson are his superiors as artists: but he is the greatest man who has written fiction.

Although he was alive but yesterday, the novel frequently awarded first position among his works, "The Ordeal of Richard Feverel," was published a good half century ago. Go back to it, get its meaning, then read the latest fiction he wrote—(he ceased to produce fiction more than a decade before his death) and you appear to be in contact with the same personality in the substantials of story-making and of life-view. The only notable change is to be found in the final group of three stories, "One of Our Conquerors," "Lord Ormont and His Aminta" and "The Amazing Marriage." The note of social protest is louder here, the revolt against conventions more pronounced. Otherwise, the author of "Feverel" is the author of "The Amazing Marriage." Much has occurred in the Novel during the forty years between the two works: realism has traveled to an extreme, neo-idealism come by way of reaction, romanticism bloomed again, the Novel of ingenious construction, the Novel of humanitarian meaning, the Novel of thesis and problem and the Novel that foretells the future like an astrologer, all these types and yet others have been practised; but Meredith has kept tranquilly on the tenor of his large way, uninfluenced, except as he has expressed all these complexities in his own work. He is in literary evolution, a sport. Critics who have tried to show how his predecessors and contemporaries have influenced him, have come out lamely from the attempt. He has been sensitive not to individual writers, but to that imponderable yet potent thing, the time-tendency in literature. He throws back to much in the past, while in the van of modern thought. What, to illustrate, could be more of the present intellectually than his remarkable sonnet-sequence, "Modern Love"? And are not his women, as a type, the noblest example of the New Woman of our day— socially, economically, intellectually emancipated, without losing their distinctive feminine quality? And yet, in "The Shaving of Shagpat," an early work, we go back to the Arabian Nights for a model. The satiric romance, "Harry Richmond," often reminds of the leisured episode method of the eighteenth century; and while reading the unique "Evan Harrington" we think at times of Aristophanes.

Nor is much light thrown on Meredith's path in turning to his personal history. Little is known of this author's ancestry and education; his environment has been so simple, his life in its exteriors so uneventful, that we return to the work itself with the feeling that the key to the secret room must be here if anywhere. It is known that he was educated in youth in Germany, which is interesting in reference to the problem of his style. And there is more to be said concerning his parentage than the smug propriety of print has revealed while he lived. We know, too, that his marriage with the daughter of Thomas Love Peacock proved unhappy, and that for many years he has resided, almost a recluse, with his daughter, in the idyllic retirement of Surrey. The privacy of Boxhill has been respected; next to never has Meredith spoken in any public way and seldom visited London. When he was, at Tennyson's death, made the President of the British Society of Authors, the honor sought the man. The rest is silence; what has appeared since his death has been of too conflicting a nature for credence. We await a trustworthy biography.

The appeal then must be to the books themselves. Exclusive of short story, sketch and tale, they include a dozen novels of generous girth—for Meredith is old-fashioned in his demand for elbow-room. They are preëminently novels of character and more than any novelist of the day the view of the world embodied in them is that of the intellect. This does not mean that they are wanting in emotional force or interest: merely, that in George Meredith's fiction

men and women live the life of thought as it is acted
upon by practical issues.   Character seen in action is
always his prepossesrion; plot is naught save as it
exhibits this.   The souls of men and women are his
quarry, and the test of a civilization the degree in
which it has developed the mind for an enlightened
control over the emotions and the bodily appetites.

Neither does this mean, as with Henry James, the
disappearance of plot: a healthy objectivity of narrative framework is preserved; if anything the earlier
books—" Feverel," " Evan Harrington," " Rhoda
Fleming " and the duo " Sandra Belloni " and " Vittoria "—have more of story interest than the later
novels.   Meredith has never feared the use of the
episode, in this suggesting the older methods of
Fielding and Smollett.   Yet the episodic in his hands
has ever its use for psychologic envisagement.
Love, too, plays a large rôle in his fiction; indeed,
in the wider platonic sense, it is constantly present,
although he is the last man to be called a writer of
love-stories.   And no man has permitted himself
greater freedom in stepping outside the story in
order to explain his meaning, comment upon character and scene, rhapsodize upon Life, or directly
harangue the reader.   And this broad marginal
reservation of space, however much it is deplored in
viewing his work as novel-making, adds a peculiar
tonic and is a characteristic we could ill spare.   It
brings us back to the feeling that he is a great man

using the fiction form for purposes broader than that of telling a story.

Because of this ample personal testimony in his books it should be easy to state his *Lebensanschauung,* unless the opacity of his manner blocks the way or he indulges in self-contradiction in the manner of a Nietzsche. Such is not the case. What is the philosophy unfolded in his representative books?

It will be convenient to choose a few of those typical for illustration. The essence of Meredith is to be discovered in such works as " The Ordeal of Richard Feverel," " Evan Harrington," " Harry Richmond," " The Egoist," " Diana of the Crossways." If you know these, you understand him. " Lord Ormont and his Aminta " might well be added because of its teaching; but the others will serve, with the understanding that so many-sided a writer has in other works given further noble proof of his powers. If I allowed personal preference to be my sole guide, " Rhoda Fleming " would be prominent in the list; and many place " Beauchamp's Career " high, if not first among his works;—a novel teeming with his views, particularly valuable for its treatment of English politics and certainly containing some of his most striking characterization, in particular, one of his noblest women. Still, those named will fairly reflect the novelist and speak for all.

" Richard Feverel," which had been preceded by a book of poems, the fantasia " The Shaving of Shag-

pat " and an historical novelette " Farina," was the
first book that announced the arrival of a great novelist.   It is at once a romance of the modern type,
a love-story and a problem book; the tri-statement
makes it Meredithian.   It deals with the tragic union
of Richard and Lucy, in a setting that shifts from
sheer idyllic, through worldly and realistic to a
culmination of dramatic grief.   It contains, in
measure heaped up and running over, the poetry, the
comedy and the philosophy, the sense of Life's riddle,
for which the author is renowned.   But its intellectual appeal of theme—aside from the incidental wisdom that stars its pages—is found in the study of
the problem of education.   Richard's father would
shape his career according to a preconceived idea
based on parental love and guided by an anxious,
fussy consulting of the oracles.   The attempt to
stretch the son upon a pedagogic procustean bed
fails disastrously, wrecking his own happiness and
that of his sweet girl-wife.   Love is stronger than
aught else and we are offered the spectacle of ruined
lives hovered over by the best intentions.   The novel
is an illustration of the author's general teaching that
a human being must have reasonable liberty of action
for self-development.   The heart must be allowed
fair-play, though its guidance by the intellect is desirable.

It has been objected that this moving romance
ends in unnecessary tragedy; that the catastrophe

is not inevitable. But it may be doubted if the mistake of Sir Austin Feverel could be so clearly indicated had not the chance bullet of the duel killed the young wife when reconciliation with her husband appeared probable. But a book so vital in spirit, with such lyric interludes, lofty heights of wisdom, homeric humor, dramatic moments and profound emotions, can well afford lapses from perfect form, awkwardnesses of art. There are places where philosophy checks movement or manner obscures thought; but one overlooks all such, remembering Richard and Lucy meeting by the river; Richard's lonesome night walk when he learns he is a father; the marvelous parting from Bella Mount; father and son confronted with Richard's separation from the girl-wife; the final piteous passing of Lucy. These are among the great moments of English fiction.

One gets a sense of Meredith's resources of breadth and variety next in taking up " Evan Harrington." Here is a satiric character sketch where before was romance; for broad comedy in the older and larger sense it has no peer among modern novels. The purpose is plain: to show the evolution of a young middle-class Englishman, a tailor's son, through worldly experience with polite society into true democracy. After the disillusionment of " high life," after much yeasty juvenile foolishness and false ideals, Evan comes back to his father's shop with his lesson learned: it is possible (in modern England) to be both tailor and gentleman.

In placing this picture before the spectator, an incomparable view of genteel society with contrasted touches of low life is offered. For pure comedy that is of the midriff as well as of the brain, the inn scene with the astonishing Raikes as central figure is unsurpassed in all Meredith, and only Dickens has done the like. And to correspond in the fashionable world, there is Harrington's sister, the Countess de Saldar, who is only second to Becky Sharp for saliency and delight. Some find these comic figures overdrawn, even impossible; but they stand the test applied to Dickens: they abide in affectionate memory, vivid evocations made for our lasting joy. As with "Feverel," the book is a piece of life first, a lesson second; but the underlying thesis is present, not to the injury of one who reads for story's sake.

An extraordinary further example of resourcefulness, with a complete change of key, is " The Adventures of Harry Richmond." The ostensible business of the book is to depict the growth from boyhood to manhood and through sundry experiences of love, with the resulting effect upon his character, of the young man whose name gives it title. It may be noted that a favorite task with Meredith is this, to trace the development of a personality from immaturity to a maturity gained by the hard knocks of the master-educator, Love. But the figure really dominant is not Harry nor any one of his sweethearts, but that of his father, Roy Richmond. I must believe that English fiction offers nothing more original than he. He is an indescribable compound of brilliant swashbuckler, splendid gentleman and winning Goodheart. Barry Lyndon, Tarascon, Don Quixote and Septimus go into his making—and yet he is not explained;—an absolute original. The scene where, in a German park on an occasion of great pomp, he impersonates the statue of a Prince, is one of the author's triumphs—never less delightful at a re-reading.

But has this amazing creation a meaning, or is Roy merely one of the results of the sportive play of a man of genius? He is something more, we feel, when, at the end of the romance, he gives his life for the woman who has so faithfully loved him and believed in his royal pretensions. He perishes in a fire, because in saving her he would not save himself. It is as if the author said: " Behold, a man by nature histrionic and Bohemian, and do not make the mistake to think him incapable of nobility. Romantic in his faults, so too he is romantic in his virtues." And back of this kindly treatment of the lovable rascal (who was so ideal a father to the little Richmond!) does there not lurk the thought that the pseudo-romantic attitude toward Life is full of danger—in truth, out of the question in modern society?

" The Egoist " has long been a test volume with

Meredithians. If you like it you are of the cult; if
not, merely an amateur. It is inevitable to quote
Stevenson who, when he had read it several times,
declared that at the sixth reading he would begin to
realize its greatness. Stevenson was a doughty
admirer of Meredith, finding the elder " the only
man of genius of my acquaintance," and regarding
" Rhoda Fleming " as a book to send one back to
Shakspere.

That " The Egoist " is typical—in a sense, most
typical of the fictions,—is very true. That, on the
other hand, it is Meredith's best novel may be boldly
denied, since it is hardly a novel at all. It is a wonderful analytic study of the core of self that is in humanity. Willoughby, incarnation of a self-centeredness
glossed over to others and to himself by fine gentleman manners and instincts, is revealed stroke after
stroke until, in the supreme test of his alliance with
Clara Middleton, he is flayed alive for the reader's
benefit. In this power of exposure, by the subtlest,
most unrelenting analysis, of the very penetralia
of the human soul it has no counterpart; beside it,
most of the psychology of fiction seems child's play.
And the truth of it is overwhelming. No wonder
Stevenson speaks of its " serviceable exposure of
myself." Every honest man who reads it, winces
at its infallible touching of a moral sore-spot. The
inescapable ego in us all was never before portrayed
by such a master.

But because it is a study that lacks the breadth, variety, movement and objectivity of the Novel proper, " The Egoist " is for the confirmed Meredith lover, not for the beginner: to take it first is perchance to go no further. Readers have been lost to him by this course. The immense gain in depth and delicacy acquired by English fiction since Richardson is well illustrated by a comparison of the latter's " Sir Charles Grandison " with Meredith's " The Egoist." One is a portrait for the time, the other for all time. Both, superficially viewed, are the same type: a male paragon before whom a bevy of women burn incense. But O the difference! Grandison is serious to his author, while Meredith, in skinning Willoughby alive like another Marsyas, is once and for all making the worship of the ego hateful.

It is interesting that " Diana of the Crossways " was the book first to attract American readers. It has some of the author's eccentricities at their worst. But it was in one respect an excellent choice: the heroine is thoroughly representative of the author and of the age; possibly this country is sympathetic to her for the reason that she seems indigenous. Diana furnishes a text for a dissertation on Meredith's limning of the sex, and of his conception of the mental relation of the sexes. She is a modern woman, not so much that she is superior in goodness to the ideal of woman established in the mid-Victorian period by Thackeray and Dickens, as that

she is bigger and broader. She is the result of the
process of social readjustment. Her story is that
of a woman soul experiencing a succession of unions
and through them learning the higher love. First,
the *mariage de convenance* of an unawakened girl;
then, a marriage wherein admiration, ambition and
flattered pride play their parts; finally, the marriage
with Redbourne, a union based on tried friendship,
comradeship, respect, warming into passion that, like
the sudden up-leap of flame on the altar, lifts the
spirit onto ideal heights. Diana is an imperfect,
sinning, aspiring, splendid creature. And in the
narrative that surrounds her, we get Meredith's
theory of the place of intellect in woman, and in the
development of society. He has an intense conviction that the human mind should be so trained that
woman can never fall back upon so-called instinct; he
ruthlessly attacks her " intuition," so often lauded
and made to cover a multitude of sins. When he
remarks that she will be the last thing to be civilized
by man, the satire is directed against man rather
than against woman herself, since it is man who
desires to keep her a creature of the so-called intuitions. A mighty champion of the sex, he never tires
telling it that intellectual training is the sure way to
all the equalities. This conviction makes him a stalwart enemy of sentimentalism, which is so fiercely
satirized in " Sandra Belloni " in the persons of the
Pole family. His works abound in passages in which

this view is displayed, flashed before the reader in diamond-like epigram and aphorism. Not that he despises the emotions: those who know him thoroughly will recognize the absurdity of such a charge. Only he insists that they be regulated and used aright by the master, brain. The mishaps of his women come usually from the haphazard abeyance of feeling or from an unthinking bowing down to the arbitrary dictations of society. This insistence upon the application of reason (the reasoning process dictated by an age of science) to social situations, has led this writer to advise the setting aside of the marriage bond in certain circumstances. In both " Lord Ormont and his Aminta " and " One of our Conquerors " he advocates a greater freedom in this relation, to anticipate what time may bring to pass. It is enough here to say that this extreme view does not represent Meredith's best fiction nor his most fruitful period of production.

Perhaps the most original thing about Meredith as a novelist is the daring way in which he has made an alliance between romance and the intellect which was supposed, in an older conception, to be its archenemy. He gives to Romance, that creature of the emotions, the corrective and tonic of the intellect. " To preserve Romance," he declares, " we must be inside the heads of our people as well as the hearts . . . in days of a growing activity of the head."

Let us say once again that Romance means a cer-

tain use of material as the result of an attitude
toward Life; this attitude may be temporary, a
mood; or steady, a conviction.   It is the latter with
George Meredith; and be it understood, his material
is always realistic, it is his interpretation that is
superbly idealistic.   The occasional crabbedness of
his manner and his fiery admiration for Italy are
not the only points in which he reminds one of Browning.   He is one with him in his belief in soul, his
conception of life is an arena for its trying-out;
one with him also in the robust acceptance of earth
and earth's worth, evil and all, for enjoyment and as
salutary experience.   This is no fanciful parallel
between Meredith and a man who has been called
(with their peculiarities of style in mind) the Meredith of Poetry, as Meredith has been called the
Browning of Prose.

Thus, back of whatever may be the external story
—the Italian struggle for unity in " Vittoria," English radicalism in " Beauchamp's Career," a seduction
melodrama in " Rhoda Fleming "—there is always
with Meredith a steady interpretation of life, a principle of belief.   It is his crowning distinction that he
can make an intellectual appeal quite aside from the
particular story he is telling;—and it is also apparent that this is his most vulnerable point as novelist.
We get more from him just because he shoots beyond
the fiction target.   He is that rare thing in English
novel-making, a notable thinker.   Of all nineteenth

century novelists he leads for intellectual stimula-
tion. With fifty faults of manner and matter, irri-
tating, even outrageous in his eccentricities, he can
at his best startle with a brilliance that is alone of
its kind. It is because we hail him as philosopher,
wit and poet that he fails comparatively as artist.
He shows throughout his work a sublime carelessness
of workmanship on the structural side of his craft;
but in those essentials, dialogue, character and scene,
he rises to the peaks of his profession.

Probably more readers are offended by his mannerisms of style than by any other defect; and they
are undeniable. The opening chapter of " Diana "
is a hard thing to get by; the same may be said of
the similar chapter in " Beauchamp's Career." In
" One of our Conquerors," early and late, the manner
is such as to lose for him even tried adherents. Is
the trouble one of thought or expression? And is it
honest or an affectation? Meredith in some books—
and in all books more or less—adopts a strangely indirect, over-elaborated, far-fetched and fantastic style,
which those who love him are fain to deplore. The
author's learning gets in his way and leads him into
recondite allusions; besides this, he has that quality
of mind which is stimulated into finding analogies
on every side, so that image is piled on image and
side-paths of thought open up in the heat of this
mental activity. Part of the difficulty arises from
surplusage of imagination. Sometimes it is used

in the service of comment (often satirical) ; again in
a kind of Greek chorus to the drama, greatly to its
injury ; or in pure description, where it is hardly less
offensive.   Thus in " The Egoist " we read : " Willoughby shadowed a deep droop on the bend of his
neck before Clara," and reflection shows that all this
absurdly acrobatic phrase means is that the hero
bowed to the lady.   An utterly simple occurrence
and thus described !   It is all the more strange and
aggravating in that it comes from a man who on
hundreds of occasions writes English as pungent,
sonorous and sweet as any writer in the history of
the native literature.   This is true both of dialogue
and narrative.   He is the most quotable of authors ;
his Pilgrim's Scrip is stuffed full of precious sayings,
expressing many moods of emotion and interpreting
the world under its varied aspects of romance, beauty,
wit and drama.   " Strength is the brute form of
t uth."   There is a French conciseness in such a
sentence and immense mental suggestiveness.   Both
his scenic and character phrasing are memorable, as
where the dyspeptic philosopher in " Feverel " is described after dinner as " languidly twinkling sto-
machic contentment."   And what a scene is that where
Master Gammon replies to Mrs. Sumfit's anxious
query concerning his lingering at table with appetite
apparently unappeasable :

" ' When *do* you think you will have done, Master
Gammon ? '

" ' When I feels my buttons, Ma'am.' "

Or hear John Thrasher in " Harry Richmond "
dilate on Language:

" ' There's cockney, and there's country, and
there's school.   Mix the three, strain and throw away
the sediment.   Now yon's my view.' "

Has any philologist said all that could be said,
so succinctly?   His lyric outbursts in the face of
Nature or better yet, where as in the moonlight
meeting of the lovers at Wilming Weir in " Sandra
Belloni," nature is interspersed with human passion
in a glorious union of music, picture and impassioned
sentiment,—these await the pleasure of the enthralled
seeker in every book.   To encounter such passages
(perhaps in a mood of protest over some almost
insufferable defect) is to find the reward rich indeed.

Let the cause of obscurity be what it may, we need
not doubt that with Meredith style is the man, a
perfectly honest way of expressing his personality.
It is not impossible that his unconventional education
and the early influence of German upon him, may
come into the consideration.   But in the main his
peculiarity is congenital.

Meredith lacked self-criticism as a writer.   But
it is quite inaccurate to speak of obscure thought:
it is language, the medium, which makes the trouble
when there is any.   His thought, allowing for the
fantasticality of his humor in certain moods, is never
muddled or unorganized: it is sane, consistent and

worthy of attention. To say this, is still to regret the stylistic vagaries.

One other defect must be mentioned: the characters talk like Meredith, instead of in their own persons. This is not true uniformly, of course, but it does mar the truth of his presentation. Young girls show wit and wisdom quite out of keeping; those in humble life —a bargeman, perhaps, or a prize-fighter—speak as they would not in reality. Illusion is by so much disturbed. It would appear in such cases that the thinker temporarily dominated the creative artist.

When all is said, pro and con, there remains a towering personality; a writer of unique quality; a man so stimulating and surprising as he is, that we almost prefer him to the perfect artist he never could be. No English maker of novels can give us a fuller sense of life, a keener realization of the dignity of man. It is natural to wish for more than we have— to desire that Meredith had possessed the power of complete control of his material and himself, had revised his work to better advantage. But perhaps it is more commonsensible to be thankful for him as he is.

As to influence, it would seem modest to assert that Meredith is as bracingly wholesome morally as he is intellectually stimulating. In a private letter to a friend who was praising his finest book, he whimsically mourns the fact that he must write for a living and hence feel like disowning so many of his

children when in cold blood he scrutinizes his off-
spring. The letter in its entirety (it is unpublished)
is proof, were any needed, that he had a high artistic
ideal which kept him nobly dissatisfied with his endeavor. There is in him neither pose nor complacent self-satisfaction. To an American, whom
he was bidding good-by at his own gate, he said:
"If I had my books to do over again, I should try
harder to make sure their influence was good." His
aims, ethical and artistic, throughout his work, can
be relied upon as high and noble. His faults are as
honest as he himself, the inherent defects of his genius.
No writer of our day stands more sturdily for the
idea that, whereas art is precious, personality is more
precious still; without which art is a tinkling cymbal
and with which even a defective art can conquer
Time, like a garment not all-seemly, that yet cannot
hide an heroic figure.

CHAPTER XIII

STEVENSON

IT is too early yet to be sure that Robert Louis Stevenson will make a more cogent appeal for a place in English letters as a writer of fiction than as an essayist. But had he never written essays likely to rank him with the few masters of that delightful fireside form, he would still have an indisputable claim as novelist. The claim in fact is a double one; it is founded, first, on his art and power as a maker of romance, but also upon his historical service to English fiction, as the man most instrumental in purifying the muddy current of realism in the late nineteenth century by a wholesome infusion,—the romantic view of life. It is already easier to estimate his importance and get the significance of his work than it was when he died in 1894—stricken down on the piazza of his house at Vailima, a Scotchman doomed to fall in a far-away, alien place.

We are better able now to separate that personal charm felt from direct contact with the man, which almost hypnotized those who knew him, from the more abiding charm which is in his writings: the

299

revelation of a character the most attractive of his generation. Rarely, if ever before, have the qualities of artistry and fraternal fellowship been united in a man of letters to such a degree; most often they are found apart, the gods choosing to award their favors less lavishly.

Because of this union of art and life, Stevenson's romances killed two birds with one stone; boys loved his adventuresomeness, the wholesome sensationalism of his stories with something doing on every page, while amateurs of art responded to his felicity of phrase, his finished technique, the exhibition of craftsmanship conquering difficulty and danger. Artist, lover of life, insistent truth-teller, Calvinist, Bohemian, believer in joy, all these cohabit in his books. In early masterpieces like " Treasure Island " and " The Wrecker " it is the lover of life who conducts us, telling the story for story's sake:

> " My mistress still the open road
> And the bright eyes of danger."

Such is the goddess that beckons on. The creed implicit in such work deems that life is stirring and worth while, and that it is a weakness to repine and waste time, to be too subjective when so much on earth is objectively alluring. This is only a part of Stevenson, of course, but it was that phase of him vastly liked of the public and doubtless doing most to give him vogue.

But in later work like " Dr. Jekyll and Mr. Hyde " we get quite another thing: the skilled story-maker is still giving us thrilling fiction, to be sure, but here it is the Scotchman of acute conscience, writing a spiritual allegory with the healthy instinct which insists that the lesson shall be dramatized. So, too, in a late fiction like " Ebb Tide," apparently as picaresque and harum-scarum as " Treasure Island," it is nevertheless the moralist who is at work beneath the brilliantly picturesque surface of the narrative, contrasting types subtly, showing the gradings in moral disintegration. In the past-mastership of the finest Scotch novels, " Kidnapped " and its sequel " David Balfour," " The Master of Ballantrae " and the beautiful torso, " Weir of Hermiston," we get the psychologic romance, which means a shift of interest;—character comes first, story is secondary to it. Here is the maturest Stevenson, the fiction most expressive of his genius, and naturally the inspiration is native, he looks back, as he so often did in his poetry, to the distant gray little island which was Motherland to him, home of his youth and of his kindred, the earth where he was fain to lie when his time came. Stevenson, to the end, could always return to sheer story, as in " St. Ives," but in doing so, is a little below his best: that kind did not call on his complete powers: in such fiction deep did not answer unto deep.

In 1883, when " Treasure Island " appeared, the

public was gasping for the oxygen that a story with
outdoor movement and action could supply: there
was enough and to spare of invertebrate subtleties,
strained metaphysics and coarse naturalistic studies.
A sublimated dime novel like " Treasure Island "
came at the psychologic moment; the year before
" The New Arabian Nights " had offered the same
sort of pabulum, but had been practically overlooked.
Readers were only too glad to turn from people *with*
a past to people *of* the past, or to people of the
present whose ways were ways of pleasantness. Stevenson substituted a lively, normal interest in life
for plotlessness and a surfeit of the flesh. The public
rose to the bait as the trout to a particularly invit-
ing fly. Once more reverting to the good old appeal
of Scott—incident, action and derring-do—he added
the attraction of his personal touch, and what was so
gallantly proferred was greedily grasped.

Although, as has been said, Stevenson passed from
the primitive romance of the Shilling Shocker to
the romance of character, his interest in character
study was keen from the first: the most plot-cunning
and external of his yarns have that illuminative exposure of human beings—in flashes at least—which
mark him off from the bluff, robust manner of a
Dumas and lend an attraction far greater than that
of mere tangle of events. This gets fullest expression in the Scotch romances.

" The Master of Ballantrae," for one illustration;

the interplay of motive and act as it affects a group
of human beings is so conducted that plot becomes
a mere framework, within which we are permitted to
see a typical tragedy of kinship.   This receives
curious corroboration in the fact that when, towards
the close of the story, the scene shifts to America
and the main motive—the unfolding of the fraternal
fortunes of the tragic brothers, is made minor to a
series of gruesome adventures (however entertaining
and well done) the reader, even if uncritical, has
an uneasy sense of disharmony: and rightly, since
the strict character romance has changed to the
romance of action.

It has been stated that the finer qualities of Stevenson are called out by the psychological romance
on native soil.   He did some brilliant and engaging
work of foreign setting and motive.   " The Island
Nights' Entertainments " is as good in its way as
the earlier " New Arabian Nights "—far superior to
it, indeed, for finesse and the deft command of ex-
otic material.   Judged as art, " The Bottle Imp "
and " The Beach of Falesá " are among the triumphs
of ethnic interpretation, let alone their more external
charms of story.   And another masterpiece of foreign setting, " A Lodging for The Night," is further
proof of Stevenson's ability to use other than Scotch
motives for the materials of his art.   " Ebb-Tide,"
again, grim as it is, must always be singled out as
a marvel of tone and proportion, yet seems born

out of an existence utterly removed as to conditions
and incentives from the land of his birth.   But when,
in his own words:

> "The tropics vanish, and meseems that I,
> From Halkerside, from topmost Allermuir,
> Or steep Caerketton, dreaming gaze again."

then, as if vitalized by mother-earth, Stevenson shows
a breadth, a vigor, a racy idiosyncrasy, that best
justify a comparison with Scott.   It means a quality
that is easier felt than expressed; of the very warp
and woof of his work.   If the elder novelist
seems greater in scope, spontaneity and substance,
the younger surpasses him in the elegancies and
niceties of his art.   And it is only a just recognition
of the difference of Time as well as of personality
to say that the psychology of Stevenson is far
more profound and searching.   Nor may it be denied
that Sir Walter nods, that there are flat, uninteresting stretches in his heroic panorama, while of
Stevenson at the worst, we may confidently assert
that he is never tedious.   He fails in the comparison
if anywhere in largeness of personality, not in the
perfectness of the art of his fiction.   In the technical
demands of his profession he is never wanting.   He
always has a story to tell, tells it with the skill
which means constructive development and a sense
of situation; he creates characters who live, interest
and do not easily fade from memory: he has exceptional power in so filling in backgrounds as to

produce the illusion of atmosphere; and finally, he has, whether in dialogue or description, a wonderfully supple instrument of expression. If the style of his essays is at times mannered, the charge can not be made against his representative fiction: "Prince Otto" stands alone in this respect, and that captivating, comparatively early romance, confessedly written under the influence of Meredith, is a delicious literary experiment rather than a deeply-felt piece of life. Perhaps the central gift of all is that for character—is it, in truth, not the central gift for any weaver of fiction? So we thought in studying Dickens. Stevenson's creations wear the habit of life, yet with more than life's grace of carriage; they are seen picturesquely without, but also psychologically within. In a marvelous portrayal like that of John Silver in "Treasure Island" the result is a composite of what we see and what we shudderingly guess: eye and mind are satisfied alike. Even in a mere sketch, such as that of the blind beggar at the opening of the same romance, with the tap-tap of his stick to announce his coming, we get a remarkable example of effect secured by an economy of details; that tap-tapping gets on your nerves, you never forget it. It seems like the memory of a childhood terror on the novelist's part. Throughout his fiction this chemic union of fact and the higher fact that is of the imagination marks his work. The smell of the heather is in our nostrils as we watch Allan's flight, and looking on at the fight in the round-house, there is a physical impression of the stuffiness of the place; you smell as well as see it.   Or for quite another key, take the night duel in " The Master of Ballantrae."   You cannot think of it without feeling the bite of the bleak air; once more the twinkle of the candles makes the scene flicker before you ere it vanish into memory-land. Again, how you know that sea-coast site in the opening of " The Pavilion on the Links "—shiver at the " sly innuendoes of the place "!   Think how much the map in " Treasure Island " adds to the credibility of the thing.   It is the believableness of Stevenson's atmospheres that prepare the reader for any marvels enacted in them.   Gross, present-day, matter-of-fact London makes Dr. Jekyll and his worser half of flesh-and-blood credence.   Few novelists of any race have beaten this wandering Scot in the power of representing character and envisaging it: and there can hardly be successful characterization without this allied power of creating atmosphere.

Nothing is falser than to find him imitative in his representative work.   There may be a suspicion of made-to-order journalism in " The Black Arrow," and the exception of " Prince Otto," which none the less we love for its gallant spirit and smiling grace, has been noted.   But of the Scotch romances nothing farther from the truth could be said.   They stand

or fall by themselves: they have no model—save
that of sound art and a normal conception of human
life. Rarely does this man fall below his own high
level or fail to set his private remarque upon his
labor. It is in a way unfortunate that Stevenson,
early in his career, so frankly confessed to prac-
tising for his craft by the use of the best models:
it has led to the silly misinterpretation which sees
in all his literary effort nothing but the skilful echo.
Such judgments remind us that criticism, which is
intended to be a picture of another, is in reality a
picture of oneself. In his *lehrjahre* Stevenson
"slogged at his trade," beyond peradventure; but
no man came to be more individually and independ-
ently himself.

It has been spoken against him, too, that he could
not draw women: here again he is quoted in his
own despite and we see the possible disadvantage
of a great writer's correspondence being given to
the world—though not for more worlds than one
would we miss the Letters. It is quite true that he
is chary of petticoats in his earlier work: but when
he reached "David Balfour" he drew an entrancing
heroine; and the contrasted types of young girl
and middle-aged woman in "Weir of Hermiston"
offer eloquent testimonial to his increasing power in
depicting the Eternal Feminine. At the same time,
it may be acknowledged that the gallery of female
portraits is not like Scott's for number and variety,

nor like Thackeray's for distinction and charm—
thick-hung with a delightful company whose eyes
laugh level with our own, or, above us on the wall,
look down with a starry challenge to our souls. But
those whom Stevenson has hung there are not to be
coldly recalled.

Stevenson's work offers itself remarkably as a
test for the thought that all worthily modern romanticism must not lack in reality, in true observation, for success in its most daring flights. Gone
forever is that abuse of the romantic which sub-
stitutes effective lying for the vision which sees
broadly enough to find beauty. The latter-day
realist will be found in the end to have permanently
contributed this, a welcome legacy to our time,
after its excesses and absurdities are forgotten.
Realism has taught romanticism to tell the truth,
if it would succeed. Stevenson is splendidly real,
he loves to visualize fact, to be true both to the
appearances of things and the thoughts of the mind.
He is aware that life is more than food—that it
is a subjective state quite as much as an objective
reality. He refers to himself more than once, half
humorously, as a fellow whose forte lay in transcrib-
ing what was before him, to be seen and felt, tasted
and heard. This extremely modern denotement was
a marked feature of his genius, often overlooked.
He had a desire to know all manner of men; he
had the noble curiosity of Montaigne; this it was,

along with his human sympathy, that led him
to rough it in emigrant voyages and railroad trips
across the plains. It was this characteristic, unless
I err, the lack of which in " Prince Otto " gives it
a certain rococo air: he was consciously fooling
in it, and felt the need of a solidly mundane footing.
Truth to human nature in general, and that lesser
truth which means accurate photography—his books
give us both; the modern novelist, even a romancer
like Stevenson, is not permitted to slight a landscape,
an idiom nor a point of psychology: this one is never
untrue to the trust. There is in the very nature
of his language a proof of his strong hunger for
the actual, the verifiable. No man of his generation has quite such a grip on the vernacular: his
speech rejoices to disport itself in root flavors; the
only younger writer who equals him in this relish for
reality of expression is Kipling. Further back it
reminds of Defoe or Swift, at their best. Stevenson cannot abide the stock phrases with which most
of us make shift to express our thoughts instead of
using first-hand effects. There is, with all its music
and suavity, something of the masculinity of the
Old English in the following brief descriptive passage from " Ebb-Tide ":

" There was little or no morning bank. A brighten-
ing came in the East; then a wash of some ineffable,
faint, nameless hue between crimson and silver; and
then coals of fire. These glimmered awhile on the sea

line, and seemed to brighten and darken and spread out; and still the night and the stars reigned undisturbed. It was as though a spark should catch and glow and creep along the foot of some heavy and almost incombustible wall-hanging, and the room itself be scarce menaced. Yet a little after, and the whole East glowed with gold and scarlet, and the hollow of heaven was filled with the daylight. The isle—the undiscovered, the scarce believed in—now lay before them and close aboard; and Herrick thought that never in his dreams had he beheld anything more strange and delicate."

Stevenson's similes, instead of illustrating concrete things by others less concrete, often reverse the process, as in the following: "The isle at this hour, with its smooth floor of sand, the pillared roof overhead and the pendant illumination of the lamps, wore an air of unreality, like a deserted theater or a public garden at midnight." Every image gets its foothold in some tap-root of reality.

The place of Robert Louis Stevenson is not explained by emphasizing the perfection of his technique. Artist he is, but more: a vigorous modern mind with a definite and enheartening view of things, a philosophy at once broad and convincing. He is a psychologist intensely interested in the great questions—which, of course, means the moral questions. Read the quaint Fable in which two of the characters in " Treasure Island " hold converse upon themselves, the story in which they participate and the author who made them.   It is as if Stevenson stood aside a moment from the proper objectivity of the fictionist, to tell us in his own person that all his story-making was but an allegory of life, its joy, its mystery, its duty, its triumph and its doom. Although he is too much the artist to intrude philosophic comments upon human fate into his fiction, after the fashion of Thackeray or Meredith, the comment is there, implicit in his fiction, even as it is explicit in his essays, which are for this reason a sort of complement of his fiction: a sort of philosophical marginal note upon the stories.   Stevenson was that type of modern mind which, no longer finding it possible to hold fast by the older, complacent cock-sureness with regard to the theologian's heaven, is still unshaken in its conviction that life is beneficent, the obligation of duty imperative, the meaning of existence spiritual.   Puzzlingly protean in his expressional moods (his conversations in especial), he was constant in this intellectual, or temperamental, attitude: " Though He slay me, yet will I trust Him," represents his feeling, and the strongest poem he ever wrote, " If This Were Faith," voices his deepest conviction.   Meanwhile, the superficies of life offered a hundred consolations, a hundred pleasures, and Stevenson would have his fellowmen enjoy them in innocence, in kindness and good cheer. In fine, as a thinker he was a modernized Calvinist;

as an artist he saw life in terms of action and
pleasure, and by perfecting himself in the art of
communicating his view of life, he was able, in a
term of years all too short, to leave a series of
books which, as we settle down to them in the twentieth century, and try to judge them as literature,
have all the semblance of fine art.   In any case,
they will have been influential in the shaping of
English fiction and will be referred to with respect
by future historians of literature.   It is hard to
believe that the desiccation of Time will so dry them
that they will not always exhale a rich fragrance
of personality, and tremble with a convincing movement of life.

CHAPTER XIV

THE AMERICAN CONTRIBUTION

I

To exclude the living, as we must, in an estimate of the American contribution to the development we have been tracing, is especially unjust. Yet the principle must be applied. The injustice lies in the fact that an important part of the contribution falls on the hither side of 1870 and has to do with authors still active. The modern realistic movement in English fiction has been affected to some degree by the work, has responded to the influence of the two Americans, Howells and James. What has been accomplished during the last forty years has been largely under their leadership. Mr. Howells, true to his own definition, has practised the more truthful handling of material in depicting chosen aspects of the native life. Mr. James, becoming more interested in British types, has, after a great deal of analysis of his own countrymen, passed by the bridge of the international Novel to a complete absorption in transatlantic studies, making his peculiar application of the realistic formula

313

to the inner life of the spirit: a curious compound, a cosmopolitan Puritan, an urbane student of souls. His share in the British product is perhaps appreciable; but from the native point of view, at least, it would seem as if his earlier work were, and would remain, most representative both because of its motives and methods.   Early or late, he has beyond question pointed out the way to many followers in the psychologic path: his influence, perhaps less obvious than Howells', is none the less undisputable. The development in the hands of writers younger than these veterans has been rich, varied, often noteworthy in quality.   But of all this it is too soon to speak.

With regard to the fictional evolution on American soil, it is clear that four great writers, excluding the living, separate themselves from the crowd: Irving, Cooper, Poe and Hawthorne.   Moreover, two of these, Irving and Poe, are not novelists at all, but masters of the sketch or short story.   It will be best, however, for our purpose to give them all some attention, for whatever the form of fiction they used, they are all influential in the development of the Novel.

Other authors of single great books may occur to the student, perhaps clamoring for admission to a company so select.   Yet he is likely always to come back and draw a dividing line here.   Bret Harte, for instance, is dead, and in the short story

of western flavor he was a pioneer of mark, the
founder of a genre: probably no other writer is so
significant in his field.   But here again, although
he essayed full-length fiction, it was not his forte.
So, too, were it not that Mark Twain still cheers
the land of the living with his wise fun, there would
be for the critic the question, is he a novelist, humorist or essayist.   Is " Roughing It " more typical
of his genius than " Tom Sawyer " or " Huckleberry
Finn "?   How shall we characterize " Puddin' Head
Wilson "?   Under what category shall we place " A
Yankee at the Court of King Arthur " and " Joan
of Arc "?   The query reminds us once more that
literature means personality as well as literary forms
and that personality is more important than are
they.   And again we turn away regretfully (remembering that this is an attempt to study not fiction
in all its manifestations, but the Novel) from the
charming short stories—little classics in their kind—
bequeathed by Aldrich, and are almost sorry that
our judgment demands that we place him first as
a poet.   We think, too, of that book so unique
in influence, " Uncle Tom's Cabin," nor forget that,
besides producing it, Mrs. Stowe, in such a work as
" Old Town Folks," started the long line of studies
of New England rustic life which, not confined to
that section, have become so welcome a phase of
later American art in fiction.   Among younger
authors called untimely from their labors, it is hard

to resist the temptation to linger over such a figure
as that of Frank Norris, whose vital way of handling
realistic material with epic breath in his unfinished
trilogy, gave so great promise for his future.

It may be conceded that nothing is more worth
mention in American fiction of the past generation
than the extraordinary cultivation of the short-story,
which Mr. Brander Matthews dignifies and unifies
by a hyphen, in order to express his conviction that
it is an essentially new art form, to study which is a
fascinating quest, but aside from our main intention.

II

Having due regard then for perspective, and trying not to confuse historical importance with the
more vital interest which implies permanent claims,
it seems pretty safe to come back to Irving and Poe,
to Cooper and Hawthorne. Even as in the sketch
and tale Irving stands alone with such a masterpiece as " The Legend of Sleepy Hollow "; and Poe
equally by himself with his tales of psychological horror and mystery, so in longer fiction, Cooper and
Hawthorne have made as distinct contributions in the
domain of Romance. Their service is as definite for
the day of the Romantic spirit, as is that of Howells
and James for the modern day of realism so-called.
It is not hard to see that Irving even in his fiction is
essentially an essayist; that with him story was not

the main thing, but that atmosphere, character and style were,—the personal comment upon life.   One reads a sketch like " The Stout Gentleman," in every way a typical work, for anything but incident or plot. The Hudson River idyls, it may be granted, have somewhat more of story interest, but Irving seized them, ready-made for his use, because of their value for the picturesque evocation of the Past.   He always showed a keen sense of the pictorial and dramatic in legend and history, as the " Alhambra " witnesses quite as truly as the sketches.   " Brace-bridge Hall " and " The Sketch Book," whatever of the fictional they may contain, are the work of the essayist primarily, and Washington Irving will always, in a critical view, be described as a master of the English essay.   No other maker of American literature affords so good an example of the inter-colation of essay and fiction: he recalls the organic relation between the Sir Roger de Coverley Papers and the eighteenth century Novel proper of a generation later.

His service to all later writers of fiction was large in that he taught them the use of promising native material that awaited the story-maker.   His own use of it, the Hudson, the environs of Manhattan, was of course romantic, in the main.   When in an occasional story he is unpleasant in detail or tragic in trend he seems less characteristic—so definitely was he a romanticist, seeking beauty and wishing to throw over life the kindly glamour of imaginative art.   It is worth noting, however, that he looked forward rather than back, towards the coming realism, not to the incurable pseudo-romanticism of the late eighteenth century, in his instinct to base his happenings upon the bedrock of truth—the external truth of scene and character and the inner truth of human psychology.

Admirably a modern artist in this respect, his old-fashionedness, so often dilated upon, can easily be overstated.   He not only left charming work in the tale, but helped others who came after to use their tools, furthering their art by the study of a good model.

Nothing was more inevitable then that Cooper when he began fiction in mid-manhood should have written the romance: it was the dominant form in England because of Scott.   But that he should have realized the unused resources of America and produced a long series of adventure stories, taking a pioneer as his hero and illustrating the western life of settlement in his career, the settlement that was to reclaim a wilderness for a mighty civilization— that was a thing less to be expected, a truly epic achievement.   The Leather Stocking Series was in the strictest sense an original performance—the significance of Fenimore Cooper is not likely to be exaggerated; it is quite independent of the question of his present hold upon mature readers, his faults of technique and the truth of his pictures.   To have grasped such an opportunity and so to have used it as to become a great man-of-letters at a time when literature was more a private employ than the interest of the general—surely it indicates genuine personality, and has the mark of creative power.   To which we may add, that Cooper is still vital in his appeal, as the statistics of our public libraries show.

Moreover, incorrigible romancer that he was, he is a man of the nineteenth century, as was Irving, in the way he instinctively chose near-at-hand native material: he knew the Mohawk Valley by long residence; he knew the Indian and the trapper there; and he depicted these types in a setting that was to him the most familiar thing in the world.   In fact, we have in him an illustration of the modern writer who knows he must found his message firmly upon reality.   For both Leather-stocking and Chingachgook are true in the broad sense, albeit the white trapper's dialect may be uncertain and the red man exhibit a dignity that seems Roman rather than aboriginal.   The Daniel Boone of history must have had, we feel, the nobler qualities of Bumpo; how otherwise did he do what it was his destiny to do?   In the same way, the Indian of Cooper is the red man in his pristine home before the day of fire-water and Agency methods.   It may be that what to us to-day seems a too glorified picture is nearer the fact than we are in a position easily to realize. Cooper worked in the older method of primary colors, of vivid, even violent contrasts: his was not the school of subtleties. His women, for example, strike us as somewhat mechanical; there is a sameness about them that means the failure to differentiate: the Ibsenian psychology of the sex was still to come. But this does not alter the obvious excellencies of the work. Cooper carried his romanticism in presenting the heroic aspects of the life he knew best into other fields where he walked with hardly less success: the revolutionary story illustrated by " The Spy," and the sea-tale of which a fine example is " The Pilot." He had a sure instinct for those elements of fiction which make for romance, and the change of time and place affects him only in so far as it affects his familiarity with his materials. His experience in the United States Navy gave him a sure hand in the sea novels: and in a book like " The Spy " he was near enough to the scenes and characters to use studies practically contemporary. He had the born romanticist's natural affection for the appeal of the past and the stock elements can be counted upon in all his best fiction: salient personalities, the march of events, exciting situations, and ever that arch-romantic lure, the one trick up the sleeve to pique anticipation. Hence, in spite of descriptions that seem over-long, a heavy-footed manner that lacks suppleness and variety, and un-

deniable carelessness of construction, he is still loved
of the young and seen to be a natural *raconteur*, an
improviser of the Dumas-Scott lineage and, even
tested by the later tests, a noble writer of romance,
a man whom Balzac and Goethe read with admiration: unquestionably influential outside his own land
in that romantic mood of expression which, during
the first half of the nineteenth century, was so wide-
spread and fruitful.

III

It is the plainer with every year that Poe's contribution to American fiction, and indeed to that
of the nineteenth century, ignoring national bound-
aries, stands by itself.   Whatever his sources—and
no writer appears to derive less from the past—he
practically created on native soil the tale of fantasy,
sensational plot, and morbid impressionism.   His
cold aloofness, his lack of spiritual import, unfitted
him perhaps for the broader work of the novelist
who would present humanity in its three dimensions
with the light and shade belonging to Life itself.
Confining himself to the tale which he believed could
be more artistic because it was briefer and so the
natural mold for a mono-mood, he had the genius
so to handle color, music and suggestion in an
atmosphere intense in its subjectivity, that confessed
masterpieces were the issue.   Whether in the objective detail of " The Murders in the Rue Morgue,"

with its subtle illusion of realism, or in the *nuances* and delicatest tonality of " Ligeia," he has left specimens of the different degrees of romance which have not been surpassed, conquering in all but that highest style of romantic writing where the romance lies in an emphasis upon the noblest traits of mankind.   He is, it is not too much to say, well-nigh as important to the growth of modern fiction outside the Novel form as he is to that of poetry, though possibly less unique on his prose side.   His fascination is that of art and intellect: his material and the mastery wherewith he handles it conjoin to make his particular brand of magic.   While some one story of Hoffman or Bulwer Lytton or Stevenson may be preferred, no one author of our time has produced an equal number of successes in the same key.   It is instructive to compare him with Hawthorne because of a superficial resemblance with an underlying fundamental distinction.   One phase of the Concord romancer's art results in stories which seem perhaps as somber, strange and morbid as those of Poe: " Dr. Heidegger's Experiment," " Rapacinni's Daughter," " The Birth Mark."   They stand, of course, for but one side of his power, of which " The Great Stone Face " and " The Snow Image" are the brighter and sweeter.   Thus Hawthorne's is a broader and more diversified accomplishment in the form of the tale.   But the likeness has to do with subject-matter, not with the spirit of the

work.   The gloomiest of Hawthorne's short stories
are spiritually sound and sweet: Poe's, on the contrary, might be described as unmoral; they seem
written by one disdaining all the touchstones of
life, living in a land of eyrie where there is no moral
law.   He would no more than Lamb indict his very
dreams.   In the case of Hawthorne there is allegorical meaning, the lesson is never far to seek: a basis
of common spiritual responsibility is always below
one's feet.   And this is quite as true of the long
romances as of the tales.   The result is that there
is spiritual tonic in Hawthorne's fiction, while something almost miasmatic rises from Poe, dropping
a kind of veil between us and the salutary realities
of existence.   If Poe be fully as gifted, he is, for
this reason, less sanely endowed.   It may be conceded that he is not always as shudderingly sardonic and removed from human sympathy as in
" The Cask of Amontillado " or " The Black Cat";
yet it is no exaggeration to affirm that he is nowhere
more typical, more himself.   On the contrary, in
a tale like " The Birth Mark," what were otherwise
the horror and ultra-realism of it, is tempered by
and merged in the suggestion that no man shall
with impunity tamper with Nature nor set the delight of the eyes above the treasures of the soul.
The poor wife dies, because her husband cares more
to remove a slight physical defect than he does for
her health and life.   So it cannot be said of the

somber work in the tale of these two sons of genius
that,

"A common grayness silvers everything,"

since the gifts are so differently exercised and the
artistic product of totally dissimilar texture.
Moreover, Poe is quite incapable of the lovely
naïvete of "The Snow Image," or the sun-kissed
atmosphere of the wonder-book. Humor, except in
the satiric vein, is hardly more germane to the genius
of Hawthorne than to that of Poe: its occasional
exercise is seldom if ever happy.

Although most literary comparisons are futile because of the disparateness of the things compared,
the present one seems legitimate in the cases of Poe
and Hawthorne, superficially so alike in their short-
story work.

IV

In the romances in which he is, by common consent,
our greatest practitioner, to be placed first indeed
of all who have written fiction of whatever kind on
American soil, Hawthorne never forsakes—subtle,
spiritual, elusive, even intangible as he may seem—
the firm underfooting of mother earth. His themes
are richly human, his psychologic truth (the most
modern note of realism) unerring in its accuracy
and insight. As part of his romantic endowment,
he prefers to place plot and personages in the dim

backward of Time, gaining thus in perspective and ampleness of atmosphere. He has told us as much in the preface to " The House of The Seven Gables," that wonderful study in subdued tone-colors. That pronunciamento of a great artist (from which in an earlier chapter quotation has been made) should not be overlooked by one who essays to get a hint of his secret. He is always exclusively engaged with questions of conscience and character; like George Meredith, his only interest is in soul-growth. This is as true in the " Marble Faun " with its thought of the value of sin in the spiritual life, or in " The Blithedale Romance," wherein poor Zenobia learns how infinitely hard it is for a woman to oppose the laws of society, as it is in the more obvious lesson of " The Scarlet Letter." In this respect the four romances are all of a piece: they testify to their spiritual parentage. " The Scarlet Letter," if the greatest, is only so for the reason that the theme is deepest, most fundamental, and the by-gone New England setting most sympathetic to the author's loving interest. Plainly an allegory, it yet escapes the danger of becoming therefore poor fiction, by being first of all a study of veritable men and women, not lay-figures to carry out an argument. The eyes of the imagination can always see Esther Prynne and Dimmesdale, honest but weak man of God, the evil Chillingworth and little Pearl who is all child, unearthly though she be, a symbol at once of lost innocence and a hope of renewed purity. No pale abstractions these; no folk in fiction are more believed in: they are of our own kindred with whom we suffer or fondly rejoice. In a story so metaphysical as "The House of The Seven Gables," full justice to which has hardly been done (it was Hawthorne's favorite), while the background offered by the historic old mansion is of intention low-toned and dim, there is no obscurity, though plenty of innuendo and suggestion. The romance is a noble specimen of that use of the vague which never falls into the confusion of indeterminate ideas. The theme is startlingly clear: a sin is shown working through generations and only to find expiation in the fresh health of the younger descendants: life built on a lie must totter to its fall. And the shell of all this spiritual seething—the gabled Salem house—may at last be purified and renovated for a posterity which, because it is not paralyzed by the dark past, can also start anew with hope and health, while every room of the old home is swept through and cleansed by the wholesome winds of heaven.

Forgetting for a moment the immense spiritual meaning of this noble quartet of romances, and regarding them as works of art in the straiter sense, they are felt to be practically blameless examples of the principle of adapting means to a desired end. As befits the nature of the themes, the movement in each case is slow, pregnant with significance,

cumulative in effect, the tempo of each in exquisite
accord with the particular motive: compared with
"The Scarlet Letter," "The House of The Seven
Gables" moves somewhat more quickly, a slight increase to suit the action: it is swiftest of all in "The
Blithedale Romance," with its greater objectivity
of action and interest, its more mundane air: while
there is a cunning unevenness in the two parts of
"The Marble Faun," as is right for a romance
which first presents a tragic situation (as external
climax) and then shows in retarded progress that
inward drama of the soul more momentous than any
outer scene or situation can possibly be. After Dona-
tello's deed of death, because what follows is psychologically the most important part of the book, the
speed slackens accordingly. Quiet, too, and unsensational as Hawthorne seems, he possessed a
marked dramatic power. His dénouements are overwhelming in grip and scenic value: the stage effect
of the scaffold scene in "The Scarlet Letter," the
murder scene in the "Marble Faun," the tragic
close of Zenobia's career in "The Blithedale Romance," such scenes are never arbitrary and detached; they are tonal, led up to by all that goes
before. The remark applies equally to that awful
picture in "The House of The Seven Gables," where
the Judge sits dead in his chair and the minutes
are ticked off by a seemingly sentient clock. An
element in .this tonality is naturally Hawthorne's

style: it is the best illustration American literature affords of excellence of pattern in contrast with the "purple patch" manner of writing so popular in modern diction.

Congruity, the subjection of the parts to the whole, and to the end in view—the doctrine of key—Hawthorne illustrates all this. If we do not mark passages and delectate over phrases, we receive an exquisite sense of harmony—and harmony is the last word of style. It is this power which helps to make him a great man-of-letters, as well as a master of romance. One can imagine him neither making haste to furnish "copy" nor pausing by the way for ornament's sake. He knew that the only proper decoration was an integral efflorescence of structure. He looked beyond to the fabric's design: a man decently poor in this world's gear, he was more concerned with good work than with gain. Of such are art's kingdom of heaven.

Are there flaws in the weaving? They are small indeed. His didacticism is more in evidence in the tales than in the romances, where the fuller body allows the writer to be more objective: still, judged by present-day standards, there are times when he is too obviously the preacher to please modern taste. In "The Great Stone Face," for instance, it were better, one feels, if the moral had been more veiled, more subtly implied. As to this, it is well to remember that criticism changes its canons with the years and that Hawthorne simply adapted himself (unconsciously, as a spokesman of his day) to contemporaneous standards.   His audience was less averse from the principle that the artist should on no account usurp the pulpit's function.   If the artist-preacher had a golden mouth, it was enough. This has perhaps always been the attitude of the mass of mankind.

A defect less easy to condone is this author's attempts at humor.   They are for the most part lumbering and forced: you feel the effort.   Hawthorne lacked the easy manipulation of this gift and his instinct served him aright when he avoided it, as most often he did.   A few of the short stories are conceived in the vein of burlesque, and such it is a kindness not to name.   They give pain to any who love and revere so mighty a spirit.   In the occasional use of humor in the romances, too, he does not always escape just condemnation: as where Judge Pincheon is described taking a walk on a snowy morning down the village street, his visage wreathed in such spacious smiles that the snow on either side of his progress melts before the rays.

For some the style of Hawthorne may now be felt to possess a certain artificiality: the price paid for that effect of stateliness demanded by the theme and suggestive also of the fact that the words were written over half a century ago.   In these days of photographic realism of word and idiom, our conception of what is fit in diction has suffered a sea-change. Our ear is adjusted to another tune. Admirable as have been the gains in broadening the native resources of speech by the introduction of old English elements, the eighteenth century and the early years of the nineteenth can still teach us, and it is not beyond credence that the eventual modern ideal of speech may react to an equilibrium of mingled native and foreign-fetched words. In such an event a writer like Hawthorne will be confirmed in his mastery.

Remarkable, indeed, and latest in time has been the romantic reaction from the extremes of realistic presentation: it has given the United States, even as it has England, some sterling fiction. This we can see, though it is a phenomenon too recent to offer clear deductions as yet. What appears to be the main difference between it and the romantic inheritance from Scott and Hawthorne? One, if not the chief divergence, would seem to be the inevitable degeneration which comes from haste, mercantile pressure, imitation and lack of commanding authority. There is plenty of technique, comparatively little personality. Yet it may be unfair to the present to make the comparison, for the incompetents buzz in our ears, while time has mercifully stilled the bogus romances of G. P. R. James, *et id omne genus*.

But allowing for all distortion of time, a creative figure like that of Hawthorne still towers, serene and alone, above the little troublings of later days, and like his own Stone Face, reflects the sun and the storm, bespeaking the greater things of the human spirit.

THE END

INDEX

333

fluence over nineteenth century fiction, 171; personal fascination upon reader, 171; death, 172; contribution to fiction, 262; *referred to,* 110, 141, 151, 152, 321; *see also, Human Comedy.*

Barnaby Rudge, by Dickens, 181.

Barry Lyndon, by Thackeray, 203, 288.

Bath, England, 103.

Beach of Falesa, by Stevenson, 303.

Beaconsfield, Earl of, *see* Disraeli, Benjamin, Earl of Beaconsfield.

Beau Nash, 153.

Beaucaire, 153.

Beauchamp's Career, by Meredith, valuable treatment of English politics, 284, 293; mannerisms of style, 294.

Becky Sharp, contrasted with Sarah Gamp, 184; comparison with Countess de Saldar in *Evan Harrington,* 287; *see also, Vanity Fair.*

Belinda, by Edgeworth, 100.

Beowulf, 3.

Beyle, Henri (*pseud.* Stendahl), introduced novel of psychic analysis, 151; followed by Balzac and others, 152; held posts under Napoleon, 152; first great realist in France, 166.

Birth Mark, The, by Hawthorne, 322, 323

Black Arrow, The, by Stevenson, 306.

Black Cat, The, by Poe, 323.

Bleak House, by Dickens, 189.

"Blackguard Parson, The," Sterne called, 86.

Blithedale Romance, The, by Hawthorne, 325.

Book of Snobs, The, by Thackeray, its satire, 200, 201.

Boone, Daniel, *referred to,* 319.

Borrow, George, *referred to,* 261.

Boswell, James, prejudice against Fielding, 51.

Bottle Imp, The, by Stevenson, 303.

Boxhill, Surrey, home of Meredith, 282.

Bracebridge Hall, by Irving, 317.

British Society of Authors, Meredith President of, 282.

Brodingagnians, The, *see Gulliver's Travels.*

Brontës, The, isolation in realistic age, 259; personal qualities and evaluation of work, 259; attitude of Charlotte Brontë toward Thackeray, 259; *referred to,* 244.

Brookfield, Mrs., friend of Thackeray, 201.

Brown, Charles Brockden, *Wieland,* 96.

Browning, Robert, age at publication of *The Ring and the Book,* 25; Meredith compared with, 293; *quoted or referred to,* 119, 156.

"Browning of Prose, The," Meredith called, 293.

Brunetière, Ferdinand, *L'Art et Morale, quoted,* 44, 54; *also,* 157.

Bulwer, Edward George Earle Lytton, Baron Lytton, comparison with Austen, 122; chronologic setting, 244; poet, dramatist, and diplo-

Comédie Humaine, La, *see* Human Comedy.

Comedy, genius for, in Fielding, 50; and broadly presented by him, 61; of Molière likened to Austen, 111; description by Meredith, 111; unrivalled in *Evan Harrington*, 286.

Congreve, William, knowledge of early literary forms, 5; visited by Voltaire, 19.

Coningsby, by Disraeli, 245.

Connoisseur, The, suggests factory for making novels, 73.

Cooper, James Fenimore, Smollett compared with, 74; romances based on pioneer life, 318; significance to literature, 318; creative power and present-day appeal, 319; portrayal of the Indian, 319; sea-tales, 320; qualities and influences as a romancer, 320.

Country Doctor, The, by Balzac, 90, 160; *see also, Human Comedy.*

Cousin Pons, by Balzac, 164; *see also, Human Comedy.*

Cousine Bette, by Balzac, 164, 166; *see also, Human Comedy.*

Cricket on the Hearth, by Dickens, 190.

Crusades, The, 140.

Cyrano de Bergerac, quoted, 119.

Dana, Richard Henry, jr., *referred to,* 77.

Daniel Deronda, by George Eliot, story subsidiary to problem, 235; author's final novel, 239; double motive

and resulting lack of symmetry, 240; merits and lessons, 240; large percentage of quotable sayings, 241; illustrates author's decadence, 241.

Dark Affair, A, by Balzac, 164; *see also, Human Comedy.*

Daudet, Alphonse, *referred to,* 173, 273.

David Balfour, by Stevenson, sequel to *Kidnapped,* 301, 307.

David Copperfield, by Dickens, represents author's young prime, 181; *Vanity Fair* compared with, 182; evaluation, 186; *also,* 177, 188.

Day, Thomas, *Sanford and Merton,* 95.

Defoe, Daniel, age at publication of *Robinson Crusoe,* 25; Richardson compared with, 46; *Moll Flanders,* 47; shows possibility of powerful story including woman, 119; Stevenson compared with, 309; *referred to,* 225.

Democratic note, in eighteenth-century novelists, 15; prevalent in *Pamela,* 30.

De Morgan, William, age limit in literary production, 25; *also,* 36.

Denis Duval, by Thackeray, plan of, found after author's death, 211.

Desperate Remedies, by Hardy, 270.

Diana of the Crossways, by Meredith, comparison with *Daniel Deronda,* 240; attraction for American readers, 290; dissertation on

INDEX

Holmes, Oliver Wendell, compared with Smollett, 74; *also*, 8.

House and Brain, by Bulwer, 249.

House of Mirth, The, by Wharton, 21.

House of Seven Gables, by Hawthorne, psychological analysis of character, 325; sympathetic background, 326; theme and plot, 326; *also*, 126.

Howells, William Dean, growth of truth in literature shown by his dialogue as compared with that of earlier novelists, 13; criticism of *Clarissa Harlowe*, 38; his opinion of Austen, 175; influence on English realism, 313; tendency toward didacticism, 277; *quoted or referred to*, 8, 54, 122, 215, 238, 257.

Huckleberry Finn, by Mark Twain, 315.

Hudson River idyls, *see* Irving.

Hugo, Victor, effect of crowded existence in, 66; dramatic power, 188; *referred to*, 190.

Human Comedy, by Balzac, early studies for, 152; place and purpose, 154; impressiveness, 155; historical period covered, 155; age of author, 156; encyclopedic survey of all classes, 156, 158; extent and partial fulfilment of definite plan, 156, 157; divided into three groups and contents of each,

158; impossible to classify, 159; various types cited, 160, 164; comparison with English contemporaries, 161, 163; *see also*, individual titles.

Humphrey Clinker, see Expedition of Humphrey Clinker.

Hypatia, by Charles Kingsley, 249.

Ibsen, Henrik, *referred to*, 190, 320.

Idealism, Modern, and readjustment of religious thought, 264.

Idyls of the King, by Tennyson, 143.

Improvisatori, Scott and Dumas natural, 129.

Indian, The, portrayal of, by Cooper, 319.

Irish types, first portrayed by Edgeworth, 100.

Irving, Washington, preceded Dickens in use of Christmas motive, 191; master of short story, 314; *Legend of Sleepy Hollow*, 316; primarily an essayist, 316; example of intercalation of essay and fiction, 317; service to later writers, 317; instinct for truth, 318; *referred to*, 200.

Island Night's Entertainment, The, by Stevenson, 303.

Italy, death of Smollett in, 74; struggle for unity depicted in *Vittoria*, 293.

Ivanhoe, by Scott, 128; *see also, Waverley Novels.*

Jack Wilton, 4.

Jamaica, Life in, first pictured in *Roderick Random*, 76.

Melodrama, Reade master of, 251.

Melville, Herman, *referred to,* 77.

Memoirs Supposed to be Written by a Lady of Quality, by Smollett, 79.

Meredith, George, description of comedy, 111; Austen compared with, 115; also mature work of Bulwer, 248; refuses classification, 265, 279; Hardy compared with, 265, 267; position as novelist and growth of novel during his time, 280; influenced by surrounding conditions, 281; noble type of women, 281; early personal history, 282; retirement at Boxhill and President of British Society of Authors, 282; philosophy of life as seen in his books, 282, 284; intellectual appeal, 282, 285, 293; comparison with James, Fielding, and Smollett, 283; use of plot, episode, love, etc., 283; characterization and evaluation of greatest books, 285; favorite task, 287; great triumph in portrayal of Roy Richmond, 288; American readers, 290; view of mental relation of sexes in *Diana of the Crossways,* 290; enemy of sentimentalism, 291; view of marriage, 292; originality in allying romance and intellect, 292; love of Italy and comparison with Browning, 293; distinction as novelist and thinker, 293; mannerisms of style, 294; causes of obscur-

ity, 296; and other defects, 297; personality, influence, and aim, 297; Stevenson influenced by, 305; and compared with, 311; Hawthorne compared with, 325; *referred to,* 141, 152, 211, 240.

"Meredith of Poetry, The," Browning called, 293.

Middle Ages, cultivation of prose romance during, 3; a view of, 143.

Middlemarch, by George Eliot, published serially, *1871-'72,* and price paid, 237; conceived as two separate parts, 237; theme, 237, 239; lack of plot, 238; product of author's brain rather than blood, 238; character drawing, 239; *also,* 221.

Mill on the Floss, by George Eliot, written under stimulus of popularity, 230; its strength, 231; *also,* 222, 281.

Miniature painting, Austen's writing likened to, 105.

Mister Gilfil's Love Story, see Scenes from Clerical Life.

Mister Jonathan Wild the Great, by Fielding, 56, 57.

Modern Love, sonnet-sequence, by Meredith, 281.

Mohawk Valley, 319.

Molière, Jean Baptiste Poquelin, his comedy likened to that of Austen, 111; *also,* 60.

Moll Flanders, by Defoe, 47.

Monastery, The, by Scott, 128; *see also, Waverley Novels.*

Monk, The, by Lewis, 96.

Montaigne, Michel, *referred to,* 308.

Montagu, Lady Mary (Wort-

Novel, Modern, sources of power, 17; psychologic and serious, 53; one characteristic of, 65; accepted length, 92.

Novel of eighteenth century, contrasted with that of to-day, 31, 35; its writing an aside, 57.

Novel *versus* romance at beginning of nineteenth century, 150.

Nuneaton, Warwickshire, early home of George Eliot, 220.

Objective method, in Fielding, 70.

Œdipus Tyrannus, Coleridge's opinion of plot, 59.

Old Curiosity Shop, by Dickens, 181, 185.

Old Mortality, by Scott, 123, 128; *see also, Waverley Novels.*

Oliver Twist, by Dickens, 180, 181.

One of Our Conquerors, by Meredith, comparison with earlier works, 280; view of marriage, 292; mannerisms of style, 294.

Ordeal of Richard Feveril, by Meredith, comparison with later works, 280; plot, characterization, and evaluation, 285, 287; *also,* 284.

Our Mutual Friend, by Dickens, 186.

Pair of Blue Eyes, by Hardy, 270.

Pamela, by Richardson, publication, 5; democratic note, 15; early study of woman, 21; first novel of analysis, 25; form and plot, 25, 26,

28; compared with modern fiction, 27; French dramatic version, 30; same motive used by Voltaire in *Nainne*, 30; sentimentality, 30; success, 33; influence upon Fielding, 48; caricature, in, 48; chronologic setting, 73, 87; *also,* 72, 161.

Paradox of literature, Amateur writing a, 104.

Paris, Artist life in, depicted by Balzac, 164.

Parliamentary series, by Trollope, 256.

Passion in the Desert, by Balzac, 157; *see also, Human Comedy.*

Patron, Freedom from the, one result of democratic note, 30.

Pavilion on the Links, by Stevenson, 306.

Peacock, Thomas Love, *referred to,* 282.

Peg Woffington, by Reade, 251.

Pendennis, by Thackeray, merits and demerits, 204, 205; strength of character drawing and organic structure, 207; *also,* 204, 219.

Père Goriot, by Balzac, comparison with Dickens as to difference between Anglo-Saxon and Celtic genius, 162; *also,* 160, 166, 168, 170; *see also, Human Comedy.*

Peregrine Pickle, see Adventures of Peregrine Pickle.

Personality, development of interest in, 6, 9.

Persuasion, by Austen, 103, 108.

Petit Chose, Le, by Daudet,

354INDEX

creasing power in drawing
women and comparison with
those of Scott and Thack-
eray, 307; witness to reality
and truth in romance, 308;
human sympathy, 309; qualities of style, 309; essays
complement of fiction, 311;
philosophy of life and religious attitude, 311; legacy
to literature, 312; *quoted or
referred to,* 80, 120, 131, 211,
232, 277, 289, 322.
Steventon, England, home of
Austen, 102.
Story-telling, its antiquity, 1,
3; three ways of, 2.
Stout Gentleman, The, by
Irving, 317.
Stowe, Mrs. Harriet (Beech-
er), started line of studies
of New England rustic life,
315.
Stuarts, The, 140.
Swift, Jonathan, Richardson
compared with, 40; chronologic setting, 87; Stevenson
compared with, 309; *also,*
57.
Sybil, by Disraeli, 245.

Taine, Hippolyte Adolphe,
conception of environment
as shaping power, 268;
quoted, 8, 41, 58, 141, 214.
Tale of Two Cities, by Dickens, evaluation, 186; dramatic study of French Revolution, 187; conditions under which it was written,
187; lack of humor, 187;
also, 125, 183.
Tales of My Landlord, by
Scott, 128; *see also, Waverley Novels.*
Tancred, by Disraeli, 245.

Tarascon, 288.
"Teacup Times," 6.
Temple Bar, London, Rich-
ardson's shop beyond, 25.
Tender Husband, by Steele, 5.
Tennyson, Alfred, Lord,
quoted or referred to, 53,
143, 200, 282.
Tess of the d'Urbervilles, by
Hardy, comparison with
earlier work, 271; fatalistic
teaching and faulty conclusion, 272; comparison with
Le Petit Chose, 273; *also,*
21, 267, 276.
Testing of Diana Mallory, by
Ward, 21.
Thackeray, William Make-
peace, master of colloquial
manner, 52; criticism of
Fielding, 70; opinion of
Dickens' *Christmas Stories,*
191; lovers of, mutually exclusive toward Dickens, 195;
comparison with Dickens,
196, 199, 205, 208, 216;
voice of late nineteenth century, 196; modern note in,
196; tests of his art and
message, 197; fluctuations in
popularity and their cause,
198; cynicism a mooted
point, 200, 202, 203; personal qualities, 200, 202;
circumstances of early life,
201; satirist of contemporary social faults, 201, 207,
213; work as essayist and
journalist, 202, 203; point
of view, 208; careless technique, 209; dramatic sense,
210; style, 211; satire, 212,
213, 216; portrayal of wom-
en, 215; attitude toward fiction, 216; comparison with
George Eliot, 218; failure

INDEX

INDEX

Yankee at the Court of King Arthur, by Mark Twain, 315.

Yellowplush Papers, by Thackeray, 203.

Zola, Emile, high-priest of naturalist school, 152; king among modern realists, 167; inheritance from preceding writers, 173; influence upon English fiction, 174; his realism contrasted with that of Dickens, 184; criticized by Anatole France, 193; theory and practice in fiction, 262; influence of scientific thought upon, 263; distinction of his work and its historical interest, 264; conception of environment as shaping power, 268; *quoted or referred to*, 151, 152, 163, 165.